THE NEW AGE OF TERROR

We have entered the new, global age of terror. Whether or not we experience it directly, we are hostages both to the nuclear balance of terror and to the massive pressure of the new weapons and new purposes of the new terrorists.

We react to the threat of mass kidnapping by hijack and skyjack, of bombs and machine guns . . . We are manipulated by terrorists skillfully creating the drama on which the mass media feed . . . Finally, there is the real threat of nuclear blackmail applied to communities or nations for purposes fanatic, political, or mad.

In this book, CRUSADERS, CRIMINALS, CRAZIES, one of the world's experts on the psychology of terrorism nakedly reveals the true source of the plague of terrorism afflicting the world.

CRUSADERS, CRIMINALS, CRAZIES
Terror and Terrorism in Our Time
Dr. Frederick J. Hacker, M.D.

CRUSADERS, CRIMINALS, CRAZIES

Terror and Terrorism in Our Time

Frederick J. Hacker, M.D.

BANTAM BOOKS
TORONTO · NEW YORK · LONDON

To my brother
and to
brotherhood

This low-priced Bantam Book
has been completely reset in a type face
designed for easy reading, and was printed
from new plates. It contains the complete
text of the original hard-cover edition.
NOT ONE WORD HAS BEEN OMITTED.

CRUSADERS, CRIMINALS, CRAZIES
A Bantam Book

PRINTING HISTORY
Norton edition published January 1977
Bantam edition | January 1978

ISBN 0-553-11458-1

Published simultaneously in the United States and Canada

Bantam Books are published by Bantam Books, Inc. Its trade-
mark, consisting of the words "Bantam Books" and the por-
trayal of a bantam, is registered in the United States Patent
Office and in other countries. Marca Registrada. Bantam
Books, Inc., 666 Fifth Avenue, New York, New York 10019.

PRINTED IN THE UNITED STATES OF AMERICA

Contents

PART IV: THE OVERVIEW

"Nothing is easier than to denounce the evil doer; nothing is more difficult than to understand him."

FEDOR DOSTOEVSKI

Preface

Terror and terrorism are as old as the human discovery that people can be influenced by intimidation. But only recently have the means become available through which time-honored fear production has grown into a menace of global dimensions. Today, we live in an age of terror. Violence, threats, blackmail, and the fear they arouse are the conditions of our daily existence. We are threatened, and we threaten. We are hostages of the nuclear balance of terror. We permit terrorists to obtain the machine guns and manufacture the bombs with which they blow us to pieces; we give them heroes' welcomes in our most prestigious institutions; we surrender to them the use of our powerful mass media; and we are entertained by the spectacle of our own destruction. By merely reacting to their actions, we dance to their tune; by leaving all the initiative and imaginative innovation to them, we have become their dupes and accomplices. We talk violence, watch violence, fear violence, and we guide our lives accordingly. Not everybody has a bomb planted in his car or has to surrender his freedom to protect his life; not everybody lives under the dictatorship of terroristic blackmail or a police state—not yet. But these things happen here and everywhere. And they can happen to any of us at any moment.

In their potent destructiveness, dynamite and high explosives are obviously more effective than daggers, gunpowder, or poison. The technological quantum jumps from the arrow to the revolver and from the gun to the Molotov cocktail have also created a qualitative change in violence. The practice of intimidation, at one time a luxury reserved for the powerful few, has now become common custom among the many would-be powerful. Readily available automatic weapons can be freely purchased both over the counter and by mail order; homemade cocktails of explosives can be mixed according to instructions found in easily available bomb cookbooks.

Terrorists today profit from the speed and anonymity of modern travel and communication. They have their own jet set and are among the best customers of telephone companies, wire services, manufacturers of electronic equipment, travel bureaus, and luxury hotels that furnish smooth service, perfect cover, and all the necessities for quick appearances and disappearances anywhere in the world. Easy access has given disgruntled small groups and even individuals a new capacity for spectacularly disruptive and destructive acts: the power to hold up large communities and whole nations.

Interdependence, complexity, and technological efficiency, which provide the terroristic tools for mobility, anonymity, and destructiveness in unprecedented excellence, make complex modern society more vulnerable than ever before to the simple threat of crudely manipulated fear. Through the help of advanced technology, the "smallness" of the groups (or individuals) has assumed an unexpected significance denied to them by the "bigness" of a deindividualizing and dehumanizing society. The big and powerful can be, and therefore *are*, successfully blackmailed and intimidated by the small and so-far powerless.

This book explores two distinct kinds of fear arousal—terror and terrorism—what they are, what they do, what they do to us, what they do for us, and what can be done about them. Terror, which is inflicted from above, is the manufacture and spread of fear by dictators, governments, and bosses. It is the attempt of the powerful to exert control through intimidation. Terrorism, which is imposed from below, is the manufacture and spread of fear by rebels, revolutionaries, and protesters. It is the attempt of the so-far powerless, the would-be powerful, to exert control through intimidation. Terror and terrorism are not the same, but they belong together, indissolubly linked by the shared belief that fear is the strongest, if not the only, effective human motivation and that violence is the best, if not the only, method to produce and maintain fear.

Terror and terrorism are twins. They hate and despise each other, yet they are very much alike. They originate from the same family background of violence with a clean conscience. They resemble and copy each other, and they depend and thrive on each other, as each claims to be necessary because of the other's existence. They are, singly and together, the greatest challenge to democratic institutions and the most dangerous threat to men and women everywhere.

Terror and terrorism aim to frighten and, by frightening, to dominate and to control. They want to impress. They play to and for an audience, and they solicit audience participation. Their appearances and disappearances are carefully staged and choreographed to get maximum attention. Grievance claims, self-display, theater, and propaganda become united in a spectacular performance. Terrorists are engaged in public relations and advertising; they are in show business. In their own interest and that of whatever "sacred" cause they represent, terrorists from above and below use all means at their disposal to intimidate their audience into submission or rebellion, paralysis or violent action, all presumably for the benefit of the terrorized. That is what they do.

Terrorists are convinced that in our desperation we need them desperately because they have all the simple answers we search for with our complex questions. By trying to compel our thinking and our actions through fear, they attempt to commit rape of the mind; they dehumanize and victimize us by treating us indiscriminately as targets, obstacles, objects, and raw material to be molded according to their conceptions. That is what they do to us.

They greatly simplify everything for us. They promise instant, radical change and relief from burdensome individual responsibility. They interrupt the dreary routines of everyday life by stimulating and entertaining us. Their spectacular violence makes for exciting, as well as commercially profitable, mass entertainment on a national and worldwide scale. The insatiable mass media crave the dramatic sensationalism that the terrorists deliver; the terrorists crave the publicity and notoriety that the mass media readily provide. Terrorism and mass media are made for each other; they would have to invent each other if they did not already exist. Terrorism, aided by the mass media, entertains and appeals to the hidden terrorist in each of us who has been terrorized by fear-arousing education, experience, and suffering. That is what they do for us.

In order to plan how best to meet their violent challenge, it is vitally important to identify the terrorists and their motivations and to deal with our own blinding fear. There are better alternatives than to respond to "wrong" violence with allegedly "right" violence, that is, our own violence, which we justify as counterviolence and which only serves to escalate the violence that we claim to abhor. This all-too-typical response demonstrates that the hidden terrorist in all of us is not so hidden. Talking first to avoid shooting is better (for everybody but the terrorist) than shooting first and then making justifications. Genuine negotiations, not morality plays or exercises in double-crossing, are always preferable to quick confrontations.

Meeting complicated challenges with simplistic solutions that have proved ineffective in the past renders us even more helpless and terror prone. Only the ignorant or the fanatics are sure that simple remedies will solve everything in a hurry. The unshakable belief in instant solutions, disallowing complexity, often makes involved problems unsolvable in the long run. Terrorists want to compel fundamental social change within days or weeks; antiterrorists proclaim that all that needs to be done about terrorism is to get tough and shoot it out. Terror from above is a short-range remedy for terrorism from below, but the powerful attraction of the terrorists' irrational solutions should not be underrated by rational politics and science.

Instead of these easy answers, we need social action and experiments with social action, teams of expert advisers, task forces, new negotiation techniques, novel approaches. We need means to curb the epidemic of mushrooming identities nationally and internationally. We need innovative techniques to counteract the deadly competition of smaller and smaller self-justified groups claiming sovereignty. We need no more self-righteous rationalizations to explain why the remediable injustices that lie at the root of most terroristic activities continue to exist in our society; we need nonviolent methods to correct them soon. We have enough budgets and weapons and support for the forces of confrontation; we need to develop the machinery for cooperation and the self-confidence to act on what we know, rather than to react to what we fear. That, for a start, is what can be done about terror and terrorism.

In my clinical and forensic practice, I have seen and evaluated every conceivable form of explosive symptomatic violence, most of which is both the cause and the effect of guilt, anxiety, and defiance. But I have also been impressed by a different kind of violence that seemingly produces not guilt but pride, not anxiety but self-confidence, not remorse but enhanced self-righteousness. I have observed and studied the "strategic" violence of mass murderers with a mission; the guiltless "defensive" violence of all nations at war; the "educational" violence of the German National Socialists, of the Russian Stalinists, of the South American dictators; and the "justified" violence of the Third World, of Arab liberation movements, of resistance fighters, of rural and urban guerrillas everywhere in South America.

No doubt violent acts often indicate sickness, emotional imbalance, or brain disorder. But more often, violence in its cruelest forms is used by the powerful or those opposed to the powerful in an effort to educate, to control, to police, to rule, to restore or to maintain balance, or as a means of protest, liberation, and revolution. To regard aggression as nothing but the expression of disturbed emotions or the manifestation of twisted brain cells is totally to misconstrue what purposeful strategic violence is all about.

By far the greatest number of violent acts with the greatest destructive effect are committed by so-called normal people who consider themselves healthy and sound and are called heroes and martyrs or villains and criminals, depending on the success of their aggressive ventures and whose side they are on.

Not only Hitler, Stalin, de Gaulle, Castro, and Che Guevara but also many American presidents and presidential candidates have been accused of having suffered from assorted psychological maladies that are nowadays quickly diagnosed—always by the opponent. The intrusion of psychiatric jargon into political language ("crazed imperialists," "demented revolutionaries," "emotionally immature, infantile rebels," "paranoid power seekers," "schizophrenic societies," and the like) perverts the medical model into a device for aggressive denunciation. The use of medical diagnosis, meant to be a guideline for treating the afflicted, turns into a putdown and a phony justification for namecalling and ridicule, for expressing distaste and disapproval in the guise of scientific objectivity.

To treat other human beings or historical figures as if they were nothing but help-seeking patients needing advice, education, and cure is a sure indication of professional aberration or, worse, of professional deceit. Social problems are mislabeled as symptoms of illnesses so that they can be ignored and perpetuated for political and ideological reasons. In truth, the antidote for oppression is liberation; the medicine for poverty in the midst of plenty is a better distribution of wealth. Injustice does not need to be treated at all, certainly not by tranquilizers; rather, it should be prevented and remedied by just measures.

The value of psychiatry and psychology for explaining and interpreting, let alone influencing, social and political events is by no means undisputed. Some critics accuse psychiatry of creating a myth in order to be able to treat it. However, mental illness is not the product of a conspiracy to discriminate against the unusual. Rather, it is a transculturally observable psychobiological reality. Because of the social consequences of disease, mental illness is sometimes either deliberately or inadvertently misdiagnosed. Occasionally, it can be feigned. That storks are said to be responsible for childbirth is an old wives' tale, a myth; but long-legged white birds called storks do exist, even if what is attributed to them does not.

Utmost simplicity is a utopian scientific ideal that more often than not is achieved by simply leaving out that part of reality which contradicts a deceptively clear conclusion. Human perception does more than mirror given facts; inner reality does not just reflect outer reality but also reflects *on* it, categorizes, evaluates, and simplifies. Therefore, the statement "a pretzel-shaped reality calls for a pretzel-shaped hypothesis" is not quite accurate, but neither are those claims that deny or ignore the existence of odd phenomena or try to straighten the pretzels for the sake of a straight and economical explanation. Complex reality requires, not the avoidance of, but the search for and toleration of the contradictions and ambiguities of the real world.

Common sense, proud of being old-fashioned, prefers to place its trust for effective protection in a disciplined police force rather than in a bunch of argumentative psychiatrists. But this is not an either-or issue. Nobody this side of sanity wants law enforcement officers replaced by professors of sociology or psychology. Clearly, the shrinks can't do the job of the government or of the police and don't want to; but they could, at least in some instances, offer their skill and knowledge in a working partnership for the benefit of the

xvi   Crusaders, Criminals, Crazies

community. It is my firm conviction that in a democracy, the ultimate decisions about matters of political impact should be made by the duly elected or appointed representatives of the people. But there is no reason why the decision makers could not make use of the best available expert opinions prior to making their decisions.

As long as the barriers of traditional mutual mistrust remain high, this is easier said than done. For too long, interest in the root causes of crime has been considered an indication of a soft approach toward the criminal and a sign of hostility toward law enforcement. For too long, the image of the mindless, brutish, corrupt, and trigger-happy policeman has been the intellectual's nightmare. New ways of working together can be found only if the old clichés are exposed to radical change in the face of real emergencies. After concrete collaboration is actually put into practice, neither law enforcement nor behavioral science can hope to remain the same.

Professional and moral choices have to be made, even if they mean the abandonment of safe routines and lifelong protective habits. Why should the expert who knows something about human motives and human experience be excluded from participating in making those decisions that he recommends to society at large? For too long, the crucial jobs of motivation and change have been left by default to precisely those individuals who are committed to the polarization and escalation of conflict and who have told us over and over again that there is no other choice but to call in the cops, the army, or whatever other practitioners of violence are available.

For anyone who believes that addiction to action or to self-righteous passivity, regardless of consequences, is the greatest threat to real security and freedom, there is clearly an obligation to act and to speak out. We have heard the noises of glamorized violence and the shrill cries of despair long enough; it is time to listen to some advice based on knowledge and experience and to develop novel approaches to meet the age-old destructiveness in its devastating new forms.

Scientific impartiality does not exclude, but on the contrary demands, a strong value commitment that needs to be stated as explicitly as possible: I abhor and emphatically disapprove of all violence as the most primitive, regressive manifestation of aggression. I believe that nonviolent (but not necessarily nonaggressive) solutions to inevitable conflicts must and can be found and that in the overwhelming majority of cases, recourse to violence represents only self-serving moral cowardice, lack of imagination, and a failure of knowledge and spirit. I have to admit that some situations—very few—permit no other solution but a violent one. But I believe that these situations, aside from the statistically infrequent examples of outright criminality or insanity, should and could be prevented by appropriate social action long before they reach the climactic stage at which violence becomes unavoidable.

I am conscious of no other preconceived notions except the definite bias for life over death that favors individual human life and human coexistence over destruction and the bias for alternatives to fighting violence with violence. These preferences are indeed the assumptions that underlie and determine my work, my ideas, and my conclusions. Everything else is, to the best of my awareness, a matter, not of cherished belief, but of empirical knowledge that can and should be scrutinized, criticized, rejected, amended, or improved. The very debate about the possibilities and limitations of combating terror and terrorism—if followed by effective action—may itself be one of the best available alternatives to unrestrained violence and counterviolence.

PART I

The
Terrorists

1

The Terroristic Enterprise

All violence is aggressive, but not all aggression is violent; there are aggressive and nonaggressive alternatives to violence. Essential and inevitable aggression manifests itself in innumerable forms, such as verbal aggression, competition, and aggressive pursuits, that are nonviolent and may be individually and collectively productive and creative.

Not every violent act is terroristic; terror and terrorism are means to an end with the purpose of bringing about certain definite changes in the action, thinking, and feeling of the public in accordance with the action, thinking, and feeling of the terrorists.

Terror and terrorism destroy without regard or scruples; in principle, they are not subject to any inhibitions or limitations. They do not stop short of the destruction of possessions, valuable goods, or human lives (either one's own or others'). Violence is simple; the alternatives to violence are complex. Similarly, intimidation is straightforward and simple, producing instantaneous responses; whereas persuasion is complex, slow, and circuitous, producing more lasting but less easily visible and recognizable results. Whenever im-

3

mediate effects are desired, polarization of conflict (whoever is not with me is against me) and escalation to violent resolution of conflict are mandatory. This vicious cycle can be started by one side, tempting or inducing the other sides to follow suit. Even in democratic societies, counterterrorist activities can, by use of electronic surveillance, clandestine infiltration, illegal searches, and similar actions, compound the violation of the values that they intend (or pretend) to protect. Inadvertently or by design, counterterrorist campaigns often adopt the tactics they presumably abhor and for the sake of efficiency become as terroristic as the activities against which they fight.

Aggression is what the other does. This aggressive, simplistic statement is inspired by a combination of many extremely complicated processes that never emerge into consciousness. Against all reason and research, action is based on evidence of this overwhelming gut feeling: It is the other who is wrong; it is the other who is aggressive or "really" aggressive. Just because the real situation is immensely complicated, self-righteousness demands a particularly extreme, stereotypical simplification.

Aggression is a species-specific, programmed disposition or proclivity elicited by a great number of socially mediated and regulated stimuli. According to the present state of knowledge, which throws some doubts on the validity of the concept of instinct, aggression is not an instinct in the strict sense of the word because there are no specific brain regions or other mechanisms and substances that, through internal stimulation, generate specifically aggressive behavior. The ubiquity of aggression in all cultures strongly suggests biological anchorage, although certainly not any exclusively or even predominantly biological determination of aggressive strivings. Of course, every aggressive manifestation is also learned behavior. The interest of modern scholars is centered on those social settings and culturally mediated symbols and other stimuli that favor, inhibit, or sublimate aggressive impulses.

Aggressive Education for Nonaggression

A simple example will illustrate some crucial issues of aggression, its stimulation, its deterrence, and its justification. A father punishes his six-year-old son with a few good whacks because the boy has beaten up his little brother. The reason for the paternal beating is to teach the boy that in civilized society one does not beat somebody smaller and weaker, yet that is precisely what the father is doing. There is an irreconcilable contrast between the educational message (don't beat) and the educational method (beating). The father, acting in consonance with his own educational experience and cultural instructions, is at no time aware that he is being aggressive. He is not angry at his son, nor does he hate him; he just believes it is his duty to teach the boy a lesson to prevent the youngster from doing to somebody else what is presently being done to him. To the father, the boy's aggressive actions and his own primitive aggressive reactions are quite different matters because the boy's beating is done for the benefit of the boy; it is educational.

Other Exceptions to the Violence Taboo

Education is one socially approved exception to the socially accepted prohibition of aggressive acts, but there are others. When the same little boy comes home complaining that he has been attacked by other boys, the parents are not likely to pity him; rather, they will advise him to hit back. Aggression is permissible and even required for self-defense, self-preservation, and self-assertion. Furthermore, the defense of higher causes—family, honor, country, God—is not just condoned but actually commanded by society.

These original exceptions to the violence taboo later on turn into the rules for any and all acts of violence. The unholy alliance of violence and its justifications starts in early childhood. From then on, justification, real or imaginary, will be found without fail;

in later life, violence will occur only when it can be justified to the satisfaction of the perpetrator.

Not all aggression results from anger and rage; it can be part of a design or the outcome of deliberate calculation. Aggression is not always an explosive and symptomatic response to intolerable frustration and pressure; aggression can be strategic, goal-directed, and intentionally employed in order to accomplish a purpose or to fulfill a function. Strategic aggression is often quite rational, serving intelligible and intelligent purposes; latent strategic aggression, often called structural aggression, is contained in social organizations and institutions, laws, and property arrangements.

Where Does Aggression Start?

After fifty-one years of debate the League of Nations and U.N. reported in over 30,000 single-spaced typewritten pages, a U.N. committee finally arrived at a definition of aggression, accepted without a vote by the General Assembly in December 1974. Its crucial article says: "The first use of armed forces by a state in contravention of the charter shall constitute *prima facie* evidence of an act of aggression."[1] This statement demonstrates no more sophistication than one little boy excusing his own aggressive acts by pointing to the opponent who has started the fight (self-defense as a justification) or another little boy who, being observed suddenly striking a playmate, remarks, "I didn't do anything wrong; I just hit him back first" (anticipatory retaliation as a justification). From the cradle to the international political arena, there is constant preoccupation with the question of who struck first or who really started it. The answer is always: not me.

There are no more ministries of war, but every country has a department of defense. Everybody merely defends himself or his country or the cause for which he crusades. Nobody is ever responsible for an attack because it is always the other who has started it; that is what *makes* him the other. The circle is closed; aggression is what the other does.

Label Swindle

Rationalization (the giving of a good reason for the real reason) and *label swindle* (calling something by a different name) are the favorite devices for making aggression legitimate, permissible, and even mandatory. Label swindle, caused by intentional deception or by hypocritical habit, is in fact the most pervasive practice of our era. By conscious effort and unconscious distortion, one's own aggression is labeled defense, necessity, duty, devotion, education, or police action; the new label miraculously conceals aggression. Initially, label swindle permits the uncontrolled employment of aggression for justifiable purposes; eventually, through habituation (getting used to and dependent on) and ritualization (establishing a prescribed order and tradition, regularly repeated) of violence, it eliminates even a lingering awareness of one's own aggression. Denial, repression, and projection help make the transition from individual, partly biologically determined aggression to collective, socially manipulable, and justifiable aggression.

Emotionally rousing, beautiful, positive labels to cover up one's own attempts to control and intimidate are always easily found. If terroristic acts cannot be represented as self-defense, as unselfish devotion to duty, or as crusades for a sacred cause, one can always resort to declaring that at this given moment there is just no alternative to violent terror as a technique of government or to violent terrorism as a revolutionary strategy. Utilizing technological perfection and psychological refinement, both terror from above and terrorism from below produce and emphasize feelings of individual helplessness in order to accustom people to resignation and despair. Taught by intimidation that the only effective way to counter intimidation is to imtimidate others, many individuals and groups have adopted the methods to which they have been subjected. From their earliest days, people have been prepared and programmed to become either victims and objects of terror or potential terrorists.

Strategic Aggression

The resurgence of terror and terrorism is not just a regression to primitive behavior that is deeply implanted in human nature, nor is it merely a return to an uncivilized stage erroneously believed to have long since been overcome by humanitarian progress. Most often, terroristic aggression is not just a symptom, a directionless explosion to relieve intolerable tension; rather, it is a calculated strategy that uses psychological means (psychoterror) to reach its goals brutally and effectively.

Terror and terrorism carefully manufacture the image of their irresistibility, which then becomes their most powerful tool. Pessimistic cynicism, posing as sober realism, has become fashionable. Hard-nosed traditionalism and radical chic join in claiming that morality and reason are merely rhetorical ornaments, basically ineffective human motivations, thus permitting terror and terrorism to become what they have always propagandistically claimed to be: irresistible forces that indeed influence, change, corrupt, and pervert the movable object of the human spirit. Terror and terrorism flourish whenever the critical intellect is ready to abdicate in favor of an oceanic sense of belonging. The frustration of felt impotence seeks escape in fantasies of unlimited omnipotence that lead to immoral acts performed in good conscience and with impunity under the cover of sanctimonious justification. The illusionary guarantee of an all-embracing identity and the promise of immediate total change, together with a general pardon for actions in the service of a good cause, are the mass-produced legitimations of the terroristic deed. Only through unlimited justification can terrorist violence become a global threat.

Types of Terrorists

Terrorists can be roughly divided into three groups according to their main motivations: the crazy, the criminal, and the crusading (the most typical variety). The emotionally disturbed are driven by reasons of their own that often do not make sense to anybody else. That is why they are called crazy, a colloquial designation I use with reluctance because of its judgmental connotation. The motives of those terrorists who use illegitimate means to obtain personal gain are understood by everybody. Criminal terrorists want nothing different from what most other people want, but they are willing to resort to socially disapproved methods in order to achieve their goals. Crusading terrorists are idealistically inspired. They seek, not personal gain, but prestige and power for a collective goal; they believe that they act in the service of a higher cause.

Of course, the pure ideal type is rarely encountered. Many criminals are severely disturbed or try to exploit various causes for personal gain. Some mentally ill individuals are irresistibly attracted to crusades or engage in personally motivated antisocial acts. Crusading terrorists often have emotional problems; some have criminal backgrounds. Just as some crusaders become more violent and criminal, splintering into smaller, more radical free-lancing units, some criminals adopt, in prison and out, the justifying and comforting identity of a cause. Convicts often feel themselves to be victims of racial, sexist, and political persecution; they believe the evil forces in society are responsible for their plight, rather than any fault within themselves. Yet, within limits, the differentiation between crazy, criminal, and crusading terrorists remains useful and valid, sometimes even vital, because the distinction determines the widely varying courses of action for meeting or treating the terrorist challenge.

The terms "criminal" and "crazy" are labels that pretend to be descriptive but often merely express disapproval. The criminal is loathed; the crazy is pitied; both are feared. Punishment is legitimate only when the offender can be blamed. The criminal can and must be blamed. Presumably, he willed his evil deed; he is bad and should be punished. The mad person cannot be blamed, for he supposedly had no free will; but that does not make him any less dangerous.

Crazy is used to describe unusual, unforeseen, and

incomprehensible conduct. In societies that by repression or ignorance are intolerant of any deviation, just being different may earn the derogatory label, empowering the community to take protective and therapeutic measures against the "guilty" person.

The typical crusading terrorist, volunteer or carefully selected, appears normal, no matter how crazy his cause and how criminal the means he uses in the service of this cause may appear. He gains his strength not only from his comparatively intact ego but from his enthusiastic membership in a group onto which he has projected and externalized his conscience. He is neither a dummy nor a fool, neither a coward nor a weakling, but a professional, well trained, well prepared, and well disciplined in the habit of blind obedience.

Anatomy of Terror and Terrorism

After differentiating between crazy, criminal, and crusading terrorists, further distinctions need to be made between motivations, the cast of perpetrators, the victims, and the objects of terror and terrorism, to which could be added the varying audience reactions such as resistance and active countermeasures.

Terrorists always feel totally justified in their actions, but what to them appears reason and justification —namely, the experienced or anticipated violence of the enemy—is very rarely the real and hardly ever the only motivation. The origins of conflict are usually shrouded in obscurity but regularly focus on an arbitrarily selected aggressive act by the opponent.

Terrorists who strike from above always require a certain degree of organization. Terrorists who strike from below may operate alone or in groups that can be distinguished by the degree and type of their organization. Crazy terrorists are often loners; criminals are mostly organized in a businesslike manner; and crusaders are generally organized in military fashion. Subdivisions can be made between the planning brain trusts that design terroristic actions but very rarely dirty or bloody their own hands, the intermediary communications staff that transmit the orders, and the actual executioners that follow instructions.

The victims are used indiscriminately but are usually carefully selected for their prominence and exchange value, often without regard to their innocence or guilt. They are used as the instruments for intimidation, fear arousal, and gain.

The ultimate objects of terror, as distinct from its immediate victims, are the true target of the terroristic enterprise. Single powerful individuals, powerful groups or families, countries, or the whole world are the terror objects, and they react in a variety of ways, ranging from complete resistance to total capitulation. The charts on pages 13–19 illustrate the points of difference.

Crazy Terrorist from Above: Big Daddy

In order to really make it and to reach the pinnacle of power, a certain degree of consistency, self-control, and ego strength is required, which most seriously disturbed persons lack. For obvious reasons, psychotic individuals do not often succeed in realizing their fantasies of becoming emperors or presidents. As a rule, overt psychotics can neither reach nor maintain themselves in top positions. Uganda's dictator, Idi Amin, may be an exception. His grotesquely irrational, bizarre actions seem to be the result of thought processes so disturbed that, in contrast with other terrorist dictators such as Hitler or Stalin, he would be considered deranged in any conceivable social setting.

British Prime Minister Harold Wilson called him "nuts" and a "neurotic paranoiac," the West German Chancellor characterized his statements as "an expression of mental derangement," and Tanzanian president Julius Nyerere described him as "a lunatic and an idiot." Amin had wired Nyerere, "I love you very much and if you had been a woman, I would have considered marrying you, although your head is full of gray hairs. But as you are a man, that possibility does not arise."[2]

High U.S. diplomats and most other observers find him "totally mad." The international press has run out of appropriate adjectives to describe the behavior of Big Daddy Idi Amin. The "mercurial" former sergeant and pugilist, who was Ugandan heavyweight champion for nine years, has been called a barbarous buffoon, a mad magician, a semiliterate lunatic, a comic figure, and a ruthless, cunning man. Idi Amin, who is said to have suffered brain damage, still loves to put on his boxing gloves occasionally; he then commands some elderly officials into the ring and beats them to a bloody pulp. He constantly feels himself threatened by enemies trying to assassinate him, and he has given as many as twenty speeches a day, in which he frequently refers to his conferences with God. His dreams provide inspirations for his political moves. In one day, he divorced three of his four legal wives for alleged association with his potential assassins. During his pilgrimage to Mecca, rain fell on the city for the first time in half a century; Idi Amin interpreted this as a divine command to expel between 50,000 and 75,000 Ugandans holding British passports, which he did the next day and also forced tens of thousands of native blacks to flee the country.

With British and Israeli support, Amin overthrew the dictatorial regime of President Milton Obote, who for years had maintained power through the army, which Amin headed. After his successful coup, Amin went to Israel on an arms shopping spree. Shortly thereafter, he expelled all Israelis from Uganda and delivered an incoherent eulogy of German national socialism, praising Hitler for the extermination of 6 million Jews. Yet he is very fond of Jews. He says, "First, I love very much the Jews. Very many of them are my best friends. General Dayan, he is my best friend. We chased Jewish women together in Tel Aviv, also with my foreign minister."[3]

TERRORISM FROM BELOW

Crazy	Criminal	Crusading
Self-centered and sacrificial	Selfish and self-protective	Unselfish and sacrificial
Thought processes: highly personal, nonrational or irrational	Thought processes: task-oriented, rational, conventional in terms of prevailing values	Thought processes: task-oriented, functionally rational.* but unconventional in terms of prevailing values
Sometimes delusional	Realistic	Realistic, often in service of unrealistic ends
Abstract goals	Concrete goals	Concrete and abstract goals
Anticipated gain: psychological and idiosyncratic	Anticipated gain: personal and material	Anticipated gain: collective, symbolic, publicity, or material
Often "incomprehensible"	Commonly "understandable"	"Understandable" to sympathizers, "senseless" to antagonists
Cry for help, self-dramatization (psychodrama), therapeutic attempt, attempt at self-cure	Materially, not psychologically, oriented	Attention-getting, ostentatious, dramatic, spectacular, publicity-conscious

TERRORISM FROM BELOW (continued)

	Crazy	Criminal	Crusading
	Amateurish M.O.**	Professional, mostly repetitive M.O.	Theatrical M.O. follows trends and fashions
	High risk taking	High risk avoidance	Indifferent to high risk
	Predominantly inward-directed aggression, intrapunitive, suicidal	Predominantly outward-directed aggression, extrapunitive, homicidal	Intrapunitive and extrapunitive, suicidal and homicidal
	Loners or small groups, not organized	Loners or organized in a businesslike (e.g., syndicates, corporations) or familylike (e.g., clan, brotherhood) manner, often subject to terror from above (Mafia)	Small or large groups, organized in armylike manner (e.g., leagues, fronts, units), with hierarchical command structure, often submissive to terror from above
	Unstable, immature, often distractible and inept individuals with weak ego and overt behavior disturbances	Detached, often dehumanized individuals, often unstable and inept but also often with seemingly intact ego and without overt behavior disturbances	Fanatical individuals, often with seemingly intact ego, without overt behavior disturbances

Conspicuous through bizarre conduct or attire	Mostly inconspicuous	Inconspicuous
Often overt sexual disturbance	No overt sexual disturbance	No overt sexual disturbance, little or no overt sexual interest
Unpredictable, vascillating, hesitating	Predictable, mostly determined, ruthless	Predictably unpredictable, determined, ruthless
Indifferent to immediate success	Exclusively interested in concrete immediate success	Predominantly interested in immediate and long-range publicity and success
Frequently imitative	Frequently imitative	Frequently innovative and violence-escalating
Eager for alliances with audience, often on any terms	Disinterested in alliances but interested in specific deals	Interested in deals and alliances on their own terms
Cannot be deterred by ordinary means, can be persuaded but not bought	Can be deterred by ordinary means, can be bought but not persuaded	Cannot be deterred by ordinary means, incorruptible

TERROR FROM BELOW (*continued*)

	Crazy	Criminal	Crusading
VICTIMS	Selection: random or according to delusional system (with attraction to the powerful and prominent)	Selection: purely instrumental (the rich and prominent for trade and blackmail value)	Selection: for symbolic and/or publicity value, often from emotional, highly charged enemy target group as instruments for barter but may become targets for brainwashing and eventual allies
	Highly endangered for short periods of time	Danger varying according to response; the more professional the criminal, the less endangered the victim	After initial phase, danger almost entirely dependent upon responses
OBJECTS (AUDIENCE)	Selection: random or vaguely defined target group, visualized as possible allies and helpers	Selection: usually small groups, such as the victim's family	Selection: largest group possible (the nation, the world)
	Recipients of moral appeals	Recipients of business propositions	Recipients of specific blackmail threats and vague moral appeals

High ambivalence	Indignation not tempered by ambivalence	High ambivalence
Merciless removal ("Kill him; he's crazy anyway") or pity (poor-devil phenomenon)	Buying offers and/or severe punishment	Extreme measures (e.g., repressive counteraction, death penalty) advocated by antagonists; understanding advocated by sympathizers
Emphasis on protection rather than punishment	Emphasis on punishment and deterrence	Emphasis on punishment for protection and deterrence by antagonists; emphasis on little or no individual punishment by sympathizers
Quick retaliation or advocacy of flexible negotiations	Advocacy of immediate negotiations, often with the use of guile and trickery	Various coping styles; show of strength (e.g., no negotiation, no concession), but negotiations obligatory if victims are sufficiently valuable

	TERROR FROM ABOVE		
	Crazy	Criminal	Crusading
MOTIVATION	Same as terrorism	Same as terrorism	Same as terrorism
CAST	Erratic, bizarre conduct with emphasis on self-aggrandizement. Untrained, often unskilled. Often manipulated	Professional conduct of administrators and executors in tight business organizations demanding discipline and submission, strict division of labor. Often well trained and highly skilled. Often manipulators	Professional conduct of generals and soldiers in military organizations demanding discipline and submission with specific rules for propaganda and image making. Often well trained and highly skilled. Often manipulated manipulators
VICTIMS	Same as terrorism	Same as terrorism	Same as terrorism

Selection: random, vague, and inconsistent, no discernible pattern	Selection: captive limited target groups	Selection: captive total population, everyone a potential victim
Wait-and-see attitude	Quick, limited response, often through manoeuvers, tricks, and without moral scruples	Ambivalent reaction according to political conviction and/or gravity of threat
Attempted exploitation of terrorist's self-destructive tendencies (give enough rope to hang)	Attempted deals and short-range accommodations, limited submission, or escape attempts, frequently, long-range accommodation and submission	Short-range escape attempts or "inner" escape by demonstrative apathy; different coping devices depending on degree and duration of "total institution"; frequently long-range accommodation, submission, and conversion (joining)
Ridicule and faked submission	Indignation and disgust	Indignation and disgust, sometimes changing to resignation or enthusiasm

---

*According to Karl Mannheim, a distinction is to be made between functional rationality, referring to the appropriate relationship between ends and means, and substantive rationality, referring to the "appropriateness" of ends.

**M.O.: modus operandi, method of procedure.

Since he assumed power, an estimated 50,000 to 250,000 of the 10 million Ugandans have disappeared. The corpses of the vanished are often found in rivers and remote places, mutilated and with their skulls cracked. On Amin's orders, all prisoners are tortured; and in the blood-drenched cells of his capital's jails, some inmates are forced to kill their fellow prisoners with large sledge hammers, to cut out pieces of their bodies, to eat the human flesh, or to stuff the severed genitals into their mouths. Reports of coerced cannibalism and other heinous tortures reach the outside world only because the prison guards, as corrupt as they are brutal, permit an occasional prisoner to bribe his way to freedom.

Idi Amin, who often surprises and directs the killings personally, also has a special way of treating his foreign ministers. Michael Ondoga, head of the powerful Christian Lugbara tribe, had been an early supporter of Amin's regime and so was given the crucial post of foreign minister. Soon, however, Amin dismissed him; Ondoga's body was found floating in the Nile. Thousands of his tribe were killed by firing squads in the subsequent purge; others were shot in the knees, doused with gasoline, and set on fire; still others were tossed alive into the Nile to be devoured by crocodiles.

The foreign minister's post was subsequently conferred upon Princess Elizabeth, oldest daughter of King Rodici of Toro, one of Uganda's four tribal kingdoms. The tall, beautiful former model had earned a law degree from Cambridge and was Uganda's first African woman barrister. She gave up her thriving movie career to serve Amin after he came to power, but she had a tough time explaining his erratic conduct. In November 1974, she was abruptly relieved of her office, accused by Amin of having had sexual relations with a white imperialist emissary in a public toilet during a fifteen-minute stopover at Orly Airport. The princess denied the allegation, claiming she would not do such a thing, and that it would have been impossible under the circumstances. Idi Amin had himself photographed with the princess when she was in her seventh month of pregnancy, presumably by him. But when he celebrated the fourth anniversary of his ascent to power, he had a nude picture of his mistress-minister published in the Ugandan papers to draw attention to the ingrate and as a warning to girls not to sell themselves.

In the international arena, Big Daddy has granted diplomatic recognition to a Scottish "government in exile" that is unknown to the rest of the world. Since Idi Amin had in the past offered himself as a peace emissary to terminate the Vietnam War and straighten out the Middle East conflict, it was not surprising that in a letter to Queen Elizabeth II he recently announced his intention to visit Britain on an official mission to advise Irish, Scottish, and other British subjects on how best to gain independence from the mother country by seizing North Sea oil deposits.

A scathing report issued by the investigating International Commission of Jurists noted that the rule of law in Uganda had completely broken down. The army and special police forces, particularly Big Daddy's personal goon squad of 3,000 (called the Public Safety Unit), the worst-trained and best-paid security force in the world, were completely out of control. This ignorant rabble in uniform tortures, loots, rapes, robs, and kills arbitrarily, without discipline or restriction. According to Amnesty International,* the atrocities committed under Amin far exceed those commonly committed under his predecessor both in brutality and in extent.

Trials are rare in Uganda, and when they occur, they take place in secret. Judges who are considered too lenient are removed and mutilated. Uganda's chief justice disappeared without a trace, as did Kamba, the Ugandan ambassador to West Germany, right after a reception given in his honor. Uganda's foreign population never knows what to expect next; the 6,000

---

*An international organization to work for the release and comfort of any person who is in prison or otherwise similarly restrained merely as a result of holding or expressing a religious, political, or other opinion that does not advocate violence.

British and 1,000 American residents are virtual hostages. Uganda is gripped by fear and practically bankrupt, but its impulsive ruler remains popular with his people. His rambling speeches, such as a recent one in which he announced ambitions to extend his country's borders, are wildly cheered by the same enthusiastic crowds who applauded the mass deportation of foreigners and citizens and the racial excesses against Asians and Europeans. His local African supporters do not share in the worldwide condemnation of Amin; they do not care if Ugandan atrocities undermine the moral justification of fighting the unjust racial system of the South African whites. Some observers believe that Amin's openly displayed insanity is at least part playacting; possibly, he's crazy like a fox. Amin says about himself: "They think I am mad, but I am not. I am very intelligent."[4] But mental illness does not preclude intelligence or cunning. Amin blackmailed the British foreign minister into a state visit to Uganda by reprieving British lecturer D. C. Hills, whom he had arbitrarily condemned to death. Amin concluded that this action proved that he is not insane. Does it?

Crazy Terrorist from Below: The Alphabet Bomber

In 1974, in Los Angeles, a man calling himself Isaac Rasim repeatedly announced in phone calls and tape recordings that the name of his Aliens of America organization would be spelled out in unforgettable fashion. The Alphabet Bomber, as he was dubbed, had issued no idle threat. He started with A for "airport," and bombs exploded at Los Angeles International, killing three people.

    The police were certain that Isaac Rasim was the same person as Yugoslav immigrant and hydraulic engineer Muharem Kurbegovic, who was followed, observed speaking into a tape recorder, and arrested at a Hollywood hamburger stand, where he had deposited the recording. In spite of seemingly persuasive evidence, Kurbegovic, who feels himself unjustly persecuted because of an alleged sexual offense, denies any responsibility for the bombing—in writing. He speaks only when he is Isaac Rasim; Mu, as he is known to his co-workers, claims to be a mute. He registered as such in 1967 when emigrating to the United States from British Columbia, and he has never said a word at his place of work, nor has he talked since being arrested. He communicates instead by expressive gestures and rapidly hand-printed messages. Mu explains his affliction as a result of abuse of his mother by Yugoslavian secret police when she was pregnant with him; he adds that he himself was abused as a boy during the Nazi occupation of his country.

Mu's last employer, concerned about the speech defect of his capable engineer, offered to send him to a specialist for diagnosis and treatment. Mu was grateful for the offer but refused. From jail, Mu wrote a letter to his former boss, begging for help in locating a lawyer who could convince the court that Mu could and should defend himself. I was consulted about how to handle this request, and I offered to see the accused bomber.

According to newspaper accounts and court reports Kurbegovic was indoctrinated in a Communist youth camp. He studied mechanical engineering in Sarajevo, Yugoslavia, then fled from what he considered intolerable Communist oppression to West Germany by hiding under a lorry. He continued his studies in Munich and earned a degree in hydraulic engineering, then emigrated to Canada. In Munich, he had sought medical treatment for self-inflicted head injuries. He had hit himself repeatedly and vehemently because of bothersome thoughts he could not get rid of any other way. He consulted a psychiatrist, who diagnosed him as brain damaged and mentally ill.

After living and working in Canada for several years, he legally emigrated to the United States, which he considered a safe anti-Communist haven. In spite of his muteness, he was gainfully employed in good positions. The conscientious engineer was well liked by his bosses and co-workers; friendly, shy Mu, who was ultrasensitive to noises, particularly the barking of dogs, had many acquaintances but hardly any close associates. Nobody at work knew about his private life. He visited taxi dance halls with compulsive frequency, and the dancing girls (to whom he did speak) were his only close friends. He took them out, bought them presents, and would live with first one and then another. But the relationships never lasted long.

In March 1971, Kurbegovic was arrested on charges of lewd conduct in the rest room of a taxi dance hall. Serving as his own attorney, he stood trial in the municipal court of Judge Alan G. Campbell. Not only did he speak well enough to be permitted to defend himself, he won acquittal and a dismissal of the charge.

In December 1971, he filed an application for a police permit to operate his own dance hall. In the subsequent hearing, he compared taxi dancers to clergymen, psychiatrists, and other members of the helping professions. He described the prospective customers of his dance hall as patients for whom he would make "nurses" available. His application was denied on the asserted grounds of his prior arrest.

Kurbegovic was outraged but didn't communicate his indignation to anybody. He began to suspect that a powerful Mafia might possibly have perverted the sacred principles of American justice. How else could it be explained that he was denied his request when he had been acquitted of the past charges? He still would not give up his fervent belief in the principles of America, so he decided to give the system just one more chance. After fulfilling the residency requirements, he made application for American citizenship. He was routinely investigated, lewd conduct arrest was discovered, and he was told that he would have to wait until further investigations could be completed. The former paranoid suspicions rigidified to paranoid convictions. Surely godless communism, hypocritical Christianity, and the Mafia must be responsible for all his troubles.

Terrorism stems from the experience of remediable injustice; Mu is convinced that he has suffered terrible injustice because he is an alien charged with a sexual offense of which he was cleared. He believes he also knows the remedy: fire, blood, and bombs. The police allege that in November 1973, Kurbegovic set fire to three different locations: the homes of three commissioners who denied his application. In June 1973, there was an unsuccessful attempt to bomb the car of one of the commissioners. On July 4, 1974, another three fires were set; and in a telephone call to a local radio station, Isaac Rasim introduced himself as a member of the SLA and threatened three more explosions in the same area where the fires had broken out. The next day, the first tape cassette was discovered outside the Los Angeles Times Building. The speaker, who said he was the leader of a powerful military group, Aliens of America, announced that he would take over the government of the world if the immigration and naturalization laws of the United States were not abolished and if the United States did not deal with Russia in a more decisive manner. In five more taped messages during the following two weeks, threats were made that highly dangerous nerve gas would be put on postage stamps and that a major bomb would be exploded at a location signifying each letter of the group's name.

On August 6, 1974, a bomb exploded in locker T223 at Los Angeles International, causing panic, considerable damage, and the deaths of three people. Subsequently, it was determined that Aliens of America, of which Rasim claimed to be the leader, did not exist except in the imagination of Mu.

Before Kurbegovic could be brought to trial for the charges that he denies, it was necessary to determine legally whether he was presently sane and able to understand the nature of the proceedings against him and to cooperate rationally with his defense. Four psychiatrists examined him and testified that in their opinion, he was mentally deranged to such an extent that he was not able to cooperate with his defense. (I did not participate in this phase of the proceedings.)

The district attorney did not call on any psychiatric witnesses. He described Kurbegovic, who had made a bizarre escape attempt during the trial, as an imposter and a fake, seeking to escape punishment.

Contrary to the unanimous psychiatric testimony, the jury unanimously found Kurbegovic legally sane and perfectly able to stand trial. The presiding judge overturned the verdict and sent Kurbegovic to Atascadero, a maximum security institution of the California Department of Mental Health, for further examination.

Criminal Terrorist from Above: The Benefactor

Among terrorists from above, outright crazies are rare, but there is no scarcity of individuals who, because of their consistent selfishness and their long criminal careers before advancing to terrorism, can safely be called criminals. Rafael Trujillo, dictator of the Dominican Republic for thirty-one years, was a thief, pimp, informer, and convicted forger before he became the benefactor of the people, genius of peace, savior of the country, protector of workers, and father of all Dominicans, as his people had to call him. A prime example of the criminal terrorist from above, Trujillo ended his career in the trunk of an abandoned car near the Dominican capital, his mutilated body a testament to three decades of dictatorial rule.

Trujillo privately owned monopolies in tobacco, oil, salt, beer, meat, milk, matches, cocoa, cement, drugs, iron, imports, shipping, air travel, insurance, and all mass media. But he left the country with 40 percent of the population unemployed, 65 percent illiterate, and 68 percent with a yearly income below $200; he also left 1,887 Trujillo monuments. The last secret balloting yielded 256,423 votes for Trujillo; invalid and not voting: none; votes against Trujillo: none.

A devout family man, Trujillo was industrious, hard working, healthy, and endowed with a good memory and excellent organizational capabilities. He was not at all the megalomaniac, sadistic monster described by his opponents, nor was he mentally ill. In truth, he was something much more dangerous: a perfectly normal common criminal.

Criminal Terrorist from Above: The Intuitive Photographer

The island of Cyprus is called Macaria ("the beatific" or "the lucky"). Yet, like the island of Ireland, it has been a historical battlefield, drenched with the blood of Phoenicians and Persians, Greeks and Romans since the beginning of recorded history. The last Phoenician descendant, Marc Antonio Bragadino, killed 8,000 attacking Ottomans before he himself was skinned alive.

Seven hundred years after Richard the Lion-Hearted, the first British conqueror of the island and later a famous hostage, Cyprus became British again in the twentieth century. (Cyprus was annexed in 1914 and made a crown colony in 1925.) However, Greek-inspired terroristic activity made the costs of maintaining British rule prohibitive in terms of effort and human lives. Under the pressure of world opinion favoring independence for Cyprus, the British withdrew, yielding the island to increased mutual terrorism and massacres by Cypriot Greeks, who made up 80 percent of the population, and Cypriot Turks, the other 20 percent.

The independent government of Greek Archbishop Makarios, established after near civil war, maintained an uneasy peace. The Greeks threatened to incorporate the island (*enosis*), and the Turks planned an invasion to protect the oppressed Turkish minority.

In July 1974, the Greek military dictatorship, which had eliminated terrorism and all opposition in their own country by a totalitarian regime of terror, gave the signal for the beginning of a long-planned operation. A Greek general, together with ten high Greek officers, commanded the Greek expeditionary corps on Cyprus to liquidate President Makarios, who managed to flee the country, although his death had been officially announced. The seat of government was occupied by Greek troops, and more than 1,000 civilians were arrested.

The Athens dictators installed their strongman, Nicholas Sampson, as Makarios's successor. The assumption of power by the notorious criminal and Turk killer, who vowed to reunite Cyprus with Greece, was the last straw for Turkey. When Turkish paratroopers landed on Cyprus, the Athens government, having lost American support, was helpless to resist the invasion. The advancing Turkish armies, presumably intervening for the protection of the oppressed Turkish minority, killed or drove out the Greek Cypriot population in occupied territories, creating a major refugee problem. Sampson was removed; his rule had lasted only nine days.

Nicos Sampson, who had adopted the English-sounding name of the biblical strongman, is the archetype of the criminal terrorist who, after a long career in ordinary street crime and terrorism from below, became ruler and wielder of terror from above. He felt that his actions had been of the sort to put him in good company:

> I fought for my country. I was a good fighter. But haven't the British and the Germans fought for their country? Why does nobody call them killers? The British, who call me killer today, have shouted with joy when French Maquis killed the Germans. And what did Churchill say when a German invasion threatened? He just asked his people to massacre the Germans, if necessary with knives and with stones. Was he a killer, a terrorist?[5]

Immediately after assuming power, Sampson had ordered large-scale killings, arrests, and torture of his opponents. He considered the manufacture and propagation of appropriate justifications his most pressing governmental task. He masterminded an elaborate mass media campaign to convince the gullible world that his kind of torture was only retaliatory and preventive. His followers, on crutches and wearing large bandages, paraded in front of television cameras, explaining in colorful interviews how they had been tortured and beaten by members of the former establishment. A few minutes later, they were observed singing, drinking, and joking—without their crutches or bandages. They had simply disguised themselves as victims in order to justify the violence that they had already started. Tools of torture and weapons presumably captured from the opponents were displayed to be used against the former "oppressors" with double ferocity to show them how it feels to be tortured.

Sampson had been a ruthless and calculating killer even before he became a devout follower of the Greek freedom movement and assistant of terrorist General Georgios Grivas. Sampson ostensibly worked for the Cyprus *Times,* and his instinct for knowing when some sensational event might happen seemed uncanny. The explanation for his mysterious intuition was simple enough: He perpetrated the atrocities himself. From the very start, he made his murders pay off for him by photographing them and selling the pictures to the international press.

In Ledra Street in downtown Nicosia, rechristened Murder Mile, Sampson had shot numerous British soldiers in the back. Eventually, he was caught and sentenced to death for twenty-five murders. After serving seventeen months in jail, however, he was freed under a general amnesty. He became a subleader of EOKA, the Greek freedom movement, and chief of its execution commando, killing not only British enemies but also Greek traitors, whose corpses he plundered for his own benefit or for that of the freedom movement. His most spectacular deed was the liberation of Igor Gaxis, second in command of the Greek freedom movement, who had been imprisoned by the British. When Cyprus became independent, Sampson wanted to be included in the government; but Makarios, whose enemies Sampson had promised to eliminate for generations to come did not trust the *trelos* ("crazy guy").

During the civil war with the Turkish Cypriots, Sampson boasted of personally having killed at least

200 Turkish women and children. The photographs of
the so-called Butcher of Amofita, showing the murdered children of Turkish Major Nehaot Itan, were
circulated around the world. Sampson cashed in on the
publicity he had arranged for the atrocities he had
performed, which in turn raised the cash value of his
personality. Sampson founded a newspaper called
Marque ("battle"), an extreme rightist sheet for which
he solicited paid advertisements through violence or
the threat of violence. Hardly anybody in Cyprus
could afford to refuse his offers. In his car there were
always two machine guns, and he was accompanied
by two bodyguards. He attempted to impress female
companions by shooting dogs from his car, just to stay
in practice. A Greek acquaintance said about him:
"Omfo [Sampson] has the brain of a child. He is not
wise and is unhesitating in everything he does."[6]

The brutal killer with the mind of a child, erst-
while professional assassin for money and publicity,
and passionate terrorist became the chief of a terror
regime installed by another terror regime. He was president for a short time only, but had he lasted longer,
he undoubtedly would have eradicated terrorism from
below by a strong, popular, patriotic, no-nonsense law-
and-order regime.

Copycats

Crusading terrorists, like their spiritual ancestors the
Crusaders, form the vanguard of terrorism. They are
the widely visible, glamorous examples to be imitated
or joined by the crazies and the criminals.

Criminals do not have much of a cause (except
their own enrichment or aggrandizement), and they
are not rebels but conformists, products of the existing
order, in which they have a function and within which
they make a comfortable living. Their mission is not
very noble, but it compensates for what it lacks in
distinction by a sort of universality; after all, nearly
everybody is imbued with the "normal" righteousness
of egotism.

Motivated by personal gain, criminals become followers and copycats of the crusaders and their tactics. They sometimes become bogus idealists, seizing the opportunity to pursue their profitable business under the cover of an all-justifying cause. There is a substantial time lapse, however, before the models and patterns of the fanatics are adopted by the disturbed and the greedy who join and imitate but do not start their own trends.

Skyjacking is one example of a crime invented by crusading terrorists and copied by those who could more accurately be described as crazy or criminal. The modern fashion of skyjacking was initiated by ideologically motivated, crusading terrorists. Between 1945 and 1950, numerous acts of air piracy, usually in the course of group escapes from countries behind the Iron Curtain, took place. In the airlift to Berlin in 1953, hundreds of thousands of flights to the beleagured city were organized and highly publicized as a spectacular defense of freedom. Then came the mass exodus of anti-Castro Cubans (by boat and all kinds of available vehicles, among them skyjacked planes) to the United States, followed from 1961 on by enforced detours in the opposite direction. The perpetrators of air piracy from the United States to Cuba were duly labeled criminals, traitors and thieves, but those who came from Cuba to the United States in exactly the same manner were described as liberation fighters. Soon the methods of these seekers of political asylum were imitated by criminals.

Criminal Terrorist from Below: The Individualist

D. B. Cooper, a highly competent criminal loner, was a typical follower who started a new fashion. The crazy act of twenty-six-year-old Canadian Paul Joseph Cini had made headlines in 1971 and initiated a more dangerous kind of skyjacking than the comparatively harmless enforced changes of destination that had been in vogue. On board a Canadian aircraft, Cini, who claimed to be a member of the Irish Republican Army (IRA), demanded a parachute and $1.5 million, threatening to blow up the aircraft if his demands were not met. Cini seemed extremely disturbed and upset; he confused a safety belt with a parachute and was overwhelmed without much difficulty. Yet his exploit was widely publicized and sensationally reported by the mass media.

Two weeks later, D. B. Cooper duplicated the deed with professional perfection. The conservatively dressed forty-year-old demanded $200,000 and four parachutes, suggesting that he might force some of the passengers to jump with him. When the plane landed in Seattle, he released all thirty-six passengers and retained only one hostess as hostage. Then, after receiving the loot and giving the pilot exact flight instructions, he jumped from the plane over Washington State and disappeared. In spite of intensive searches, Cooper has never been found.

Overnight, the daring adventure became a popular legend, and the mysterious Cooper became a minor folk hero. Bowling alleys announced D. B. Cooper sweepstakes, and shirts were sold with the inscription "D. B. Cooper, the only way to fly." But there were those who became outraged; one pilot even threw the bullet-ridden corpse of a twenty-four-year-old who had attempted a skyjacking out of his plane. Los Angeles Police Chief Davis suggested installment of portable gallows at airports so that skyjackers, after summary trial and sentencing, could be hanged on arrival.

Cooper's act, imitated five times during the following week and dozens of times thereafter, introduced a spate of skyjackings featuring the taking of hostages, extortion of ransom, and parachute jumps. This novel style of skyjacking not only provided an outlet for the disturbed and the bored by affording catharsis for feelings of protest and revenge but also was great entertainment for the public. And it was profitable.

Criminal Terrorists from Below: Syndicates and Families

Most criminal terrorist activities are performed, not by individuals, but by groups that are at times so well organized for highest profit that what started as terrorism from below becomes terror from above.

In the United States, criminals interested in their own enrichment discovered the establishment's hypocrisy and vulnerability long before the revolutionaries or the flower children. They also discovered that tight organization is the secret of business success in the modern world, whether that business is legitimate or illegitimate. Organized criminals are neither idealists nor moralists. They are realists, and they mean business, aiming for maximum return on minimum investment. They deal in gambling, prostitution, labor racketeering, narcotics, or anything else that makes money, just as other syndicates deal in cigarettes, alcohol, sugar, oil, and similar commodities. By supplying highly desired consumer goods, organized crime fills the gap left by the establishment's reluctance openly to provide satisfaction for those strong public needs that are officially disapproved and denounced as illicit and immoral.

Organized crime does not overtly fight big business; it imitates big business, working toward alliances and deals that define mutual toleration and each other's territorial integrity. Crime syndicates do not want to change the weaknesses of human nature; rather, they seek to exploit these weaknesses for their own material benefit. Therefore, they cater to and reinforce vanity, greed, and corruption to take all the better advantage of their partners' and victims' vulnerability.

Organized criminals profit from the existing social order. They are conformists to society's ultimate goals, deviating only in their use of legally forbidden means. These criminals do not want to overthrow the establishment; they want to make accommodations and profitable deals with vested interests in order to acquire vested interest. They have no cause except that of their own profit. Although they exploit the crusading and gambling proclivities of others, organized criminals usually are not crusaders or gamblers themselves. They prefer, not to bomb, but to bribe police officers, judges, and officials. They know that the reputation for respectability is the best cover for illicit operations and that apparent legality is the best way to hide and organize illegality.

Within the larger society, crime syndicates are terrorists from below; but in terms of their internal structure, they are organizations of terror from above. They demand blind obedience, unquestioning loyalty, and total dedication from their members, who in return can expect total protection, legal aid, insurance, heroes' funerals, and a strong sense of belonging to a family. Everything is permissible in the family's service; only the mortal sin of disloyalty cannot be forgiven. Actual, potential, and suspected traitors are mercilessly executed as punishment, warning, and example.

The boss, father, papa-pope, God, and godfather is totally ruthless, unrestrained, and cruel toward all outsiders; but to his loyal family members he is the kindly, caring, concerned, paternalistic protector. Overt violence is necessary in the power struggle to establish the regime; when firmly entrenched, terror from above prefers to use attention-getting aggression sparingly and selectively. Once the irresistible striking power of the organization and the helplessness of the potential victims are accepted as facts of life, occasional spectacular reminders are sufficient to maintain domination by terror, which employs threats, hints, or even innuendos instead of naked violence. The more entrenched the terror regime, the more it can afford to replace force with politeness because the terror victims and terror objects cannot afford to refuse any offers.

Bloody gang killings characterize the early-competition phases of actual warfare between rival terror regimes; after supremacy is established in a conquered territory, the real work of the terroristic businesslike organization and criminal governmentlike administration for producing and increasing profits can start. Jurisdictional and territorial agreements are concluded with the authorities, who are given a piece of the action for looking away and not interfering with the syndicate's sovereignty. Target groups and individuals made docile by fear, intimidated by bombings, burnings, killings, and other spectacular acts, are more than willing to accept the lesser evil of paying a tax or a protection fee to the outlaws, who simultaneously provide both the need for and the guarantee of protection. The gangster's most effective weapon is terror propaganda, which advertises the organization's striking ability and success in order to obtain the cooperation of the authorities and the compliance of terror victims and objects. If the use of crude violence becomes necessary, professional executioners, who often do not know their victims, carry out their orders without inhibition while the responsible crime directors, usually far away, never bloody their hands.

This kind of criminal terrorism is well organized and strictly confined to reasonable targets: their own people or competitors, plus occasional spectacular warnings and examples that serve rational (i.e., financially lucrative) purposes. Cruel calculation, rather than rage or hatred, determines the bureaucratically planned and administered actions of the organized criminals. Kidnapping, extortion, the taking, exchanging, and killing of hostages belong to their ordinary repertoire. But since collusion and cooperation with the authorities are necessary for the profitable operation of mob enterprises, certain limits are never overstepped. Clever operators, putting business success above all other considerations, will not jeopardize their profits and their existence by making exaggerated demands or by arousing too much public indignation. The mobsters never openly demand the release of convicts, nor do they defiantly call for radical changes in prison systems or alterations of the social structure. They respect the sovereignty of those from whom they want similar respect. They will not openly interfere with the authorities' business because they do not want any interference with their own. They are very easy to get along with if they are left alone to do their criminal business, which consists of making enormous profits from stimulating and gratifying the demand for consumer goods not sufficiently provided or adequately distributed by the morally inhibited, although clandestinely indulgent, establishment.

High prices are paid not just for ordinary commodities but for alluring images and exciting fantasies. Gangland's most precious homegrown merchandise is glamorous danger and dangerous glamour, kicks and thrills for entertainment and as a way of life. In a drab and dreary world, the gangster bosses and their families offer simple conduct models and impressive opportunities for identification. Surrounded by a well-advertised old-fashioned halo of romantic heroism, the mobsters manufacture, sell, and represent excitement, unconditional dedication, and the adventure of risky action, together with appropriate justifications. Their most brutal deeds, performed without qualms because they serve the higher cause of family loyalty, are applauded, envied, and imitated by the disenchanted and alienated. Terrorism from below turned into terror from above is good business for the terrorists, good consolation and vicarious gratification for the immature and irresponsible, and when observed from a distance, good family entertainment for everybody, terrorists and terrorized alike.

Crusaders

Aggressive youngsters and perpetrators of apparently motiveless violence used to be called "rebels without a cause." Recently, some of these alienated juveniles have found a cause to channel and justify their uncontrollable aggression; they swell the ranks of the crusading terrorists, who are rebels with a cause.

Motivated by unselfish ideals, crusaders are the real terrorists, the genuine article. Crusading terrorists from above justify their existence as an antidote to terrorism from below. They may be czars or kings or inquisitors, but more often they are the former terrorists from below who came to power by means of the very terrorist tactics they now try to obliterate. Thus it is that terror from above incites further terrorism from below, which in turn sometimes serves as training for future terror from above.

Stalin robbed banks to finance Bolshevik terrorism before he became dictator and practiced state terror;

many Nazi bomb throwers later became police chiefs, governors, and high government security officers when their party came to power. Several veterans of the Chinese Long March, of the Cuban Revolution, and of Third World uprisings now occupy security positions or perform high government functions either nationally or internationally. The leader of the Mau Mau terrorist campaign in Kenya, which was unusually cruel and grotesquely brutal even by terrorist standards, occupies a high place in the cabinet of his country's president, Jomo Kenyatta. Menachem Begin, brilliant theoretician and practitioner of Irgun terrorism against the Arabs and British during the British mandate in Palestine, became the respected leader of the Israeli rightist opposition in Israel's parliament, the Knesset. Algeria's Bouteflika was a member of the FLN (Front de Libération Nationale), whose motto was "My Brothers, do not kill only, but mutilate your adversaries, pierce their eyes, cut off their arms, and hang them," before he became foreign minister and president of the UN General Assembly, where he gave Yasir Arafat, the terrorist leader of the Palestine Liberation Organization (PLO) and provisional head of the as-yet-nonexistent Palestinian state, a hero's welcome. Totalitarian dictators like Hitler and Stalin, African tyrants and despots, South American fascist and Eastern European Communist regimes, Spanish and Greek generals, South African and Third World rulers are all examples of crusading terrorists from above, their unifying cause being the suppression of terrorism from below.

The crusading rebels and revolutionaries who oppose them have made terrorism the international issue that it is today. From all over the world, they demand recognition and justice by their growing numbers and increasingly sophisticated methods. We must not be deaf to their voices, or we will surely continue to hear their bombs.

2

Terrorists
with a Cause

A specter is haunting the world, the specter of international terrorism. During one week, members of the Japanese United Red Army raided the French embassy in The Hague. A man wearing a South Vietnamese army uniform hijacked a plane; when the pilot refused to fly to Hanoi, he blew it up, killing all seventy-one people on board, including himself. In Northern Ireland, the IRA (Irish Republican Army) killed two judges, one in the presence of his daughter. In Paris, a young man threw a hand grenade, killing two and injuring thirty-four. And in Argentina, a businessman and a chauffeur were killed, and two other businessmen were kidnapped. That was in September 1974 at about the same time that, according to the Institute for the Study of Conflicts in London, at least eighty-six extremist movements were operating around the world. Some of these groups, which reflect innumerable nuances of radical views ranging from anarchist to neofascist, have several thousand members; others, only a hundred or less.

At the end of 1975, six terrorists of mixed nationalities, among them one woman, probably German, invaded the Vienna headquarters of the Organization of Petroleum Exporting Countries (OPEC) and took sixty hostages, including eleven oil ministers from Arab countries, after killing three guards and officials. In the same week, three masked gunmen shot and killed an American CIA official in Athens; 500 left-wing urban guerrillas attacked an army arsenal in Buenos Aires, and one hundred of the guerrillas were killed in the subsequent battle with the Argentine army, bringing the death toll in Argentina close to 1,000 for 1975.

Neither the escalation of terroristic violence without end in sight, nor the now-regular participation of women in such violence, cause any surprise. In 1971, glamorous Lila Khaled had been a unique sensation as the only prominent female in terroristic skyjacking, an activity up to then reserved for men only. The grotesque slayings of Sharon Tate and her friends had shocked the world; the active participation of the "Manson girls" in acts of such ferocious brutality was acknowledged with incredulity and even a sense of unreality because women were not believed capable of such extravagant excesses of aggression. Since then, the participation of women in leading or supporting roles in all forms of crazy, criminal, or crusading terrorism has escalated to become almost commonplace. Several important SLA (Symbionese Liberation Army) members were female; the leader of the Japanese Red Army is reported to be a woman; the West German anarchist Baader-Meinhof group was led by Ulrike Meinhof and had many women members, one of them, Angela Luther, still at large; both would-be assassins of President Ford were women; and one of the six guerrillas attacking OPEC in Vienna, a petite teen-age girl (described as looking less than twenty), shot an Austrian police officer.

All over the world, women are clamoring for an authentic identity of their own; they refuse to remain confined within the narrow and oppressive role definitions imposed upon them by exploitative or thoughtless men. In the context of their rising identity expectations, the "virtues" of flexible submission and comfortable dependency become the vices of spineless passivity and cowardly helplessness. No violent terroristic act has been performed specifically to advertise or further the cause of women's liberation, but women obviously are increasingly willing and even eager to release their long-pent-up frustration and rage in the service of causes that permit them to assert their equal claim to symbols of liberation and to a fair share of terroristic action.

Until very recently, all available evidence indicated that terrorism has international links but no global organization; the conspiracy theories of the terrorized have some basis in reality. In Dublin in 1973, the Sinn Fein arranged a widely advertised festival of international solidarity with the struggle of the Irish people, intended to attract representatives of terrorist groups from all over the world. The much-ballyhooed anti-imperialist rally simply fizzled out. Nevertheless, from 1973 on, a loosely connected network of mutual aid and technical assistance has existed among various terrorist groups. Palestinian training programs attracted apprentice terrorists from Western Europe, Japan, Scandinavia, and the United States. The IRA, operating in Northern Ireland and in England, maintains close ties with the Basque separatist group in Spain responsible for the killing of Spanish Prime Minister Carrero Blanco. Four thousand South American guerrilla groups have allegedly created a junta for revolutionary coordination.

At a secret convention in Trieste, Italy, in 1974, various ethnic groups, including Croats, Corsicans, Basques, Irish, and Welsh, met with representatives of terrorist organizations. In mid-1975, the French connection linking terrorist groups with several foreign intelligence services of certain sovereign nations was discovered after the successful flight of terrorist Carlos, who ran a Paris clearing-house for liberation movements including the Uruguayan Tupamaros, the Canadian Liberation Front, Ireland's IRA, Germany's Baader-Meinhof people, Japan's Red Army, Yugoslavia's

Croatian Separatists, Turkey's Liberation Front, and Lebanon's Palestinians.

In all probability, Carlos surfaced again in the attack on OPEC in Vienna in December 1975. Some hostages identified him from photographs; others did not recognize the pudgy Latin American leader of the coup as "the Jackal" (the nickname given by the British press to Carlos, "the most wanted terrorist in the world").[1] Venezuelan-born Carlos (whose true name is Ilitch Ramirez Sanchez, after Lenin's middle name, Ilitch), son of a Colombian lawyer, trained at Moscow's Patrice Lumumba International Friendship University, acquired some of his international connections as an attractive playboy in London before he became the terrorist leader who is credited with planning and attempting to execute the killing of Jewish leaders all over the world and, aside from conducting the attack on the French embassy in The Hague, collaborating on the massacre at Israel's Lod Airport, participating in various bombings in Paris and London, and in all likelihood engineered the OPEC caper.

The Vienna raid, whether planned and led by Carlos or by somebody who resembled him, and many other recent terroristic episodes indicate growing solidarity among the comrades in terrorism wherever they may be. Arrangements for mutual aid and comfort are bound to multiply as terrorism spreads and becomes ever more successful. Even the most diverse terrorist groups consider themselves engaged in a common struggle, although not necessarily against the same enemy. They will continue to provide weapons for each other, to train each other's recruits, and on occasion to serve as hired guns for each other; they will also continue to function as agents for superpowers and their satellites. So far, this limited system of mutual cooperation based on a feeling of comradeship has not grown into a tight organization with a common platform, a common strategy, or an integrated command structure. In all likelihood, a terrorist international does not exist as yet.

Crusading terrorism's purposes are always the same, but like fashions, the preferred methods change, strongly influenced by mass media requirements for novelty, variety, and ingeniousness. The vast discrepancy between the giant terroristic image exaggerated by fear and the comparative insignificance of terroristic reality is a measure of the terrorists' success and is precisely the reality that they want to produce. In this reality, mighty governments have to negotiate and compromise, an inordinate amount of social and security resources have to be diverted for protection against terrorist attacks, convicts may have to be released or ransom paid, and law enforcement can be forced to abandon its function and can be discredited, ridiculed, and best of all (from the terrorists' viewpoint), humiliated. The Robin Hood type of terrorism, extorting money from the rich and powerful (countries, companies, families) and redistributing the wealth to the poor, is an overt attempt to gain the sympathy and support of the masses, who are everywhere poor and potentially greedy. Terrorism then can assume a moralistic stance, representing itself as the harbinger of a new era that will replace an old order which proves unable to satisfy man's legitimate needs and can no longer claim to be moral in terms of consciousness and purpose. Crusading terrorism aims to redefine radically the material and transcendental needs for community and morality that culminate in the ardent desire for identity.

Modern terrorism from below is varied and multifaceted. In South America it is directed against oppressive national governments; in the Third World, against colonial regimes and their vestiges; in Ireland, against fellow Irish of different religious faiths and against the British oppressor; in the Middle East, and exported from there to Western Europe, against the state of Israel and all Zionist allies and sympathizers around the world. Basques, Croats, Puerto Ricans, Armenians, Greek Cypriots, South Moluccans, and Irish strive for national independence; the Palestinians, for a state of their own; Japan's Red Army, Germany's Baader-Meinhof people, and some Palestinians, for global liberation; and all of them, for more justice and for genuine identity, to be proved by exclusive sovereign control over their own territory.

Identity and the Philosophy of Crusading

Identity is the answer to the question "What am I really?" It defines the individual as part of a higher and larger whole. You belong; therefore, you exist. Some individuals, deprived of close emotional ties in childhood, are unable or unwilling to identify with anybody or anything intensively or for long periods of time. Unsatisfied identity needs may be manifested by restless shifts of identity (shopping for identity) or by insatiable hunger for identity expressed in the rage to belong and extreme fanaticism. Some people maintain a lifelong attachment to the same identity; identity Don Juans constantly change their loyalties. Neurotics are often unsure of what they are and to what and to whom they belong; in identity crises, they will reproach themselves for not fulfilling the demands of their identity-inspired role definitions.

Everybody belongs to many natural and acquired communities, and yet identity diffusion or the simultaneous fulfillment of various role definitions is downgraded as a sign of immaturity and an inability to make commitments. Lacking or insufficiently strong identity engagement is denounced as a sin by the identity group and is experienced as guilt by the individual; being condemned to the exile of one's own self, through exclusion or by expulsion from the identity peer group, is considered the worst social disgrace.

Biological "Rights"

Belonging to the human species is a biological fact, but the discovery that such biological belonging confers certain basic rights is a historical and social accomplishment. "Just" claims derive from being part of a community (human, national, racial, sexual, age, and so forth). Social rights and claims transcending mere biological existence stem from such belonging. The human being grows into a real person only as representative of humanity (or nationality) after he becomes aware of his human (national) rights and is at the same time willing to submit to certain restrictions and obligations demanded by the community.

Community will turn into identity if and when belonging to the community is acknowledged as imposing duties and conferring rights. By sacrifice, by the restraint of egoism and narcissism, by postponing and blocking impulse gratification, the human being's biological fate of belonging becomes his cultural achievement of identity.

Identity is the subjective feeling of continuous, developing sameness, the sense of unitary personal existence and at the same time of belonging to a durable, unchangeable, and immortal wholeness. Identity is experienced as a mysterious, supernatural something, a mixture of sensations, sentiments, insights, memories, and certainties. By transcending rationality through identity, one recognizes one's self and is recognized by others. Identity constitutes and creates its own morality, its own beauty ("Black is beautiful"; "Italian is beautiful"), and its own truth.

This certainty of belonging provides not only plausible, moral, and utilitarian justifications but also spiritual inspiration (which is different from mere interest or intellect) for every action and for existence itself.

One's own identity is experienced as great, beautiful, valuable, deep, creative, wonderful, unique; all existing high values are lumped together. Following the pattern of the original mother-child relationship, identity signifies the primary, basic trust in the uniting wholeness that promises healing, complete security, and instant salvation.

Identity is no thing, no location, no substance, no fluid, no independent force or power, no real person or object that exists independent of the wishes, needs, and fantasies of the identity seeker and finder. But identity is a very powerful abstract love object. Every love object's attractiveness is enhanced by the lover's imagination and fantasies. The charisma and significance of the love object are partly in the eyes of the beholder; the lover has projected his or her desires and idealized expectations of self (ego ideal) onto the love object. The need for love has to find the appropriate love object; by the same token, the need for belonging has to find an appropriate identity to which an independent, objective existence can be attributed.

Identity, representing not just what one is but what one's "real self" ought to be, is the remedy for anomie, alienation, and isolation. It provides permission for aggression, liberation from individual responsibility, and satisfaction of the needs to belong and to transcend the self.

Identity expresses a hope for the future based on past memories (or illusions) of a lost paradise that should be restored.

Thus, the subjective feeling of belonging, experienced as genuine, does not necessarily refer to an actual community; it is the other way around. The individuals in need of belonging seek, find, or partly invent those communities and commonalities that gratify their individual dreams and expectations. Individual identity searches often produce the identity, which is experienced as objectively existing.

Slaves do not rebel; they submit. Total slavery is characterized by the slave's lack of recognition that it exists. Rebellions and revolutions occur only when the oppressive conditions have sufficiently improved so that the rebelling groups can become subjectively conscious both of oppression and of the possibilities of throwing off the yoke. Only those who are partly emancipated will demand the end of all oppression.

The recognition of jointly suffered oppression welds isolated, impotent individuals into a potentially powerful unit capable of combating the injustice to which they have been subjected. This, in turn, affects the individual's self-esteem and self-understanding. The old (powerless) self, "me," discovering that just rights have been unjustly withheld, becomes a demanding "me, too" that, in order to acquire the denied rights, produces a new "we" awareness. A strongly positive value is given to the very identity distinctions that formerly served as rationalizations for discrimination and oppression (female, black, Jewish). Through the new "we" feeling, a new individual personality is created, a more powerful and richer "me."

Identity has to be found at all costs, even if it must be imagined or invented. Identity is the device by which individual hopes and desires can be experienced as supraindividually inspired commands and demands. The sum total of individual expectations is projected as communal conscience. The self-image has been elevated to the model of being and becoming; egoistic righteousness and self-aggrandizement have triumphantly returned to their point of origin via the detour of identity.

Privileged groups develop strong identity feelings to protect and defend their inherent, inherited, or acquired rights. But this claim to superiority will provoke uniting identity feelings in other groups, who will regard anybody's privileges that restrict their rights as arbitrary, provocative, and unjust. Identities are based either on the claim of superior strength and virtue, which "naturally" calls for higher rewards, or on the claim that in spite of existing but so-far-unrecognized merits, rewards have been unjustly withheld. Aren't men "really" superior to women? Haven't women "really" been deprived? Hasn't "real" injustice been inflicted by the Jews on the Arabs and by the Arabs on the Jews? Weren't colonizers "really" superior in knowledge, skill, and education? Weren't the colonial people "really" deprived and exploited? Just ask the men and the women, the Arabs and the Israelis, the whites and the blacks, the rulers and the ruled, the entrepreneurs and the workers. No identity group, no matter how large or small, will have any difficulty in staking claims for their legitimate rights and in providing the justifications with which they are satisfied. Identity, they feel, entitles them to use whatever means they deem necessary for the realization and defense of their reasonable demands. In extreme situations, the identity of the privileged is defended by terror, and that of the underprivileged is awakened and realized by terrorism.

The spokesmen and prophets of identity serve to awaken and direct the formerly absent, deficient, or false identity consciousness by constant admonitions, reproaches, appeals, and reminders. The new, correct identity consciousness then provides its own interpretations of the past, in which previously overlooked elements of community are discovered, and supplies a comfortably simplified model of the future as a continuing struggle between the forces of light and darkness, between right and wrong.

The feeling of identity seems to flow from a mystical, eternal belongingness. It is usually not experienced as a response to external threat and danger, but identity does serve to provide prime justification for violence and for regression in the service of aggression. Identity denotes and connotes that community in whose defense aggression can and must be mobilized when threats arise. Even crude violence is always considered fully justified and is soon experienced, not as violence, but as inevitable necessity.

Identity legitimizes aggression customarily denied to the individual, thus liberating him from anxiety, inhibition, and guilt concerning his formerly restrained or repressed aggressive impulses. Terrorists draw their inspiration from the real or imagined experience of remediable injustice. Terrorists from below are injustice collectors who use terror from above as their model and seek remedy for injustice through unrestrained sovereignty and legitimation of all means in the service of their sacred cause. Terrorists are at their most dangerous, not when they behave like children or lunatics, but when they act like sovereign states.

The existence of a shared identity diminishes or eliminates conflicts among the followers through group identification in the service of a cause, cements the group into a coherent whole, and permits precise role definitions and role ascriptions in relation to and in the service of the cause.

The lofty morality of the group code transcends

the narrow boundaries of individual egoism, but only in order to confirm and strengthen the more powerful group egoism that satisfied the hunger for the unlimited exercise of power and stills the thirst for dependent submission. Identity is the group institution and symbol under the cover of which the individual can gratify his most elementary, infantile, and grandiose desires for omnipotence, omniscience, narcissistic satisfaction, and aggressive release. The all-deciding and all-justifying group is often only the concrete product of the member's need to belong; the group ideal to which the members have sworn obedience reflects only their own hopes and fears. They seem to serve a cause, but in fact the cause serves them and their own wishes. They often die in its service, victims of self-deception and puppets of their own illusions and delusions.

Nationalism

Contrary to rational predictions, facilitation of communication, free trade, international travel, and economic interdependence have not led to automatic progress, mutual interdependence, and world peace. All those who stressed the exclusive importance of economic and sociological factors, discounting anthropological and irrational psychological elements, have been wrong. The presumably obsolete, transcendental authorities of tradition and intuition manifested in radical nationalism and radical socialism have shaped and determined our contemporary world more decidedly than the supposedly more progressive forces of tolerance, mutual understanding, and an identity that would embrace the whole human species.

Metaphysically intoxicated barbarians will dominate the world, Heinrich Heine predicted a hundred years ago, and it is indeed nationalistic passions, with or without socialist reforming zeal, that seem predominant all over the globe. In the twentieth century, nationalism, originally elitist and later adopted by the bourgeoisie, grew into mass movements that culminated in demands for political self-determination, cultural independence, and absolute sovereignty. Religious, feudal, and tribal loyalties became less important because of industrialization, urbanization, and mass communication. In a more secular and democratized world, nationalism was transformed into the inspiring, consoling, and activating motivation of the modern have-nots. Although chauvinism belongs to the ideology of establishments that have exploited and humiliated their victims, national identity has become the battle cry of the disinherited and dispossessed, as if the interests of the oppressed were identical to those of the oppressors. Coercion and arbitrariness, resisted by all means available when imposed by foreigners, are accepted and willingly obeyed when exercised by one's own people.

If oppressors and oppressed are united by national identity, compulsion can be labeled a necessary discipline, a requirement of national security, or a condition for liberation and national sovereignty. The newly liberated slaves and emancipated masses who have thrown off the yoke of colonization and foreign oppression are not satisfied with a redistribution of material goods; they want to belong to a sovereign nation and be recognized as free, self-determining human beings. Although nationalism is, of necessity, antiuniversalist, exclusive, and antagonistic, it is often coupled with social identity claims that demand global revolution and worldwide changes in the social structure. The demand for self-determination and freedom of action is combined with the desire to restore national spontaneity and the dignity of simple origins. Nationalism and certain forms of radical socialism often advocate the return to small, "natural," controllable, more human units and express opposition to large, impersonal, anonymous, universal authorities that ignore racial, regional, and individual differences.

Territoriality

National identity claims demand possession of and total sovereign control over a certain territory for obvious practical reasons and in order to express and strengthen the feeling of belonging. The macro-individual nation exerts the same sovereign rights within its territory as the individual within his house, which is his castle; that is, defends it against any outside interference. Yet the needs of one identity for sovereignty and territorial possession necessarily create similar needs among other identities, and these needs must become antagonistic and irreconcilable precisely because they are based on the same structural principle. But there are no more unoccupied territories to satisfy the multiplying demands of identity explosion. The identity claims of the have-nots seeking sovereign control (through use of violence, if necessary) over a territory that belongs to somebody else are as sacred and unnegotiable as the right of the possessor to defend his own sacred soil (also acquired by violence), drenched as it is with the blood of past and present identity comrades.

Sovereignty

Sovereignty, characterized and expressed by control over a certain territory, used to be reserved for the very powerful. Only the largest industrialized nations, the strongest armies, and the most gigantic industrial corporations succeeded up to now in realizing the widely desired monopoly of sovereignty; everybody else was excluded from the club. But today, the general availability of cheap yet sophisticated technological products, the access to instantaneous worldwide communication through the mass media, and the implications of newly found or invented identities have changed all that. Now, nearly everybody can play the power game of sovereignty. The formerly powerless have gained access to power through the systematic use of the weapons of the weak: terrorism, guerrilla warfare, self-sacrifice, and identity. Your identity is not just what you are now but what you really are, that is to what you are entitled.

Identity implies imperative claims to a catalogue of unfulfilled demands. The feeling of belonging makes all the difference when "me" becomes "we." Identity miraculously transforms the egotistical narcissism of the greedy individual into altruistic service for a higher cause, which is, of course, one's own, disguised as a collective concern. Identity imitates and mimics divine, moral, and secular sovereign rights; it is pseudoreligious and quasi-sovereign, the modern opiate and "speed" for the masses, consoling illusion and stimulating activator all at the same time.

Formula for Violence

Aggression by individuals or small groups is, as a rule, restrained and confined by other individuals, by hierarchically higher and more powerful control agencies (state, church, family, and so forth), and last but not least, by the person's mortality. Public safety and general security in any society are guaranteed by the refusal of the collective to grant total sovereignty to any individual. Even in the ideal democracy, in which the individual is or should be free, he is not completely sovereign; there are definite limits to his freedom erected by the interests of others or of the community and by universally accepted, binding values. Established agencies beyond his control will draw the line between license and freedom and will enforce independent judgment on the extent and justification of the individual's aggression for self-assertion and self-defense. But no such limits exist for certain units (such as some states or religions) that represent themselves as infallible, ageless, and immortal, claiming complete sovereignty and the inalienable right to be and to remain the ultimate arbiters in all matters of vital concern.

When the abstract identity of ever smaller groups expresses itself in demands for unrestrained sovereignty and for specific territorial possession, peaceful coexistence of competing identities must end because obviously the territorial claims of one identity can be fulfilled only at the expense of another, which feels itself equally justified and sacred. When belonging to a group assumes the spiritual force of identity, and when simultaneously identity claims can only be satisfied by territorial acquisition or possession, the age of innumerable holy miniwars has started, all of them fought with uncompromising ruthlessness.

Violence becomes uncontrolled in principle and near universal when each individual or small group claims sovereignty and is able to construct a value system justifying its own aggression. This is exactly what is happening now.

The denial of any valid and binding universal morality did not lead to the disappearance or relaxation of morality (or pseudomorality); instead, it led to particularization and fragmentation. No rational, humanistic control took over where religious authority left off; the authoritarian superego was not abolished but broken up, and each part put in uniform.

After God was proclaimed dead, many new national, parochial, provincial, racial, and even private gods, all providing inbuilt justification for aggression and a good conscience for their followers, began competing with each other for supremacy in the Babylonian chaos of nonnegotiable identity claims. Identity is the goal and the holy land of modern crusaders; and identity plus sovereignty plus territoriality is the modern formula for unrestrained violence.

The International Menace

PALESTINE: SPECTACLE IN THE DESERT   The Palestine popular front, under the leadership of Dr. George Habash, was responsible for the coordinated, simultaneous skyjackings of four airplanes in September 1970. The triggering event was the tentative acceptance by Jordan and Egypt of a peace plan worked out by U.S. Secretary of State William Rogers. The Palestinians feared that treacherous Arab governments might conclude peace treaties at the expense of Palestinian national and revolutionary demands.

Right after takeoff, an El Al Airlines 707 from Amsterdam was skyjacked by the so-called Che Guevara Commando, which consisted of the veteran skyjacker Leila Khaled and an accomplice (who was subsequently killed by Israeli security men disguised as stewards). Khaled was wounded, arrested, and detained in London by the British authorities. At the same time, a Pan American World Airways 747 was hijacked shortly after takeoff from Amsterdam on a flight to New York. The plane was directed to Beirut, Lebanon, where the hijackers were joined by a band of armed comrades, including explosives experts who wired the plane for destruction. Fifteen minutes later, a Trans World Airlines 707 was skyjacked right after takeoff from Frankfurt, Germany. Around the same time, a Swissair DC-8 was hijacked right after takeoff from Zurich. The wired Pan American plane was commandeered to Cairo and, after the passengers and crew members had been released, demonstratively blown up. The TWA and Swissair planes were directed to Zorka, a desert airstrip in Jordan, which was transformed into a landing field.

The Popular Front for the Liberation of Palestine had set a seventy-two-hour deadline for the release of terrorists imprisoned in Great Britain, Switzerland, and Germany. Although the Swiss and German governments quickly agreed, the British hesitated; two days later, a BOAC plane was hijacked over the Persian Gulf and forced to land at the Jordanian airstrip alongside the two other airplanes. The plight of the terrified hostages in the unbearable hot planes became increasingly desperate. Great Britain, together with West Germany and Switzerland, yielded. Breaching their own principles of law, they surrendered their convicted or otherwise legally held prisoners, including the just-arrested Leila Khaled, in exchange for the release of the hostages in Jordan. In a supercolossal extravaganza, the Palestinians blew up the three giant planes and had themselves photographed on the debris, waving and shouting victory.

Within twenty-four hours, four airplanes had been hijacked, and 751 passengers had been taken hostage, with no casualties. Israel had declined all concessions, regardless of the consequences. Instead, 450 Arabs

in the occupied zone of West Jordania and the Gaza
Strip were jailed. It was denied that these arrested
Arabs were intended to serve as counterhostages to be
exchanged for Israeli and American passengers, and all
of them were released.

The Swiss, German, and British governments were
severely criticized in their own countries for not having shown more firmness, even though such a response
might have meant sacrificing hundreds of innocent citizens. One had to draw the line someplace, the critics
said. If legitimate governments felt free to violate their
own laws, what would happen next? Once the precedent was set, crime and disorder would certainly sweep
over those countries that had invited lawlessness by
breaking their own laws. So far, these dire prophecies
have not come true.

BLACK SEPTEMBER The Black September, a nu-
merically small Palestinian splinter group of Al Fatah,
derives its name from the memory of a massacre of
Palestinians by Jordanian troops said to have been
bribed and terrorized by Israelis. Credit is claimed by
the Black September for the assassination of the Jordanian prime minister in Cairo and for an assassination
attempt on the Jordanian ambassador to Great Britain
in London in 1971, for the killing of five Jordanians
suspected of collaboration with Israelis in Germany in
1972, as well as for various acts of sabotage in German and Italian machine shops and pipelines and for
the skyjacking of a Sabena airplane at Lod Airport.

Black September gangs are specialists in exported
terrorism; they are fiercely nationalistic international
operators. In small units of seven to ten, they strike
unexpectedly, wherever their targets may be. Organized in small cells, the secret clan has good contact
with leftist underground organizations in many countries; but Black September has no headquarters, no offices, no flags, no definite ideology. On short notice,
terrorists are recruited ad hoc for certain tasks; then
they disband. The various participants know only a

few of their comrades personally; they are familiar
with their superiors but with very little else. They are
dedicated fanatics, but they function as hired killers.
They appear independent, uncontrolled, and uncontrollable. They do not just talk about the destruction
of Israel; they work at it. And as a fringe benefit,
they eliminate Arab moderates and outright traitors
by quick execution. Their unruly autonomy creates the
impression of incorruptibility and dynamic mobility.
No agent or spy has been able to penetrate their organization.

Arab states and official Arab organizations frequently disavow the clandestinely supported Black September when its deeds provoke unfavorable comment.
But when its actions are applauded by world opinion,
Black September represents the vindictive and implacable collective Arab conscience.

Every action of crusading terrorists is a link in the
interminable chain of precedents and consequences. After the Japanese mercenaries had staged the massacre
of twenty-six innocents at Israel's Lod Airport, the
Arabs were accused of cowardice for letting other nationals do their dirty work. The Black September attack on the Israeli athletic team at the Munich
Olympics (see Chapter 9) was planned as a rehabilitation effort, as proof of Arab courage.

The Lod slaughter was meant to be revenge for
the attempted hijacking of a Sabena plane at Lod, during which Israeli security officers disguised as mechanics had killed the attackers and one passenger.
The Israelis had been very proud of how energetically
they had handled matters on that occasion. In a detailed radio and television speech, the minister of defense had contrasted the superior Israeli guile and
toughness with the inferior Arab naïveté and ineptness. The public dissection of the Sabena episode was
perceived as a smear and a challenge by many Arabs,
particularly by the Black Septembrists, who decided
to take bloody revenge.

After Munich, the Israelis lashed out at Lebanon,

punching deep into fedayeen land with tanks and airplanes. And in Cairo, the guerrilla radio blared: "All
glory to the men of September, the gold medal they
had won in Munich was for the Palestine nation."
The United States cast a veto when the U.N. Security
Council resolution condemned only Israel for its retaliatory strike without mentioning the Arab terrorist
attack that had provoked the retaliation. Then came
the retaliation for the retaliations and the Zagreb follow-up of Munich, followed by innumerable acts of
anticipatory and retaliatory terrorism and counterterrorism.

IRELAND: CHRISTIAN TERRORISM   "They count their
bullets instead of the pearls on their rosary; their Ave
Maria and the Lord's Prayer are their bursting bombs
and the rattling of machine gun fire. Gasoline is their
holy water and a house in flames is their mass." Irish
poet and playwright Sean O'Casey wrote these sentences more than half a century ago. They still apply
to the condition of a deeply split people who have
condemned themselves to inhumanity and incessant
strife.

    "Religious fanaticism is handed down from gen-
eration to generation like a hereditary disease," stated
Northern Irish writer Andrew Boyd. A fifteen-year-old
Protestant pupil commented in a school paper that he
would make life intolerable for the Catholics so that
they would all leave. A Catholic priest described a
holy crusade against people who lack all human dignity. On the occasion of Christianity's celebration of
peace, the IRA sent Christmas cards depicting a war-
rior, with the inscription: "No peace in unliberated
Ireland." A Protestant minister, preaching against the
Roman faith, literally hit presumed traitors with his
Bible.

    Ireland, which at one time had Christianized
large areas of Europe, is said to suffer from too much
Christianity and not enough Christians. Religious fer-
vor competes with fierce nationalism, producing
bloody massacres in the name of the sacred cause.

Irish history is one long battle of brute force pitted against equally brute counterforce.

Originally, the Irish island was inhabited by Firbolgs, who fought each other; later, they were massacred by the invading Vikings and Danes. Later still, Britain's King Henry VIII punished his Irish subjects for not wanting to be liberated from Roman influence.

In the seventeenth century, Oliver Cromwell terminated an uprising of two years' duration with a bloodbath in the east Irish port of Drogheda; there were hardly any Irish survivors. Crushed and decimated, the remaining Irish were either sold as slaves to the West Indies and Virginia or kept as slaves in their own country. In subsequent rebellions, hundreds of thousands of Irish were killed or starved. At the end of the nineteenth century, 1 million Irish emigrated to the United States; these emigrants became the nucleus of the Irish freedom fighters, who returned to the old country as the Sinn Fein. With the IRA as their activist frontrunners, Sinn Fein fights for sovereign Irish independence and reunion with the six Ulster counties of the North.

The rebellious IRA is split into two factions: the Marxist, comparatively moderate Officials and the ultranationalist, conservative Provisionals (often called Green Fascists), who are primarily responsible for the bombings and killings on the Catholic side. Although the Eire government and most respectable Irish citizens disapprove of their methods, even the most bitter critics of violent tactics have to concede that deep in most Irish souls there is some admiration for "the boys." Irish tradition has it that a fellow Irishman on the run must be sheltered and protected; when 19 Provisional prisoners recently escaped from jail, 600 policemen and soldiers, assisted by helicopters, dogs, and planes, failed to catch even one of them.

The Protestants, whose activist groups are organized in the paramilitary Ulster Defense Association (UDA), also engage in spectacular terrorist activities. The Catholic minority in the North are reduced to second-class citizenship. They are denied homes, jobs,

and votes; humiliated and discriminated against; and
when it is deemed necessary, put in concentration
camps and tortured.

In 1969, nearly all top government officials in
Northern Ireland were Protestant. In the North, unemployment is three times higher in Catholic than in
Protestant counties, and government support from
London predominately benefits the Protestants, who
distribute the bounty. As a result of discrimination
and oppression, a new Catholic family structure seems
to have emerged there, strikingly similar to the alleged
structure of the black American ghetto family. The
family is often dominated by the mother, while the unemployed father, deprived of his authority, drinks ex-
cessively, works irregularly or not at all, and often
engages in brutal conduct.

The Protestant majority of Northern Ireland want
English assistance in protecting their religion, their
higher standard of living, and their very lives. Indeed,
they are afraid that if British troops ever left, their
countrymen from the South would slaughter them by
the thousands.

When, in 1969, the Catholic Ulster Defense
League demonstrated against oppression and discrimination with peace marches and protests, the Protestant
majority became violently provoked, and the Northern
Irish police lost control of the situation. British troops
were sent to Northern Ireland to protect the Catholic
minority, and even the IRA cooperated with their alleged protectors for a short while. Soon, however, the
British army stopped acting as a neutralizing force and
became the partisan police instrument of the Northern
Irish government. The UDA and the IRA, bitter enemies on all other points, are united in regarding the
British soldiers as foreign invaders, interfering with
Irish sovereign rights. The vast majority of Irish and
Northern Irish disapprove of violence in principle but
advocate violent means to resist the imperialist British
forces, whose presence nevertheless safeguards the
properties and lives of the Northern Irish.

NICARAGUA AND THE SUPERPOWER Nicaragua has achieved what many other countries have sought without regard to cost or means: stability. Since the early 1930s, the country has been under the uninterrupted leadership of the Somoza family, father and sons. At present, effective power is exercised by Anastasio Somoza, who at American insistence adopted a hard-line no-ransom policy toward terrorism. Numerous hostages were killed because the Nicaraguan government refused to yield to or even negotiate with terrorists. However, the Somoza government and its secret police were tough not just with terrorists but with everybody threatening the government's stability.

Torture is routinely applied to prisoners, and most of it takes place in the quarters of the national guard or in the presidential palace itself. Prisoners are exposed to bright electric lights shining directly into their eyes; or their hands and feet may be manacled while they are nearly drowned; or they are caged up in close proximity to wild animals in the presidential garden. After serving six months without trial, as provided by law, prisoners are often released only to be rearrested within minutes. Strikes are prohibited; four trade-union leaders asking for better wages and working conditions were arrested in 1974 and held for four months. But in spite of the stability of the strict law-and-order regime, there is restlessness and widespread discontent in Nicaragua.

The Sandinista National Liberation movement, an extreme leftish organization, provides the terrorism from below to challenge U.S.-supported Somoza's terror from above. In the early 1930s, Augusto Cesar Sandino, violently opposed to the U.S. ownership rights to a proposed Nicaraguan canal, organized a rebellion and, with strong support from the local population, successfully held off 2,000 marines and 4,000 Nicaraguan soldiers until President Franklin D. Roosevelt ordered the withdrawal of U.S. troops. According to official reports, Sandino was executed by a Nicaraguan machine-gun squad. In fact, an assassination team, op-

erating on Somoza's orders, shot the guerrilla leader as
he left a dinner engagement at the presidential palace.
The chief assassin, Abelardo Cuadra, claims to have
opposed the suggestions made by the generals (representing Nicaragua's power) who eagerly advocated
time bombs and kidnapping. "Of course I was opposed," he said later, "but what could I do? If I had
not gone along, they would have killed me that same
night."[2] The subsequent official investigation of the killing was headed by none other than Cuadra himself.

On December 27, 1974, in Managua, the Nicaraguan capital, a band of Sandinistas invaded an elegant party given in honor of the U.S. ambassador, who
had just left the gathering. While gaining forcible entrance, the terrorists killed four people, including the
host, and captured more than a dozen guests as hostages, including Nicaragua's foreign minister, the
Nicaraguan ambassador to the United States, a U.N. ambassador, and the mayor of Managua. President Somoza immediately declared martial law and ordered
the site of the attack surrounded by the military, but he
withdrew the troops in exchange for the release of
some female hostages. After sixty hours of siege and
intensive negotiations, in which the terrorists agreed
to a reduction in ransom from a few million to a few
hundred thousand dollars, the terrorists' request was
granted. Eight masked guerrillas, still carrying machine
guns, together with eighteen political prisoners freed
from Nicaraguan jails and twelve hostages, kept to
protect the terrorists against a change of mind, were
flown to Cuba. Young Nicaraguans at the capital's airport cheered wildly as the Sandinistas departed. Upon
safe arrival in Havana, the hostages, including the three
high diplomats and a Roman Catholic archbishop who
had also been forced to accompany them, were permitted to return to Managua.

Because of the high rank of the numerous hostages, President Somoza had to negotiate and yield;
nevertheless, he continued to boast of his uncompromising hard-line policy toward terrorists. Because Nicaragua and Cuba do not maintain diplomatic relations,

the Spanish government acted as intermediary, making the necessary arrangements with Cuba to receive the guerrillas and their freed comrades. After his release, Nicaraguan Foreign Minister Aguilla complained that he hadn't been able to bathe for three days, but he stated: "They treated us very well; they were nice and kind."

At that time, an American official commented that the problem in fighting terrorism on an international scale was that governments which believe in the rule of law as America does can't do much when other governments disregard that rule. Political assassins and kidnappers cannot be eradicated when they are readily released back into the marketplace. Undoubtedly true; international terrorism would indubitably cease to exist if all (or even most) governments of sovereign nations agreed not to organize, support, finance, or grant sanctuary to terrorists. But what of governments that came to power by and through terroristic methods? What if they are compelled to continue the employment of terroristic methods in order to maintain their power? What if the outward display of their sovereignty depends on the goodwill of superpowers who make their support contingent on the suppression of political opponents, who, in turn, become terrorists to shake off the yoke of this suppression?

THE SOUTH AMERICAN WAY OF LIFE Abductions and killings of U.S. officials and diplomats have been increasingly commonplace in various Latin American countries, including Guatemala, Brazil, Uruguay, Argentina, Mexico, Haiti, and the Dominican Republic. Latin America, from whose fertile soil many guerrilla movements have originated, has been the modern testing ground for innovative terroristic tactics; the Robin Hood type of kidnapping has proved its propagandistic effectiveness in several South American states; yet only in Cuba were guerrillas successful in overthrowing the government and assuming and maintaining power. In all other countries, guerrillas have demonstrated that large-scale urban guerrilla activities can be carried out in cities for a long period of time, but they have not been able to command widespread popular support or to seize the government.

The Latin American brand of terror from above is not the product of the sadistic inclinations of unrestrained warlords; it is government routine, used as an instrument of policy to assure a regime's stability.

Government spokesmen point out that torture and other forms of repression have been in use long before the current regime; indefinite imprisonment without charge or trial, brutal extortion of confessions, and the elimination of political opponents by the government are common practices and are accepted as inevitable facts of life. Counting on the population's willingness to support all, even the most violent, extralegal government measures to avoid being frightened and inconvenienced by terrorism, many South American regimes have practiced ruthless terror from above (usually carried out by the military rather than by police forces, according to Brian Jenkins)* long before large-scale terrorism from below began to dominate the scene. People have accepted totalitarian dictatorship as the lesser of two evils.

URUGUAYAN TUPAMAROS   In the early 1960s, the ultraleftist urban guerrilla movement of the Tupamaros became a tightly organized and effective striking force for terrorist activities in Uruguay. In the late 1960s and early 1970s, the Tupamaros were able to embarrass the government with their superior operational skill and to attract national and international attention with enormous ransom demands for charitable purposes designed to win them local popularity. Within one hour, they carried out successful kidnappings of prominent diplomats at different places, and they ab-

---

*Brian M. Jenkins has prepared various studies on terrorism as a staff member of the Rand Corporation of Santa Monica. (Reproduced in *Hearings . . . Terrorism*, Part 4; see p. 345, Chapter 10, n. 1.)

ducted and killed American public safety adviser Dan
Mitrioni. Finally, the government, incapable of curb-
·ing the increasingly violent events, called in the army
to crush the guerrilla movement. The military succeeded in smashing the Tupamaros, but in the process,
they also eliminated the government and established a
military dictatorship.

PERÓN COUNTRY Modern Argentina is the most Eu-
ropean-appearing South American country, with a
much higher per capita income than its neighbors and
an educational system that has all but eliminated il-
literacy. Life seems sweet in Buenos Aires, the worldly Argentinian capital, full of crowded luxury restaurants, elegant shops, and well-dressed, promenading
couples.

But the reality behind this appearance is another
matter. An average of one major kidnapping takes
place every eighteen hours. In 1973, between 500
and 600 people were kidnapped; in 1974, the number
approximately doubled. Although 90 percent of the
victims are Argentinian, it is the captured officials of
multinational corporations who command headlines all
over the world. A ransom of $14.5 million, demanded
and paid for the release of Exxon executive Victor E.
Samuelson in 1974, has set a world record.

For foreign business executives and for many
prosperous local people, life in Argentina has changed
radically. Buenos Aires still offers a wealth of creature
comforts and diversions, but the carefree enjoyment of
a normal existence is gone. After commenting on the
weather, it is customary to hear people ask, "Who was
killed today?" Many foreign firms have transferred
their executives to other countries. The remaining
families stay in their homes, which have become for-
tresses. Fear is pervasive; kidnappings can occur anytime and anyplace—on beaches, in rush hour traffic,
in restaurants, homes, shops. Neither women nor children are safe from terrorist attacks. Ironically, the
number of bank robberies has decreased in Argentina.

Criminals, too, have jumped on the kidnapping bandwagon, imitating the techniques developed by crusading terrorists.

In the mid-1970s, terrorism from all sides has been stepped up and become significantly more brutal and dangerous. Terrorism used to specialize in spectacular Robin Hood kidnappings; but recently, large-scale retaliation attacks and revenge murders have become daily occurrences. Stepped-up security precautions have not prevented kidnappings, but they have made hostage capture more bloody and led to an inflationary rise of ransom demands. Negotiations with kidnappers, now declared illegal, have not stopped but carry a greater risk for the victims.

By the end of 1974, more than 180 persons had been killed since the death of the *líder,* Juan Perón, in July. His third wife, widow, and successor to the presidency, Maria Estella (Isabel) de Perón, appealed to the people in bold speeches against terrorism and took firm measures, such as censorship and more severe penalties (because of its ineffectiveness as a deterrent, the death penalty is alternately introduced and abolished), reinforced by large posters proclaiming: "Isabel is sovereignty," "No to treason," and "Everything unites us; nothing and nobody separates us." In March 1976, an ailing inept Isabel Perón, who had been ruling Argentina for twenty-one months after her husband died, was whisked into an enforced retirement in spite of the living memory of the catastrophic results of military terror in recent Argentine history. The generals had taken over to battle run-away inflation, to restore confidence, and to terminate the open gang wars that claim more victims in Buenos Aires than the fighting in Belfast.

The life and career of Juan Perón is a study in the merging of terror from above and terrorism from below. The young Argentinian military attaché in Rome had been impressed by Italian dictator Benito Mussolini, who had mobilized the masses, not just to consent to but fervently to desire modern fascism. After coming to power in 1943 as head of a military junta, Perón, together with his second wife Evita, mobilized the impoverished masses of the descamisados ("the shirtless"), who enthusiastically supported his wasteful and oppressive rule. His grandiose promises regarding revolutionary land reforms, resistance to foreign imperialism, and redistribution of wealth were never kept. But he did permit his followers to engage in spectacular symbolic actions, such as the burning of the aristocratic Jockey Club, and he did introduce a system of minimal social protection, with higher wages, social security, and medical care.

Perón never succeeded in liberating his people from oppression (which, on the contrary, he imposed on them) or from poverty, but he managed to instill in them a strong new sense of identity. Even his adversaries admit that he was the first to give the Argentinian people the feeling that they were human beings with inalienable rights, who could be proud of their heritage and of belonging to the Argentinian nation.

After nine years of semifascist reign, Perón's rule of terror from above (mitigated by some democratic trimmings) became increasingly corrupt and oppressive. In 1952, three years after his wife Evita died of cancer, he was deposed by a military conspiracy. The discredited dictator, who was accused of sexual misconduct with minors, had transferred his personal fortune, estimated at between $200 and $300 million, to foreign countries. He took up residence in Madrid and from there organized political and terrorist activities in Argentina.

For over eighteen years, Perón kept his influence alive from afar, partly through the activist wing of his former supporters, predominantly Catholic leftist Peronistas who came to be known as the Montañeros. These urban guerrilla fighters became more terroristic after the military seized power in Argentina in 1963, but the exiled dictator's political convictions, a deliberately vague mixture of notions about social justice, economic independence, and national sovereignty, appealed to other, more radical leftist groups. The Marxist People's Revolutionary Army (ERP) emulated and soon topped the Montañeros' terrorist activities against the military regime. From exile, Perón encouraged the terrorists with money, practical advice, and inflammatory speeches: "If I were younger, I would be with you in Argentina, throwing bombs and helping with my own hands, so that justice prevails."

An interminable series of so-called direct actions by his supporters eventually brought Perón back to power in Argentina, which had become ungovernable as a result of the terrorist-inspired *violencia*. Perón supporter Dr. Héctor J. Campora who, on being elected president, immediately declared an amnesty for all political prisoners and arranged for the triumphant return of the exiled "leader" Perón was welcomed with boundless enthusiasm by his nostalgic followers. Perón thanked his faithful supporters, promised to unite the whole country behind him, and prohibited any further direct actions.

Soon, the ERP and other leftist groups who had hoped that Perón would create the promised homeland of socialism denounced him as a traitor. He, in turn, denounced them: "Their acts are expressions of pathological barbarism unleashed as part of criminal and terrorist plans against the nation." (Perón speech)

Masses of the most fervent former Perón supporters were arrested as traitors, interrogated by torture, and mutilated. During the nine months of Perón's second reign, more than 200 persons were killed in the pitched battles between fascist execution platoons supported by conservative government and union officials and various leftist terrorist groups. Since Perón's death, the epidemic of assassinations has spread.

A new antisubversion bill puts all attempts to alter or suppress the institutional order and social peace of the nation under criminal sanction of up to eight years in prison. Press coverage of terrorist acts that was not sympathetic to the police was forbidden. By officially enforced label swindle, words such as "guerrilla," "Montañero," and "Marxist" had disappeared from the newspapers and have been replaced by "terrorist," "outlawed organizations," and "extremist."

The new legislation was also directed against profiteering, strikes, hoarding, and drug abuse. The parliamentary opposition, fragmented into small parties, had criticized the government for limiting freedom of the press and arresting countless innocent people.

Latin America's first woman president had laid the cornerstone for a vast mausoleum in which the bodies of the country's great are to rest, regardless of their political persuasion. The bodies of her husband and his former wives are to lie there peacefully side by side with all the others who, according to their different convictions, have contributed to Argentina's greatness. The dead will be reconciled at "the country's altar." Meanwhile, the living wonder what alternatives there are to the escalating turmoil of machine-gunning rival gangs except terror from above, which promises to restore peace and quiet, the tranquillity of the cemetery.

BRAZIL'S "NAZIS"   On his arrival in Algiers, the sixty-year-old leader of the Brazilian Revolutionary Communist party, who had been one of forty prisoners exchanged for kidnapped German Ambassador Ehrenfried Von Hollenberg, said that having lived under a Nazi dictatorship, the German people will understand why Brazilian revolutionaries must resort to kidnappings in order to free their tortured brothers.

The ruling clique of Brazilian generals keeps about 15,000 political prisoners behind bars. According to numerous reliable reports, police in Brazil, as in post-Allende Chile, torture prisoners routinely, not to obtain information, but for purposes of intimidation. The regime has given Brazilians a strong feeling of national identity, a sense that they share in the building of a new superpower. (The new Chilean rulers have the same goal in mind.) "Brazil, love it or leave it," say the bumper stickers.

Brazil's "restrained democracy," which does not permit any free elections, periodically stages an election farce in which more than 50 percent of the voters have been known to cast blank ballots. For some ultrarightists, even these trimmings of parliamentary democracy and the remnants of judicial process, which are kept alive to appease the international community, seem like intolerable restraints. Vigilante-type self-help organizations in Brazil (and in Uruguay and Guatemala) take matters into their own hands, executing sentences that the official system of justice refuses to impose. Pride in national sovereignty forbids any investigation into the workings of these death squadrons, which are led by off-duty policemen in civilian clothes. They work swiftly and efficiently; without delay of cumbersome legal technicalities, they kill suspected terrorists or suspected criminals of any sort, anybody they consider dangerous or just do not like.

The governments, which secretly support the activities of the vigilantes, claim that the death squads are a propaganda invention of the terrorists and their Communist allies. In 1973, the estimated number of victims of the nonexistent death squads was 1,300.

JAPAN'S EXPORT TERRORISM The United Red Army of Japan is the most advanced, best-organized group aiming to bring about a simultaneous and permanent worldwide revolution. The "soldiers of the revolution" consider themselves members of an international army of terrorism, and they are pledged to participate in all revolutions anywhere in the world through exemplary acts. Since 1970, when they skyjacked a JAL jet going to North Korea, they have taken credit for successful attacks in Israel, Europe, and Asia and for the massacre of *twenty-six* tourists at Lod Airport in Tel Aviv.

This ultraleftist fringe group was founded in 1969. After splintering off from a rebellious student organization, they began engaging in urban guerrilla activities, attacking police stations, holding up banks, and the like. In keeping with their international revolutionary doctrine, the hierarchically organized group, run by a central committee that directs the execution squads (usually consisting of five people), sought bases in North Korea and Latin America, but only the Palestinians responded favorably. The mastermind behind the organization is thought to be a twenty-eight-year-old Japanese woman, a former bar hostess, who is variously described as a kindhearted person ready to help whenever a worthy cause needs a champion, and as "a ruthless revolutionary." Allegedly, her reply to the charge that the Red Army is a plague was: "If that is so, we must infect the whole world. I'm the germ of the plague."[3]

WEST GERMANY: INTELLECTUAL TERRORISTS In the late 1960s, following the Berkeley pattern, leftist students at West German universities organized peaceful protest marches, provocations, sit-ins, and occasional building occupations, mostly in protest against the Vietnam War. At a demonstration against the visiting shah of Iran, clashes occurred between rival Persian student groups in Berlin, and one German student died, killed by a police bullet. His death served as a signal to various leftist student groups, who escalated their actions and, in an effort to symbolize the napalm bombing of Vietnamese villages, fire-bombed two empty West German department stores. Some group members were arrested, among them Andreas Baader.

The official birth date of the Baader-Meinhof gang is May 14, 1970, when sociology teacher Ulrike Meinhof and several others liberated Baader by shooting it out with police at a library where Baader had been permitted to borrow books for use in the preparation of his defense. In the course of this confrontation, one police officer was severely injured. Baader and Meinhof went underground, and for one and a half years, they terrorized the West German population by ever more extravagant threats and various assassinations and assassination attempts. During an intensive nationwide search for the group, at least three police officers were fatally injured when the Red Army Faction, as the Baader-Meinhof gang called itself, changed its tactics to bombing.

The police had killed three young Baader-Meinhof members, among them Petra Schelm. In May 1972, an American colonel was torn to pieces by a bomb as revenge for the death of Schelm, and seventeen people were injured at the bombing of the Springer Press Building in Hamburg. Three American soldiers died in a Heidelberg bomb attack on the headquarters of the U.S. army.

Innumerable other killings and bomb attacks were attributed to the Baader-Meinhof gang, who apparently enjoyed the support of large numbers of student, intellectual, and political sympathizers. An overwhelming majority of Germans, increasingly panicky and outraged, demanded extreme countermeasures. Law-and-order advocates accused everybody with progressive sympathies of complicity and demanded firm military measures. The accused then accused the accusers of fascist tendencies, prompting Nobel Prize winner Heinrich Böll to warn his countrymen against popular hysteria.

Several weeks after the bombing attack on U.S. army headquarters, gang members Holger Meins and J. C. Raspe were arrested in Frankfurt. A little later Gudrun Ensslin was taken in Hamburg, and Ulrike Meinhof was captured in Hanover. They expressed their conviction that the domination of international imperialist monopoly capitalism could be broken only through violence and by liberating deeds. Baader, Meinhof, and the others remained in German jails for several years, awaiting trial. It proved very difficult to fix responsibility on the individual group members for their participation in collectively planned and executed criminal acts.

In prison, the Baader-Meinhof gang caused the German authorities almost as much trouble as they did while they were free. Mostly well-educated and well-connected university graduates or teachers, they used every means granted them by the democratic rule of law in West Germany to irritate, provoke, and battle the system. Sympathizing leftist defense lawyers smuggled messages in and out of jail, and a series of complaints, disciplinary actions, and appeals occupied the prison officials and courts, distracting them from the frequently postponed main trial. Various plans for escape attempts became known, and numerous threats were received. This resulted in the Baader-Meinhof people being classified as extreme security risks and confined in isolation cells with minimal privileges. Through various grapevines, they nevertheless managed to communicate with each other and to organize a highly effective collective hunger strike. Shortly after Ulrike Meinhof was finally tried, found guilty, and sentenced to eight years for her participation in Baader's liberation four and a half years earlier, her comrade Holger Meins died in jail of self-starvation. (Meinhof, incidentally, was operated on for a brain tumor several years ago, a fact that she refused to use as part of her defense.) Several hours later, one of the highest German judges, who personally had had nothing to do with the Baader-Meinhof trials, was assassinated in reprisal by an executive command of the Red Army Faction. The assassins went to the judge's Berlin apartment bringing flowers for his birthday, opened fire, killed him, and disappeared.

The series of trials against Meinhof and her comrades continued. In May 1976 Ulrike Meinhof hanged herself in her Stuttgart jail cell, in spite of the strictest supervision and security measures. Her suicide was attributed to feelings of growing hopelessness or to her unbroken rebellious desire for spectacular self-sacrifice.

Scattered groups expressed their "abhorrence of the tragic end of Ulrike Meinhof";[4] some others suspected murder by the authorities and demonstrated through protest notes and staged street violence. In West Berlin numerous persons were injured in brawls with the police in Munich and Wuppertal. In Rome, Toulouse, and Zurich fire bombs exploded, and in Frankfurt a thousand demonstrators attacked riot police with gasoline bombs in unprecedented frenzy.

ITALY: TERRORISTS IN SEARCH OF AUTHORITY Numerous Italian coalition governments succeeding each other at an alarming rate have not been able to avert the probability of economic disaster in Italy. Fast-growing terrorism from the Left and the Right plays a significant part in undermining public confidence in a parliamentary system that is unable to control the political antagonists, who are united only in their joint rejection of democratic procedures.

Two groups, representing the opposite ends of the political spectrum, identify with the glamorized antagonists of World War II. Black terrorism expresses the nostalgia for fascism, when there was law and order and no terrorism from below; Red terrorism identifies with the Allies, particularly the Soviet Union, who were fighting fascist terror from above. Both groups feel betrayed by the big economic interests that presumably govern the Italian republic. Characteristically, they not only complain of oppression and exploitation by the system but also seem frustrated by authority's lost omnipotence.

Like youngsters unable to accept dependence on their parents yet recognizing them as their sole providers, the terrorists blame the system for its lack of power, the very power they regard as unjust and oppressive. They object to authority having yielded its absolute sovereignty to democracy, and through terrorism, they hope to establish an all-powerful ideal order that they believe has vanished in the modern world. Black or Red, they try to realize their fantasies of total domination and total subjugation. The paradise lost is to be regained with bombs and bullets.

CANADA: *Contestation Non, Changement Oui* Only a few years ago, the terrorist organization FLQ, born of the separatist and socialist ferment in Quebec colleges and universities in late 1962, committed spectacular atrocities and attracted banner headlines all over the world. The FLQ (Front de Liberation du Quebec), drawing its inspiration from the successful Algerian and the Cuban national liberation movements, attracted young French Canadians impatient to separate Quebec from the rest of Canada.

Terrorists always engage in name-calling as a preface to blame-calling. "English domination" was the name for the oppression that had to be destroyed; "liberation" was the magic word that promised complete change for the economically underprivileged and discriminated-against of Quebec. The French-Canadian revolutionary clichés expressed the struggle for independence as a fight of the young against the old, the pure against the corrupt, the courageous against the cowardly, and the liberated against the enslaved. Schoolchildren chanted on the streets: *"Shakespeare non, Molière oui";* and students vowed to eliminate all those who collaborated with the English "enemy." The angry youth refused to tolerate the frustration of their French identity claims, and they became increasingly terroristic because their demands were not immediately met. Between 1965 and 1972, 250 bombings occurred, usually after advance warning. Then the FLQ announced that having done everything in their power to convince the population of the justice of their claims, they would have to alter their methods, regardless of sacrifices in human lives.

British diplomat James Cross was kidnapped, and the liberation of twenty-three political prisoners and a ransom of half a million dollars were the price of his release. Then the Canadian minister of labor and immigration was kidnapped to reinforce the unmet demands. The governments of Quebec and Canada refused to release the prisoners, and the FLQ responded with the announcement that "Pierre LaPorte, Minister of Unemployment and Assimilation [sic] was executed at 6:18 tonight by the Dieppe Cell (Royal 22nd); we shall conquer. FLQ."[5] A short time later, LaPorte's body was found stuffed in the front of a car; he had been strangled with a thin gold chain that held the picture of a saint.

In the wake of general public outrage, strict countermeasures were enacted by Parliament and vigorously enforced. The terrorists had proved that a handful of determined fanatics could exploit the vulnerability of modern pluralistic society and could intimidate a whole country temporarily. But the effectiveness of their spectacular methods contrasted sharply with their spiritual impotence and their inability to change the people's attitude. The informed population of a democratic society senses that terrorism from below, substituting bombs and assassinations for discussion and clarification, contains the germs of terror from above. Terrorism has virtually disappeared in Canada.

The combination of firmness in enforcing democratically agreed upon rules with simultaneous readiness to make reasonable compromises in order to avoid the pitfalls of conflict polarization and escalation (as, for instance, indicated by the election of a French Canadian Prime Minister) pays off. Old generals and terrorists wither away when, after conflict defusion and conflict deglamorization, there is no longer any need for their spectacular services. In England terrorism imported from Ireland has escalated because Britain has not found a feasible way as yet to extricate itself from an imperial heritage which included colonial terror. The U.S. has been remarkably free of political terrorism because the U.S. institutions for conflict resolution and justice redress, available to everyone, were believed to be working by and large in a satisfactory manner. All this may have changed recently; the mood of the country as expressed in the popularity of certain politicians, in court decisions and in the ascendancy of law and order feeling, suggests that some modified terror from above is no longer an option beyond the pale of imagination. An increase of all kinds of terrorism in the U.S. is therefore quite probable.

3

Crusader and
Anticrusader Beliefs

Crusading terrorism from below is often a curious mixture of mythical inspiration and barbarous pragmatism manifested in ambiguities and contradictions. Terrorism appeals to the public's feelings of decency and solidarity although the same public stands accused by the terrorists of dishonesty and treachery. In order to protect inhumanity and dehumanization, the terrorists treat their victims in a dehumanized manner. Violence is used to promote the causes of nonviolence and mutual understanding. Deploring exploitation and the ravaging of innocence, the terrorists ravage and exploit innocent victims to further their own aims. Proud of operating outside the system that they attack and denounce, they depend on national and international pressure from the same system to help them reach their goals. In order to promote the cause of liberation, they deprive innocents of their freedom and imprison and coerce their victims. Yet the terrorist mystique has considerable attraction for alert, intelligent, capable individuals of all age groups in many countries.

Misconceptions About Crusaders

The man in the street (and in government offices) harbors some amazingly persistent illusions about crusading terrorists. The Irish situation provides several examples for the persistence of obsolete, yet tenacious myths that should be relegated to the wastebasket of history.

Contrary to widespread belief, terroristic violence is *not* always futile and ineffective in transforming reality. If it had not been for IRA terrorist activities, the Republic of Ireland never would have come into being; this is also true of independent Cyprus, Algeria, Tunisia, and possibly Israel. Statues and plaques are erected in honor of Eamon de Valera, a former terrorist and first prime minister of the independent republic; in 1974, Sean McBride, former IRA leader, received the Nobel Prize. Is Arafat next? Every blackmailer, it seems, holds the olive branch of peace in one hand, which he will deliver when his demands, underscored by the gun in the other hand, are fulfilled.

Terrorism often is *not* confined to outlaws and the dregs of society (riffraff theory); it is supported by responsible citizens and organizations, either openly or in secret. Modern terrorism, even when it is officially denounced, is by no means peripheral to the historical process and the social fabric. In Ireland, Algeria, Tunisia, and many other places, terrorism has expressed the most important social, religious, and historical forces.

Terrorists are *not* all part of a Leninist-Marxist conspiracy. The IRA, particularly its activist Provisional branch, is actually conservative, patriotic, nationalistic, and rightist, and is denounced by opponents as a bunch of fascists and "crazy drunkards."

The peacefulness of the Christian message does *not* protect against violence. The IRA's and UDA's brand of vehemently avowed Christianity, which they want to impose on their violently reluctant brothers, does not prevent them from throwing bombs indiscriminately and often, even without the customary advance warning.

PARTICULARIST AND OTHER FALLACIES   Whether the series of bombings, shoot-outs, mass arrests, pitched street battles, and assassinations in Ireland should be attributed to the flare-up of a smoldering civil war or to terrorism is open to question. Since 1969, more than 1,000 people have died in sectarian fighting that started after British soldiers searched a house in Belfast for IRA weapons and were attacked with bullets, nail bombs, and Molotov cocktails. Social revolutionary motives merge with nationalism and religion to stimulate the self-sacrificial devotion of the fanatics, who feel that they and they alone can solve the Irish problem.

Nowhere is the particularist fallacy more popular and more clearly an essential part of the conflict than in Ireland. The Irish, inordinately proud of their heritage and identity, are firmly convinced that no one but the Irish can conceivably comprehend or help to solve their "own" problems. But the projection, polarization, and escalation of the problems that they consider typically Irish obviously follow general patterns including the staunchly maintained belief in the incomparable uniqueness of their struggle.

The particularist fallacy, overemphasizing the specifics of a local situation while ignoring the decisive general, even universal, patterns of conflict, tends to make any conflict "unsolvable." Characteristically, no outside arbitrator or judge is accepted by any of the parties, who disagree on everything except the rejection of any impartial intervention.

Shrinking and Expanding Identities

The differences among the Irish, comparatively small to the outside observer, seem enormously significant to the Irish themselves. The brothers who passionately hate and love each other join in passionately hating the interfering foreigner. They are forever ready to fight their traditional civil war and to combat the equally traditional British enemy with homicidal rage, a rage that represents outward-turned self-destructiveness, usually manifested by torturing self-doubts, depression, alcoholism, and suicidal preoccupation. Personality structure both reflects external conditions and creates them by projection of inner conflict. Witnessing and living the tragic spectacle of battling identities, nobody, least of all the Irish themselves, can tell whether the Irish problem is really religious, national, economic, personal, or all of these. Large parts of the outside world, baffled by the Irish struggle, are willing to settle for the explanation that says "the whole country is crazy."

The Northern Irish have no doubt that their Catholic countrymen will make the transition from terrorists to executors of state terror with no difficulty. They therefore victimize in order not to become victims. Thus national, religious, and social identities melt into each other and separate again, expand and shrink: all Irish against the British, Northern Irish against Southern Irish; Provisional wing against Official Marxist wing, and so on. Violence on all sides escalates and becomes habituated; otherwise decent people are heard making jokes while mutilating, maiming, and shooting other human beings. The world is shocked, mystified, and eventually bored by the continuous uproar of Christian terrorism created by the life-and-death battle of various identities, all claiming territorial sovereignty and the unrestricted right to violence.

The Irish Catholics are unjustly persecuted in retaliation for the oppression of Catholics in the North and the denial of Irish unification and sovereignty. The Northern Irish are unjustly persecuted and their lives jeopardized by IRA terrorism and by the uncompromising identity claims of the Irish Catholics, whom the hardworking, achievement-oriented Protestants consider primitive papists and unregenerate barbarians; the birth of a united Irish nation may mean individual death to the Irish Protestants. The British, drawn into the conflict against their will, cannot find any decent way to get out of it. They are persecuted by the devastating IRA terrorism in British cities and by the wholesale slaughter of British soldiers sent to Ireland to keep the warring factions apart and to protect the lives of Northern Protestants. Everybody feels wronged, deceived, and unjustly injured; each party feels that this injustice, inflicted by the other parties, is remediable only by violence. All parties suggest remedies that are diametrically opposed in content yet identical in their recommended method; all parties are, or have become, terroristic.

Palestinian Neo-Zionists

Crusading terrorists feel obligated to explain. When I visited Lebanon after the Munich Olympics tragedy, all I needed to say was that I came from abroad and had written a book, and I immediately got an appointment at the PLO headquarters in Beirut. After a long chat, I was invited on a guided tour of a Palestinian refugee camp. In the next few days, I made two more visits, to be greeted each time by heavily armed youngsters. Our conversations in English and French were animated, at times impassioned. The people, all young, all male, drifted in and out. They offered coffee freely and wanted me to be at ease, but they never let go of the guns casually held in their laps.

Every conversation started with a vehement denunciation of Israel. The fedayeen talked over and over again about Israeli atrocities from which the Arabs, particularly the Palestinians, had to suffer: about the "sneaky" invasion of Arab territory by Zionist settlers, about Zionist terrorism, and about the establishment of a foreign state and outpost of imperialism on stolen soil. They deplored the expulsion of the Arabs in various wars, leading to territorial expansion and the indiscriminate Israeli bombings that killed thousands of innocent women and children. For the terrorists and for many others, the Israelis were the Prussians of the Middle East. They had imposed their foreign values of dehumanizing industrialization and ruthless militarism by sheer terror; they had committed genocide by either killing and expelling the indigenous Palestinian population or depriving them of their traditional culture.

The terrorist youngsters did not use the phrase "identification with the aggressor," but this is what they meant: the Jews, having been subjected to the Nazis' genocidal fury, now inflict on the Palestinians what was inflicted on them; they, who had been expelled or had seen their innocent people killed, now expel and kill innocent people. Not surprisingly, the Palestinians called the Jews Neo-Nazis. More surprisingly, they half ironically and half seriously referred to themselves as Neo-Zionists. Of course, the Palestinians passionately hate the Zionists. The intensity of their rage against everything Jewish may even suggest some underlying ambivalence, some repressed inner attachment to the implacable foe.

The Palestinians' admiration for Zionist methods, or rather what they believe to have been Zionist methods, and their determination to imitate them is not clandestine, but quite conscious and outspoken. According to the Palestinians, the success of the Zionists was due to a combination of three factors: the insistence on the realization of a dream of national independence on a certain "holy" territory; the determination to pay no attention to adverse opinions, including those of one's own people; and the unrestricted employment of all means to realize the dream of territorial independence.

Theodor Herzl, the intellectual Viennese founder of Zionism, is also one of the Palestinian terrorists' heroes. They quote from his works, they admire his visionary zeal and the "unrealistic" tenacity with which he held on to his visions against all odds.

At the First International Zionist Congress in 1897 in Basel, Switzerland, Herzl had been insulted and ridiculed. Both the Jewish and the non-Jewish world agreed that he was a boastful buffoon and a dangerous fool. His Jewish opponents, proletarians and many powerful "money Jews" alike, suggested that this theater critic and writer apparently could not distinguish between life and literature; he looked at serious reality, of which he knew nothing, as if it were grand opera, with which he was familiar. But Herzl and a small group of determined followers remained undaunted. There never would have been an Israel without the Zionists' visionary dream, stubbornly defended against all resistance and ridicule for over fifty years.

The Palestinians say that some detachment, some turning away from today's reality is necessary to bring about the ardently desired, thoroughly justified reality of tomorrow. The Palestinians are willing to wait as long as it takes them to realize their dream, as long as the Zionists waited or longer, even a hundred years. They will settle for nothing less than full national independence on Palestinian soil. Like the Zionists of old, they have unbounded faith in the justice of their cause.

According to the Palestinians, the early Zionists could not have cared less what the world and other Jews thought or said about them. Friends could be betrayed, foes could be cajoled, promises could be broken, and any brutality could be justified if the interests of the cause demanded such ruthlessness. Good grades in conduct are the concern of obedient schoolchildren, not of revolutionaries. The Zionists willingly accepted all political and financial help from wherever it came, without any obligations on their part. The Zionist cause, and nothing but the Zionist cause, commanded total and unconditional loyalty. In the Palestinians' estimation, the Zionists were totally uncompromising, blindly partial, monomaniacally one-sided, and totally committed. For their tenacity, single-mindedness and devotion they were reprimanded by the whole world, including most other Jews. But they got Israel.

To the Palestinians, the lesson of Zionism is that the noble end justifies all means, particularly the use of violence whenever and wherever necessary. Changes in the status quo, established and maintained by powerful forces, can be accomplished only by carefully organized violence. The Zionists were masterful teachers, ingenious innovators, and expert practitioners of terrorism. Eventually the British had to withdraw from their mandate, exhausted by the constant terrorist bloodletting, officially disapproved of but secretly supported by the Jewish population. The Palestinians are convinced that just as the Zionists were able to create Israel through terrorism, Palestinian terrorism will bring about an Arab Palestinian state.

In many crucial respects, the analogy is spurious, and the comparison does not fit at all. Obviously, the early Zionist settlers never dreamed of martial conquest, hoping only to transform a desolate desert into a productive, flourishing area through peaceful means. Arabs never had to undergo worldwide persecution, expulsion, and a genocidal holocaust; and terrorism was never approved Zionist policy and never achieved the crucial, almost exclusive importance that Palestinians want to assign to such violence. Yet, for the Palestinians, the comparison is intellectually convincing, emotionally moving, and spiritually inspiring. The mortal enemy is to be defeated by his own method. The Zionists succeeded by irrationally insisting on the realization of a dream, by ignoring all adverse public opinion, and by ruthless terrorism; the Palestinians intend to achieve their goal by exactly the same means.

Imitation is the most extravagant form of flattery. Identification with the aggressor turns humiliating passivity into invigorating activity. The aggressors' most obvious and most striking (his worst and most aggressive) characteristics are internalized and copied, not just in retaliation and for cathartic relief, but also to demonstrate that the formerly oppressed can now afford to act like the oppressors. Arbitrariness and cruelty are the last remedies of the desperate, but they are also the luxury items of conspicuous power consumption. Unrestricted sovereignty or the illusion of sovereignty is like hard drugs; for the identity fanatic who demands unrestrained sovereignty, no sacrifice is too great if it gets him his high. The seemingly lucky enemy, or rather the stylized, distorted, and exaggerated caricature of the enemy, provides a model of success that is admired without bounds. The enemy represents the negative identity of a value system diametrically opposed to one's own beliefs, but he is also the screen onto which parts of one's own ego ideal have been projected. The enemy is envied and hated for having what it takes to succeed. To become like him is the price of victory. One can safely eliminate the model only after it has been firmly recreated within oneself.

Terrorists, actors, gamblers, and fanatics are drawn to high risks; they are counterphobically seeking the excitement of danger, despising the safe routines of regular hard work and slow advancement. The desire for fundamental change combines with an insatiable thirst for adventure at ever higher stakes.

Mussolini said: "The deed is our doctrine." Indoctrinated terrorists hooked on easy success obtained by surprise and contempt for conventional morality soon need no doctrine to spur them on. They act for acting's sake. As the deed replaces the justifying doctrine, the terrorists become action addicts.

Scenarios for Aggression

Terrorists and their sympathizers have no trouble in convincing themselves not only that they are right but also that they are innocent. And they will try their best to convince the rest of the world as well. During my trip to the Middle East, I visited Jerusalem and Cairo. The generally shared Israeli point of view was clearcut and easily comprehensible. For Israel, the building of military strength was a matter of survival. The Israelis had not needed Munich to convince them that at the slightest lapse of vigilance, the implacable Arab enemy would attack and kill them. Most Israelis realize that even following a tough line which does not allow for compromise does not guarantee more than their day to day survival, but they are convinced that anything less would surely lead to their immediate destruction.

In Cairo I obtained an introduction to Mohammed Heikal, intimate friend of President Nasser, adviser to President Sadat and editor in chief of the most powerful Arab newspaper, *Al Ahram*. I presented myself as an Austrian-born American psychiatrist who had written a book on aggression and who was interested in all the aspects of the Munich event. Heikal invited me to a fascinating seminar on violence and terrorism. The participants, in addition to Heikal, included fourteen Arab professors, diplomats, and journalists, all of whom spoke fluent English. I offered my theories on aggression, which were well received. Agreeing with my finding that one's own aggression is experienced as inevitable self-defense against outside aggression, the Arabs immediately proclaimed the Israelis to be aggressors who use the rationalization of self-defense to conceal and justify their aggressive acts, their former terroristic activities, their robbery of Arab land, and their provocative disobedience of U.N. decisions.

A professor of sociology said that it was indeed very difficult, yet possible in principle, to distinguish between legitimate and illegitimate aggression. There were psychosocial thresholds that could be objectively determined, he said. Any group, deprived of its land by robbery; denied its legitimate claims for independence, identity, and security; and forced to live under substandard conditions was certainly using thoroughly legitimate violence to terminate the inhuman, unjust, and intolerable state of affairs imposed upon them by arbitrary violence. The Palestinians simply had no other choice; the legitimacy of their rights, self-defense, and self-assertion could be scientifically proved. The Olympic Games in Munich had been the vulgar power display of satiated sovereign states who form the world establishment. The terrorists had only proved that there is not and should not be any security in a world which permits nations to be oppressed, dispossessed, and deprived of their sovereign rights by brute force. The Munich event had awakened the world and finally forced the indifferent to acknowledge the truth. The responsibility for the deplorable tragedy and the loss of human lives rests with those who create and perpetuate conditions that make violence a necessary reaction.

Another speaker went further; according to his version, the Arab terrorists had only used defensive aggression when returning the fire of the German police, who had acted under Israeli pressure. I pointed out that two Israelis had been killed many hours before by the Arabs when they invaded the Israeli quarters. True, my opponent conceded, but these killings had not been planned; they had just "occurred" unintentionally in the course of the occupation of the building. This was not aggression; if it was, one would also have to call all casualties of traffic accidents, wars, and natural or man-made catastrophes victims of aggression.

After a prolonged discussion in which Jewish-dominated world opinion was frequently blamed for labeling all Arabs as cowards and brutal criminals, the proponent of the Arabian nonaggression hypothesis finally conceded that if aggression were defined in purely descriptive terms (i.e., free of value judgments and ahistorically), then the killing of the two Israelis could be considered an act of aggression, although unplanned and unintended. But in that case, it was necessary to devise two scenarios in order to arrive at the correct understanding of the total situation. The first scenario was preliminary, concerned with the action from the planning stage up to the occupation of the Israeli quarters. Then, and only then, the second scenario began: with the negotiation between the terrorists and the authorities. And during the entire second scenario, the Arabs had not initiated any violence at all, either against the hostages or against the negotiators.

History is distorted if it is made to begin at a point chosen by an interested party. By the simple device of introducing a second, all-important "real" scenario, arbitrarily made to start with an act of Israeli or German aggression, this highly educated Arab justified the aggression of the Arab intruders. For the Arabs, the current phase of the Israeli-Arab conflict starts with the "terrorist invasion" of the Zionists, with the "original sin" of Israel's founding, with the "unprovoked imperialist aggression" in the Suez War of 1956, or with the "unprovoked attack" in the Six-Day War of 1967. For the Israelis, the history of the same conflict starts with the expulsion of Jews from their territory in biblical times; with worldwide anti-Semitism, climaxed by the German holocaust; or with the many violent Arab attacks aimed at preventing the return of Jews to their homeland.

The More It Seems to Change, the More It Remains the Same

It is always the same thing; the justification mill continually grinds out the same stereotyped legitimations, producing the same desired results. The important mechanisms involved, conscious or unconscious, deliberate or intuitive, manipulated or spontaneous, are as clear-cut and simple as can be: One's own aggression is denied or represented as reactive and defensive only; by label swindle, one's aggression is called necessity, duty, or heroism. The opponent is (and always has been) actively aggressive; he has (or could have) started the conflict. The "real" history of the conflict is made to start with one or more acts of enemy aggression that are readily apparent. In the tangled interplay of actions and reactions, certain events or episodes can always be singled out to prove the opponent's original real aggression, so that everything that follows can be interpreted as self-defense. Appeals are made to disinterested third parties (such as arbitrators, psychiatrists, courts, and international organizations) and also to reason, truth, history, and the like in the hope of finding support for one's own point of view; but if such support is not forthcoming, for whatever reason, the third party is discredited for lacking impartiality, knowledge, or integrity.

The justifications on either side are indistinguishable from each other. The leader of the Popular Front for the Liberation of Palestine, Dr. George Habash, stating that Israeli mass graves are blueprints and stimulants in the war against Israel and imperialism, continued: "We'll fight and strike at our enemies, wherever they are." An Israeli spokesman stated: "We prefer that other countries control, hunt and expel the terrorists, but what they won't do, we will do. And we will do it anywhere in the world that we must."

Both parties are equally indignant when the essential similarity, if not the identity, of their patterns is alluded to or pointed out. Each side feels that there are enormous moral and factual differences that should be abundantly clear to any impartial observer. One young Zionist executed for the assassination of British Minister of State Lord Moyne stated at his trial: "Our deed stemmed from our motives; our motives stemmed from our ideals, and if we prove that our ideals are right and just, then our deed was right and just."[2]

Menachem Begin, rightist Israeli politician and former leader of the Zionist Irgun, proudly exclaimed: "A new generation grew up that knew no fear. We fight, therefore we are." For the political existentialism of crusading terrorism, the extreme risk, the risky life, and the life risked are the sole valid proof of existence and value; only the exposed and endangered self can be fully realized. Terrorism had exactly the same meaning for some former Zionists that it has for present-day Palestinians: discovery and confirmation of the real self, active participation in a newly found collective identity, and liberation from thousands of years of passive resignation. Begin also said: "Our enemies called us terrorists—but our friends knew that we were ahead of history. They gave us a much simpler Latin name; they called us patriots. In truth, we were anti-terrorists." This statement of the former Zionist terrorist could have been made in exactly the same manner by any Arab terrorist.

These are the patterns, not just in the Near East, but everywhere: unconditional and uncompromising self-righteousness on the one side produces mirror-image aggression on the other side (if it was not already present).

Conflict polarization and escalation always follow the same rules. To have violence, three successive moves must be made: The enemy must be considered aggressive and guilty; yourself, only defensive and innocent. The start of hostilities must be attributed to one or more of the opponent's aggressive acts, making him responsible for all subsequent aggression on either side. You must insist on retaining full sovereign jurisdiction over matters of vital importance.

These three commandments for the production of violence are the prohibitions, the don'ts in the search for nonviolent, rational, civilized solutions to conflict. Violence can be prevented up to a point. There *is* a choice, particularly the freedom to choose not to let it come to the point where violence is the only remaining option.

One's own violence is always experienced as counterviolence, as aggressive antiaggression. It is always the others who have started or could have started; it is they who are wrong and therefore carry all the responsibility for their terrorism and for one's own terroristic antiterrorism.

4

Blurred
Distinctions

Terroristic Children

The strange story of the Doukhobors ("spirit wres-
tlers") is not set in the Middle Ages; it unfolds dramatically in our own century in friendly, democratic
Canada. From their beginnings in eighteenth-century
Russia, the Doukhobors emerged as a heretical sect intent on fighting, not with the weapons of war, but
with the spirit of truth. To that end, they teach their
children from early childhood that Christ is in the
spirit only and that obedience is essential for a life in
Christ. They also fervently believe that only the
law of God has to be followed; the law of man can and
must be ignored. Worldly education is impure and
hence to be distrusted; the Doukhobors refuse to send
their children to school, insisting on educating them
themselves in the only true faith, which calls for total
dedication, unquestioning obedience, and self-sacrificial disregard for all the suffering inflicted by nonbelievers. The loyalty of the Sons of Freedom, an elitist
activist group of Doukhobors, has to be constantly
proved by ostentatious defiance of man-made laws;

from their earliest days, the children are brought up
to bomb and burn not only government possessions
and the dwellings of their opponents but also their own
homes and those of their leaders in order to prove
their disdain for worldly possession. After particularly
spectacular actions, young and old unite in macabre
nude dancing.

Like several other groups, the Doukhobors emigrated to the comparatively empty North American
continent at the end of the last century to build their
own utopia according to the precepts of Tolstoy and
early Christianity. Originally, the simple Russian peas-
ants abided by a Quaker-like religion of love and a
creed of "toil and peaceful life." But what began
with fundamentalist dedication to nonviolence and
nonresistance became in the twentieth century the
breeding ground for the raising, training, and justification of bizarre and cruel youthful terrorists. The Sons
of Freedom are responsible for more than 1,100 bombings and burnings in the first half of this century,
which resulted in several dozen deaths, many hundreds of injuries, and enormous property damage.

Burning and bomb-throwing Freedomites enjoyed the sympathies of the passive majority of Doukhobors. A small but influential group of Canadians
and foreign journalists and scientists accepted at face
value the Doukhobor explanation that all their terrorist
acts were protests against religious persecution. For
several decades, the Canadian government was nearly
helpless against the fanatically indoctrinated children
and their fanatically indoctrinating parents and relatives.

Royal Canadian Mounted Police tracked down
the terrorist children, most of them under the age of
eight, who played with bombs and explosives the way
other youngsters play with marbles. But arresting the
children only increased popular sympathies for the
merciless terrorists. Local and federal Canadian governments tried to spread "the real truth" that "a huge
crime syndicate of at least 2,500 people was operated

by a backwoods Mafia-like organization that victimized everybody, particularly their own children."[1]

On March 6, 1962, a huge power transmission tower servicing East Kootenay in Canada was blown up by nine Doukhobor terrorists, six of whom were captured and imprisoned. In the wildest reprisals of Kootenay history, numerous courthouses and homes were bombed, and the suspected leader of the uprising was torn to pieces when his own bomb exploded.

Twenty-two-year-old Paul Edward Podmorrow, a Doukhobor terrorist, was brought up in total rote obedience to his elders. He did not exactly know what a government was except that it was to blame for everything. "He did not know why he had to fight government, but he hated it, was certain it was persecuting him and depriving him of freedom of religion," according to Simma Holt.[2] Together with several friends, he bombed a highway bridge and was caught and arrested. In jail, Podmorrow and his comrades started a hunger strike, and he died of self-starvation in the latter part of 1963. Marches by psalm-singing protesters could not be stopped at the funeral. Podmorrow's family wanted the Canadian public to see how their boy was murdered by the government; weeping and wailing children mourned their courageous, martyred leader.

When interviewed by radio and television crews, the children did not hide their hatred of the government and its laws. The hardened little terrorists had no hope for their future; they were convinced that they would be kept cold and hungry and made to die like Paul Podmorrow. Are these children (and their parents) crazy? Are they criminals? Or are they crusaders?

The Criminal and the Ill

With foreseeable regularity, the perpetrators of violence are called crazy, criminal, or both by their opponents and victims, and the violence-prone justify their deeds as having been dictated by sacred causes as part of a crusade. Most human actions have many mixed motives, making several equally valid explanations possible for any given action.

Labels often tell more about the emotions of the name-caller than about the alleged motives of the perpetrators. Nevertheless, it is of great practical importance to distinguish among different groups of terrorists, but it should be kept in mind that neat categories often overlap in complex reality.

The determination of sanity that decides a defendant's fate is made, not by disinterested parties, but by community representatives who have their own rational and irrational needs for safety, protection, and retaliation. If the community is not too frightened of the offenders and accepts the sincerity of their story, they are classified mentally ill and treated accordingly. But if the nature of their acts makes them too scary or horrible, they are disbelieved, classified as criminals, and disposed of accordingly.

TEST CASE: MC NAGHTEN   In 1843, David McNaghten, an Irish Protestant suffering from paranoid delusions and hallucinations, became convinced that British Prime Minister Robert Peel was the representative of the devil, conspiring with the pope and the Jesuits to destroy the British Empire. He planned to assassinate the prime minister, but in attempting to do so, he mistakenly shot and killed Peel's secretary instead. The judges found the defendant, who firmly believed that he was fulfilling a holy mission, to be suffering from "lunacy" (at that time, still attributed to the influence of the moon); and because he was not in possession of the necessary mental powers to make a valid distinction between right and wrong, they decided to acquit him.

Parts of the community were outraged that a dangerous criminal was not given his just punishment, and many Whigs and protectionists (members of an opposing political group) felt that somebody trying to get rid of a Tory (which the intended victim was) could not be all that crazy. The judges explained their verdict in a long dissertation that has remained the guideline for Anglo-Saxon law. But almost since its inception, the McNaghten rule has been criticized on scientific grounds for putting all the emphasis on the purely cognitive aspects of knowing the difference between right and wrong. Nevertheless, mentally ill individuals so deluded that they are unable to tell right from wrong should, according to law, be acquitted by reason of insanity.

Yet all such insanity rules and fine legal distinctions are not of much help to the defendant if his offense is considered particularly dangerous, repulsive, or contemptible. Terrorists who seize upon important occasions and well-known personalities fare badly in the courts unless they are judged by sympathizers, in which case they are rarely tried or punished at all. Usually, the magnitude of a terroristic crime and its consequences call for harsh self-protective punishment, regardless of the offender's mental condition. When the crime exceeds the ordinary in importance and publicity, the enraged public often insists on enforcing its right to retaliation, even though there is no doubt about the offender's bizarre delusions and psychotic derangement.

PRESIDENTIAL ASSASSINS AND THEIR ASSASSINS On July 2, 1881, forty-year-old Charles Guiteau, usually referred to as a "disappointed office seeker," shot President James Garfield. Several of Guiteau's immediate family members were mentally ill and had died in asylums; he himself had belonged to religious sects and utopian fringe organizations experimenting with sexual and economic equality. Most of his adult life he had spent looking for a cause or an organization to which he could devote himself completely. He was an identity seeker without personal identity.

Claiming to be employed by the strongest, most competent firm of the universe, by Jesus Christ and Company, he purchased an expensive pistol so that he would not have to be ashamed if the weapon was displayed in a museum. Prior to the deed, he ordered a cab to bring him to jail immediately afterward. Claiming to the very end that he had acted as an authorized agent of God, he was found sane and guilty and hanged in front of a large, wildly cheering crowd.

In September 1901, Leon Czolgosz shot President William McKinley after shaking his hand. Czolgosz had been a conscientious worker and a faithful practicing Catholic until he suffered a nervous breakdown, during which he believed himself to be the target of a conspiracy and persecution by priests. Turning away from the church, he attended several anarchist meetings and decided to kill the president because he believed that no single individual should receive so much attention.

After the assassination, vigilante committees searched out many hidden anarchists. Newspapers reported anarchist plots, and Congress passed prohibitive laws against the immigration of anarchists.

Czolgosz was declared legally insane by examining psychiatrists. Refusing to testify, he confined his defense to the statement that he regretted nothing because the president had been an enemy of all good people. After being found sane and guilty, Czolgosz was executed in the electric chair.

Jack Ruby, who in 1963 killed President John Kennedy's assassin in front of the nation's television cameras, was diagnosed by several psychiatrists as suffering from mental illness. He was found sane and guilty. Sentenced to death, he died of cancer in prison.

CONSPIRACY? The search for meaning in historical developments finds or imagines reasons for the world-shaking event. That a great man, a leader and hero who symbolizes a great cause, could be the victim of chance, martyred by the delusions of a lunatic nobody rather than by an elaborate conspiracy of enemies, is hard to accept by all those who want to make some sense out of what happens in this world.

The Dutch Communist Marinus van der Lubbe, who set fire to the German Reichstag in 1933, was believed by the Nazis to be the executive of a large

Communist conspiracy. No proof ever existed, and conjectures that he was a Nazi agent also proved to be without foundation. The mentally deficient, confused, and deluded arsonist was declared sane and guilty and was executed.

Doubts have arisen about whether Sirhan Sirhan, who shot Senator Robert Kennedy in the pantry of the Ambassador Hotel in Los Angeles, acted alone. Similar rumors have linked Lee Harvey Oswald, President Kennedy's murderer, and James Earl Ray, the killer of Dr. Martin Luther King, Jr., with conspiracy plots.

So far, no convincing evidence has been unearthed to support conspiracy theories in the assassinations of John and Robert Kennedy. It appears that Lee Harvey Oswald and Sirhan Sirhan were confused, emotionally disturbed loners acting on purely personal inclinations and without political motives. After his arrest, Sirhan Sirhan eagerly accepted the martyr role of ideologically inspired assassin that public opinion thrust upon him. But Sirhan's rambling diary (excerpts of which were presented at his trial) contains no clues to conspiracy, only much evidence of immature resentment, aggressive fantasies, and murderous preoccupation. Some examining psychiatrists found Sirhan Sirhan insane; others did not. Sirhan, after having been found guilty and sane, was sentenced to death.

LONER IN SEARCH OF A VICTIM   Arthur Bremer's 113-page diary showed that this severely disturbed young man had for a long time planned to assassinate somebody of great importance. He had made meticulous preparation for the killings of several important persons. (Similarly, Lee Harvey Oswald had made an attempt on the life of ultraconservative General Edwin A. Walker before shooting President Kennedy.) Bremer had wanted to assassinate President Richard Nixon, but his confusion and inability to concentrate made him postpone his spectacular plan until, inspired by the film *A Clockwork Orange,* he carried out his murder attempt on Democratic presidential contender Governor George Wallace.

Because of the political significance of the victim, political motives for Bremer's act were immediately suspected. But the white, Protestant youngster with the crew haircut did not belong to any of the target groups Wallace blamed for the decay of the country in his public speeches. He was neither black nor a long-haired hippie. Rather, he was a paranoid schizophrenic who had adopted violence as the only means left to escape his pervasive sense of failure. "I just had to kill somebody," he said; "that is how far I have gone and I hope that my death will make more sense than my life."[3] In reply to the district attorney's summation at his trial, Bremer smiled and stated: "The district attorney says society has to be protected from somebody like me. I would have preferred that society would have protected me from myself."[4] Bremer, after being found guilty and sane, was sentenced to thirty-three years in prison.

HARD LUCK   A crazed killer was on the loose, a disfigured loner (one eyelid permanently closed, one corner of his mouth drooping) easily recognized by his oversized head and the inscription "Hard Luck" tattooed on the back of his hand. He roamed freely in Oklahoma and California, terrorizing sizable parts of the population for several weeks.

William Cook, perfectly typecast as the public's idea of monstrous fiend and debased mass killer, was born to abject poverty and deprivation. One of many children, he grew up in a rural district in Oklahoma. He was six years old when he and the other children were witnesses to their father's murder of their mother. After the father was taken to jail, social agencies picked up the children and placed them in various orphanages and foster homes. But they overlooked little William, who in panic had hidden from the authorities in nearby caves.

For the next three years, he lived in nearly total isolation. Nobody wanted the child-fugitive; nobody missed him. Like a wild beast, he depended for sustenance on whatever he could find or steal. He acquired what were later called the "instincts of a ferocious animal"; he became a hardened criminal, hatefilled, totally alienated, and totally independent long before he reached puberty. He was first arrested at the age of ten. Thereafter, he spent most of his life in penal institutions. He was convicted of thefts, robberies, and increasingly brutal assaults and murder attempts.

Released from a penitentiary after serving several years, he went hitchhiking, stopped a passing car, and at gunpoint forced its five occupants, a Mr. and Mrs. Mosser and their three children, to follow his orders. He compelled them to drive him around for six days, seemingly without aim or definite destination. Then, one afternoon, he ordered them to stop the car, pointed his gun, and cold-bloodedly killed them, later burying their bodies in the same abandoned caves where he had hidden as a child.

Cook continued his crime spree. He seized, gagged, and bound a sheriff and commandeered his car. Using the red lights of the official vehicle, he stopped a traveling salesman in California, shot and killed him for no apparent reason, and continued his travels in the dead man's car. By that time, the gruesome discovery of the buried bodies had been made. He was identified by the sheriff and many other witnesses who had seen him on various occasions in the company of the Mosser family. With his monstrous looks, he was not easily forgotten.

Intensive searches went on everywhere; yet for many weeks, Cook eluded his pursuers. In the meantime, he held up two migrant workers and forced them at gunpoint to accompany him in the murdered salesman's car. Soon, however, he no longer had to use his gun or any other threats; his new victims had either accepted their fate or joined him voluntarily. In any case, the three of them traveled around California, then crossed over into Mexico, where they spent two weeks. When they ran out of money and things to do and Cook became tired of the whole thing, he returned to the United States and was promptly arrested at the border.

Traveling with the Mossers through several states made their murder a federal crime. At the trial in Wichita's Federal Court, all psychiatrists, and for that matter other witnesses, agreed that Cook, a fairly intelligent individual, was explosively dangerous, exceedingly brutal, and severely psychotic. His total lack of regret or guilt, as well as his stolidly maintained indifference to his own fate, seemed to confirm that he was mentally ill. But it was for the courts to decide if this psychiatric condition amounted to legal insanity. Prominent doctors from the Menninger Clinic (where Cook had been examined) testified, and a federal judge sentenced him to 300 years in a maximum security prison, excluding any possibility of probation or parole during his lifetime.

But the State of California would not be satisfied with any verdict other than the death penalty. Cook was brought in from Alcatraz to be tried in the California courts at El Centro for the murder of the salesman. On request of the defense, I volunteered my services and examined the defendant in custody.

Cook, an athletic, stocky little fellow who had been in Alcatraz for several months, was escorted by four officers and seated in the middle of a heavily barred cell block. I was placed opposite the defendant, who was immobilized by heavy iron chains. Four sheriffs seated on each corner of the cell block, barely outside earshot of a whispered conversation, had their automatic weapons trained on us, presumably for my protection. No doubt they were scared of him, in spite of his exemplary behavior in jail, which had been the only home he ever knew. His evil charisma prevailed even behind bars; as long as he was alive, he remained a terrible threat. The overkill potential of the community had to be mobilized and displayed, not for protection but for reassurance. Cook knew all that very well. He knew that sooner or later he would be killed, one way or another, accidentally or to thwart the escape attempt he never planned to make. He was lost; he wanted to get it over with quickly.

He did not regret his deeds, but he had no hate for his victims. The shooting of the salesman had been an "accident" in the process of stealing his car. The Mosser family he had executed deliberately. But he claimed that he had come to like them quite well during their long journey. They were all nice people, and he had been particularly fond of the youngest boy, who reminded him of himself at that age. Therefore, he had shot him first; he wanted to spare him the hardship and disappointment of life.

In my testimony to the court, which had also been transformed into an armed camp, I confirmed the diagnosis of my Menninger colleagues and stressed my conviction that this defendant "did not know the difference between right and wrong and should be considered legally insane." The jury returned a verdict of sane and guilty. Cook was sentenced to death and died on December 12, 1952, in the San Quentin gas chamber.

Before his last trial, Cook had accepted an offer of a sizable sum of money for the rights to his adventurous story. The movie "The Hitchhiker" is based on his experiences. He could come into possession of this money only if he were judged sane, which meant certain death. If he were found insane and permitted to live, he would not be considered legally capable of receiving the money. He collected and was executed.

CORPSES FOR CASH   In 1956, a series of senselessly brutal murders of children terrorized California. The buried victims, often sexually abused, were found gruesomely mutilated with slit-open stomachs and severed body parts. After an intensive manhunt, Stephen Nash, white, intelligent, good-looking, homosexual, with a long criminal record, was arrested. Not only did he readily confess to the three murders with which he was charged; he also claimed that he had committed eight more, making the body count eleven to one in his favor. The state, he reasoned, could take only his one life; whereas he had taken eleven. The unbelieving authorities thought he was bragging, but he gave them the location of another one of his victims in return for a sizable sum of money. When the child's body was found at the indicated place, Nash offered to sell information about another victim for an even higher price. (He intended to use the money to buy burial ground for himself in a Catholic cemetery in order to prove the venality and corruption of Christian churches.) Another corpse was found, but by then the authorities had had enough; Nash was indicted for five murders. Nothing is known about the fate of the other six victims; perhaps they existed only in his imagination.

I interviewed Nash twelve times and testified at his trial, which he frequently interrupted with gleeful descriptions of incredibly brutal deeds and long speeches in which he insisted that he was perfectly sane. Nash claimed that he knew not only what he was doing but also why. He was abandoned as an infant by his unknown parents. Because of this, he had been victimized by three humiliating circumstances: First, his religious foster parents had subjected him to circumcision; second, they had placed him in a religious school; third, his reason had been destroyed by Christian sacraments. These steps had been taken without his consent, robbing him of the opportunity to exert his democratic rights. He therefore had become the reincarnation of Jesus as a symbol of nonsexual love, belief in reason, and Jesus' holy wrath, with which he chased the money changers out of the temple. Now, he had to destroy three groups of people—sailors, children, and women—killing them in successive bunches of three from each category.

Nash considered himself the center of the universe, supreme in his power to liberate people from their suffering. He could see no contrast between his sadistic deeds and Christ's message of love, which he endorsed and claimed to represent. He was performing a service of charity for his victims by sparing them the disappointments of life. He himself had been rejuvenated by his deeds, which gave him "complete inner peace" from his former tension and fear.

Nash, an avid reader of Hitler's *Mein Kampf* and Tolstoy's *War and Peace,* had acquired considerable legal knowledge. He frequently recited the state's definition of insanity word for word, intending to prove that he was sound and fully responsible. He wanted to die, imagining that his execution would be a big public event attended by important persons. He was afraid of nothing except being deprived of his last spectacular opportunity by being declared incompetent or insane. He need not have worried. After being found guilty and sane, a jury sentenced him to death.

As one jury member later said privately, they believed him to be "nuttier than a fruitcake" but they did not want to take a chance on having this dangerous monster around. The governor pocket-vetoed the suspension of the death penalty, suggested at the time by the California legislature, and Nash was executed in the gas chamber.

SANITY UNQUESTIONED Charles Manson, the ghoulish organizer of a terroristic plot to bring about an Armageddon between blacks and whites, engineered the brutal slaying of Sharon Tate and four of her friends. His "family" of followers, held together and exploited by strict control measures, had many of the trimmings of a terror regime. In spite of or because of his cruelty and detachment, Manson was adored, venerated, and blindly obeyed by the family members, to whose lives he had given meaning and direction and on whom he had conferred a sense of belonging and a new identity.

Prior to his conviction for first-degree murder, no examination was made to determine Manson's sanity. Psychiatrists might have found something slightly unusual in the thought processes of a small-time criminal preoccupied with esoteric mysticism, the kings of eternal life, and the angels of the abyss, who was firmly convinced that he could bring about a world conflagration between the races. After his conviction for first-degree murder, the sanity trial was anticlimactic. Having been found guilty and sane, Manson received the maximum sentence.

ENVIRONMENTALIST MASS MURDER   Police and fire departments are usually busy on Halloween night when, according to time-honored custom, juveniles enjoy the partial suspension of society's taboo on aggression and are permitted to perform all kinds of pranks if the treats extorted by the threats of tricks do not come up to expectation. Often, youthful exuberance oversteps the limits. Every Halloween, thousands of automobile tires are slashed, innumerable windows are broken, and several hundred homes are burned. In 1974, an old Mexican was kidnapped by young tricksters and killed "just for fun."

On Halloween 1970, the elegant Santa Cruz home of prominent ophthalmologist Victor M. Ohta was set on fire. The fire department found the corpses of the doctor, his wife, his secretary, and his two children floating in the swimming pool. They had been strangled with men's ties and riddled with bullets. Soon afterward, twenty-four-year-old John L. Frazier was arrested and confessed to the murders. In confused speeches, sometimes under the influence of hallucinogenic drugs, he had frequently announced that great things were about to occur. Police had found Frazier's handwritten note placed on the windshield of the murdered doctor's car.

> Today World War III will begin as brought to you by the people of the free universe. From this day forward anyone and/or company of persons who misuses the natural environment or destroys same, will suffer the penalty of death by the people of the free universe. I and my comrades from this day forth will fight until death or freedom, against anything or anyone who does not support natural life on this planet. Materialism must die or mankind will.[5]

In his defense, Frazier continued to justify the
"execution" of the ophthalmologist's family as a symbolic act for the liberation of mankind and for the
preservation of natural beauty against dirt and pollu-
tion. Frazier did not belong to any group or movement; his comrades, the liberators of the universe, were
alive only in Frazier's delusions and hallucinations.
Frazier, found guilty and sane, was sentenced to life
imprisonment (the death penalty was in abeyance at
that time).

COMMONSENSE SANITY DETERMINATION   Customarily, fanatics and mentally ill offenders are completely
convinced of the justice of their cause, feeling themselves legitimized by the code of the group they represent. If this group is totally imaginary, or if the
means employed have no conceivable rational connection with the proclaimed ends, the persons committing
these atrocities are very likely deranged.

Frazier's murders for the purity of the environment, Nash's campaign of revenge against a society
that had circumcised him as an infant and put him in
denominational schools without his consent, and Manson's helter-skelter attempt to instigate a decisive world
battle between blacks and whites are so bizarre in
their justification that little doubt exists about the
severely disturbed minds of the instigators. Yet, in spite
of their insanely brutal deeds, Manson and Nash and
the Doukhobor children were convinced that they used
mercy killing violence for ultimately peaceful purposes
only and that they were reincarnations of the Savior.

Recognizing a person as mentally disturbed is easy
as a rule, but the community's acceptance of an obligation to provide adequate care for such a person, to
help him rather than to punish him, is traditionally
quite a different matter.

Psychological Profile of the Skyjacker

Not all skyjackers display the same personality characteristics, but they do have many traits in common,
according to Texas psychiatrist Dr. David G. Hubbard,

author of *The Skyjacker*. Most of the fifty-two skyjackers he examined were disturbed, inadequate, often physically weak, frustrated, egotistical daydreamers, frequently with deep-seated, overtly manifested sexual problems. They were depressed, with suicidal fantasies and strong tendencies toward dissociation. Practically all were paranoid to some degree, and many of them suffered from paranoid schizophrenia.

Almost without exception, the men were self-punishing, passively oriented, and ineptly striving to placate their wives, who reviled and cuckolded them. In their youth, the skyjackers typically had many flight and fall dreams; and throughout their development, most of them displayed infantile fantasies of omnipotence and megalomanic ideas that often reached the intensity of delusions. The skyjacking usually followed a frustrating professional or personal experience and was motivated by revenge for injustice or by rage over failure. Hubbard also suggests that a subtle disturbance of the inner ear, affecting the skyjacker's body image and sense of gravity, is a distinguishing factor.

My own experiences and investigations, some of them made in collaboration with the Aberrant Behavior Center in Dallas, confirmed many of Hubbard's findings. Among the crazy and criminal skyjackers I examined, the highly pathological family structure, resulting in the formation of an infantile, undifferentiated, inept personality with depressive, suicidal, and paranoid tendencies, often amounting to delusions and hallucinations, occurs with amazing frequency. In my own case material, about equally divided between experienced and inexperienced pilots and parachutists, flying represented a symbol of sexual potency, suggesting the supreme ability to triumph over limitations of space and gravity. In the patient's imagination, the aircraft (usually a big jet plane) was pictured as a sovereign, independent community subject only to the orders of the omnipotent pilot. Fantasies about finding ultimate asylum, rest, and possibly death in the airplane were curiously mixed with expectations of achieving omnipotence by replacing the pilot and with notions of unrestricted release of aggression. Exhibitionistic publicity expectations regularly provided crucial motivations, and the satisfaction of having brought about an exciting, possibly even a world-shaking event pervaded the thought processes of the skyjackers, attracted by the mystique of sovereignty, in which the airplane represented the home or territory of an independent, tightly knit community under the command of an all-powerful leader. Risking his own life, the skyjacker experienced the short-lived dramatic realization of his fantasies as a striking denial of all the previous failures in his life.

Expectations of punishment, particularly the death penalty, serve as attractions rather than deterrents because of extremely strong aggressive tendencies that are directed against the self, culminating in suicide fantasies.

All patients examined by Hubbard and by me were severely neurotic or psychotic individuals, with or without criminal tendencies. Most of them were outright mentally ill, a few were outright criminals, and the majority represented a mixture of these two. None belonged to the crusading variety. Obviously, not every crusading terrorist is mentally healthy either, but hard-core crusading terrorists are psychologically miles apart from this group of individuals.

In-depth data from clinical experiences with crusading terrorists are rare and not likely to become more available in the near future. Yet, judged by their performance and method of operation, crusading terrorists can be expected to be competent, realistic, sober, and determined; they are quite different both psychologically and actually from the sorry bunch of their psychotically criminal or criminally psychotic imitators.

DIVINELY INSTRUCTED SKYJACKER After the breakup of his marriage, William Herbert Greene III, a thirty-year-old unemployed movie cutter, had displayed rather peculiar behavior for several months. He firmly believed that he had been bewitched by black magic, that several people in his environment had plotted against and persecuted him, and that he had to participate in a life-and-death struggle between God and the devil. His family made him consult various psychiatrists, but he never agreed to psychiatric treatment.

In April 1972, he left his job and from then on wore only women's clothes, in accordance with a divine order communicated to him by a song he had heard on the radio. Several days later, he left Los Angeles, again following God's command as contained in a song. In a stolen automobile he drove to San Diego, then to Mexico, and then back to San Diego for no apparent reason. Suddenly he decided to fly to New York to visit his sister. When the plane landed in Chicago, he grabbed another passenger's bag in front of a crowd of people. To his disappointment, he was not arrested; the passenger only demanded the return of the bag and did not pursue the matter. Greene continued on to New York, spent the night with his sister, and the next day committed two more thefts on the subway, again failing to get himself arrested.

Next Greene was commanded by God via a television movie to visit the space center at Cape Canaveral. Complying with the order, he flew to Florida and planned to steal a police car in Palm Beach. But he noticed a big sign saying "Delta is ready when you are," and recognized this message as another divine order. Accordingly, he boarded a Delta plane and, when it was in flight, gave the hostess a handwritten note claiming that he had a pistol and that he wanted to be flown to the Bahamas and to be given half a million dollars. The pilot suggested to Greene, who never left his seat, that they return to Chicago and permit the passengers to disembark. Greene calmly agreed, and when the plane arrived in Chicago, he was arrested without resistance. He did not possess a gun, nor did he have any idea what he wanted to do in the Bahamas.

Greene, who had no criminal record, was considered mentally ill by various prominent psychiatrists;

doctors in several clinics diagnosed him as paranoid schizophrenic. He was judged guilty and sane and sentenced to thirty years in prison.

A CRAZY CRUSADER TAKES TO THE AIR   Thirty-seven-year-old Mexican immigrant Ricardo Chavez-Ortiz, married for seventeen years and father of eight children, lived in the Los Angeles barrio. Working on and off as a short order cook, he had not been able to support his family adequately. They were crammed together in broken-down quarters and often went hungry. Yet even this standard of living seemed luxurious to Ortiz in comparison with the bitter deprivation of his childhood in a Mexican village and his first years in the United States.

Chavez-Ortiz had never been in any trouble with the police, but on two occasions welfare social workers had sent him to psychiatrists who had diagnosed him paranoid schizophrenic and had treated him with drugs and psychotherapy for several months. During his psychotic episodes, good-natured, passive Chavez-Ortiz believed that his co-workers and his children, whom he dearly loved, were plotting against him. After psychiatric treatment, which had helped him overcome his delusions, he seemed quite normal again.

Chavez-Ortiz had applied for a job as a police officer in Tijuana, but he never received an answer to his application. Once again he lost his job as a cook; and once again he believed that this was because of the plotting of his co-workers. He told his wife that he intended to go to Mexico to find a job as a police officer and then used the last of his earnings to purchase a ticket to Albuquerque under a false name.

Arriving in Albuquerque with light luggage and a guitar, Chavez-Ortiz felt desperately ill and decided that he was not well enough to look for work. While purchasing medicine for his stomach, he observed all kinds of weapons on display in an adjoining sporting goods store. He bought a gun and some ammunition, which he hid in the closet of his hotel room, and the next morning boarded a plane. He enjoyed the takeoff and the beautiful view, but suddenly, when the charming hostess offered him a drink, he became overwhelmed by the contrast between his happiness and the plight of Mexican children and all the children of the world. He decided that right then and there something had to be done to help them. He politely requested the hostess to permit him access to the pilot's cabin; then, he asked the pilot to surrender his cap, which Chavez-Ortiz put on, and to fly to Los Angeles. The pilot tried to persuade him to desist from his plan and to drop the pistol (which was not loaded), but Chavez-Ortiz refused politely and deferentially, saying he had to do his duty toward the children of the world. Constantly expressing his great concern for the safety of the passengers and the airplane, he apologized for inconveniencing them. Although as he told me, he was "half expecting to be killed," the prospect did not upset him because he believed it would confirm his sacrificial intentions and help children.

Chavez-Ortiz at no time asked for or received any money or other benefits for himself; he demanded only the opportunity to deliver a message to the world on radio in Spanish. His request was granted after landing, and he delivered a somewhat rambling two-and-a-half-hour speech in which he asked for peace on earth and better educational opportunities for Mexican and all other children. Smiling, he then surrendered and was taken into custody.

Prior to his trial, I had expressed some doubts about the defendant's ability to participate rationally in his defense, as required by law, and particularly to give informed consent to changes of legal representation that had been suggested and clearly imposed on him by a local Mexican group that had paid his bail. Chavez-Ortiz, who was totally disinterested in any legal strategy but who had written a letter to President Nixon demanding either the death penalty for himself or acquittal, was found capable of rationally assisting in his own defense. Because there was hardly any dispute about what had actually happened, the trial was undramatic except for the battle of experts, causing the judge to question the scientific reliability of psychiatrists who offered differing opinions. As usual, the psychiatric disagreement centered on the evaluation and labeling of the various signs and symptoms.

I presented the results of psychological tests and clinical impressions based on thirty-two hours of intensive psychotherapeutic interviews, an evaluation of Chavez-Ortiz's history, and hospital observations and concluded that Chavez-Ortiz was suffering from an episode of recurring paranoid schizophrenic illness similar to those he had undergone at least twice in past years. At those times, when he was not accused of any crime, this condition had been diagnosed by two physicians and intensively treated by one psychiatrist, who, after another lengthy interview with the defendant, fully confirmed his previous and my present diagnosis.

During this episode of his illness, Chavez-Ortiz did not hallucinate, but he was considerably confused and showed signs of delusions and serious misrepresentation of reality, accentuated by impulsive destructive and self-destructive acts.

Chavez-Ortiz frequently knelt down in front of strangers; he invariably kissed the hand of every person he met. His intention to sail around the world in a rowboat in order to prove the courage of Mexicans, his bizarre skyjacking feat, and his grotesque behavior during that attempt appeared to indicate a psychotic disturbance, particularly in view of his previous history and psychological tests.

This type of conduct, which was confined to the periods of his acute disturbance, seemed to indicate more than just an innocuous cultural deviation. Yet, previous episodes of violence and bizarre impulsivity in this mild-mannered, compliant man were interpreted by the defense and the government as either minor or insignificant, perhaps even culturally determined departures from Anglo norms. In any event, they were viewed as nonpathological, possibly exaggerated, and misguided expressions of a deviant social philosophy. The government's psychiatrist noted that the defendant was entirely independent of any social organization and that he was "somewhat confused, emotionally disturbed and mentally ill." He diagnosed "paranoid trends manifested by extreme sensitivity to rejection," and he observed "exaggerated responses and a tendency to misinterpret, personalize and exaggerate the rejection of others." Commenting on the defendant's fantasies of violence and self-aggrandizement, he attributed these "fantasies with a flavor of adolescence" to "immaturity rather than to the bizarreness of a psychosis." Considering Chavez-Ortiz's "simplistically held beliefs," he maintained "that because his motives were not wrong (from his subcultural point of view) and that he was hijacking the plane solely for the purpose of dramatizing a social protest, that he did not feel he really committed a criminal offense."[6] He concluded that he could not discover any sign of psychotic illness and was unable to concur with my opinion.

In my opinion, I wrote:

> Every human behavior is largely culturally determined. There is no difficulty in finding cultural coloring and cultural (as well as subcultural) habituation in many, if not all, of the defendant's actions. That these actions contain, as they must, come cultural and/or social determinants does not necessarily imply that they are therefore normal and not expressions of severe, even psychotic psychopathology. There is severe mental illness in every culture. Unless it is assumed that behavior shown by this defendant, culminating in the hijacking of an airplane for purposes of advertising the plight of the people and the children, lies within the subcultural frame of reference valid for Mexican immigrants subject to prejudice and deprived living, this defendant's actions have to be considered the expression of personal psychopathology beyond any normal behavior acceptable by his or any different subculture.[7]

Political and religious rationalizations and expressions are characteristic of many forms of psychotic illness, serving sometimes consciously, sometimes unconsciously to excuse and justify criminal and/or psychopathological behavior. On the other hand, not all deviant political or religious views, regardless of how unsound they may seem, are necessarily expressions of either criminality or psychopathology. In other words, exaggerated concern and even preoccupation with social and religious issues does not in and of itself indicate psychopathology.

In view of the defendant's personality pattern, his type of delusional reasoning, and his previously diagnosed mental illness, there seems to be little reasonable doubt that his social-political activities and convictions were expressions of mental disturbance, even though they were codetermined by his personal, social, and cultural experiences.

Chavez-Ortiz was found guilty and sane and was sentenced to thirty years in prison; this was later reduced to twenty years.

The issues were quite clear-cut. The prosecution wanted Chavez-Ortiz to be classified as a criminal terrorist so that he could be punished and serve as a deterring example. The defense seemed to place the interests of a cause over those of an anonymous, confused, and resourceless defendant. It seemed as if they wanted him to be labeled a crusading terrorist so that his vague message of world peace and improved opportunity for children could be more effectively used for propagandistic political purposes. Aren't Mexican immigrants discriminated against, exploited, and persecuted? Aren't Mexican children deprived of many educational opportunities? What is so crazy about bringing this consistently ignored and sad state of affairs to the attention of the public? Is every attempt to remedy social indignities by publicity to be denounced as crazy and thus thwarted?

The prosecution wanted a long prison sentence because Chavez-Ortiz was a common criminal. The defense probably wanted a sentence that would make him a martyr, a symbol of injustice and persecution perpetrated on a whole group. Chavez-Ortiz did not understand his symbolic significance; he wanted simultaneously to die, to live on a remote island, and to try traveling around the world in a rowboat. He did not care which as long as he was treated like a gentleman.

Mental illness is neither a social rubber stamp nor a cop-out; it is a crosscultural psychological reality. I believe that Chavez-Ortiz was mentally ill, a crazy terrorist with crusading overtones. Indisputable signs of mental disturbance, past and present, governed his conduct, or as the law expresses it, substantially impaired his capacity to guide and evaluate his own conduct.

The determination of punishable guilt or the possible exculpation of offenders because of mental illness are social, not medical matters. The representatives of the community differentiate between bad and mad, thus deciding whether the offender should be punished or treated. The medical experts only explain, advise, and suggest; they do not decide. Whatever psychiatric opinion, legal provisions, and humane considerations may dictate, most people do not want to keep skyjackers or presidential assassins in hospitals or allow them to be treated and helped regardless of their motivations.

PART II

The Victims

5

Poor Devils

Indifferent to innocence and human suffering, terrorism recognizes no rules or limits imposed by decency or pity; it can strike anybody, anywhere and does so with increasingly foreseeable, yet unpredictable, regularity. Crusading and crazy terrorists of a bygone era chose their victims for what they were or what they represented: kings, archdukes, members of a hated establishment or an enemy target group; criminal terrorists confined their victim selection to the powerful and wealthy. But nowadays, everybody is a potential victim. The horror of modern terrorism is precisely expressed by everybody being helplessly exposed at random: the train or plane passenger; the customer or employee in the bank or drugstore; the man, woman, and child on the street taking a walk or a ride in a car—all of them doubly innocent, free of guilt, and free of involvement. Often, the terrorists do not know whom they will hurt, and they could not care less. Nothing seems important to them except they themselves and their cause. In planning and executing their deeds, the terrorists are totally oblivious to the fate of their victims. Only utter dehumanization permits the ruthless use of human beings as bargaining chips, bargaining instruments, or objects for indiscriminate aggression.

Yet after the deed even the most dehumanized killers cannot help developing feelings; their emotions, no matter how odd, testify to a humanity that their actions denied. The extreme situation brings out extreme feelings and thoughts. The victims, cruelly and indiscriminately singled out, also display their emotions, some of them unexpected and strange.

William Cook, the cold-blooded mass murderer, and only incidentally a crazy terrorist, had acted out his ferocious compulsion to inflict on others what had been done to him in the merciless reprisal of indiscriminate killing.

Cook's twisted personality and the motivation for his bizarre crimes could be explained by his unusual and extraordinarily traumatic childhood experiences. But what motivated his victims? Two migrant workers at first accompanied him only under duress, then semivoluntarily, and finally, completely voluntarily for fourteen days. They testified that he was a nice guy, although he did not talk much, kept to himself, and never got close to them. They knew that he had had a hard time in life and never had a break. They were not afraid of him, although they had heard radio reports about the many murders he had committed. But then, they themselves were unstable, barely literate, friendless people. Birds of a feather?

But what about the thoroughly respectable middle-class family who traveled with Cook for six days? Could they actually have wanted to remain with him? No one knows for sure; he killed all the victims before they could tell. The reconstruction of events has to depend on what witnesses observed and on Cook's own statement. Cook had little reason to lie. He had nothing to lose, and he wanted to die. He described in detail how the family were frightened out of their wits the first night and day. He watched them very closely, threatening them with instant death if they made a wrong move. But later on, as they began to know each other, they got along very well. For many days, he did not brandish his gun at all. They chatted with each other, he telling them of his life and they of theirs.

The youngest boy came as close to being his friend as anybody ever had. The two talked a great deal, and on several occasions, they took little exploratory trips through the forest, leaving the other four in the car. Toward the end, they were quite chummy.

The family and Cook ate together in restaurants. A dozen times, they stopped for fuel at gas stations, and Cook left them to use the rest room. Each night, he slept deeply for several hours. There were many opportunities for the family members, together or separately, to escape or draw attention to their plight. But either they were too intimidated or Cook was right in assuming that they had also come to like and even trust him a little. Paradoxically, just because of this developing closeness, Cook told me, he felt compelled to kill them as soon as they aroused his sympathies. Ashamed to show any emotion, he quickly corrected himself: "I killed them just so, for no particular reason."

Apparently the Mosser family had, to their misfortune, become convinced that the devil was really only a poor devil. In the eyes of the victims, the brutal aggressor had been transformed into a victim himself, to be pitied and protected, rather than feared and condemned.

Captors and Captives

There is no doubt that strange feelings of camaraderie, closeness, empathy, friendship, even love often develop between hostages and captors, between victims and victimizers. Many years after the brutal mass murderer's execution, the poor devil phenomenon would attract popular and scientific attention under the name "Stockholm Effect," so called after the curious, yet characteristic series of events that took place during and after a bank robbery in Sweden.

In August 1973, Jan-Erik Olsson, a recently escaped convicted felon, strolled into the headquarters of the Kreditbank in the middle of Stockholm, fired several shots into the ceiling, and captured four hostages—three attractive females and a male bank clerk:

blackhaired Kristin Enmark, twenty-one; blonde Elizabeth Oldgren, twenty-three; Brigitta Lundblad, thirty-one, mother of two, employed at the bank for ten years; and Sven Saefstrom, twenty-five years old.[1] Olsson demanded that a friend of his, Clark, imprisoned in the jail from which he had escaped, be allowed to join him. This request was immediately granted. Clark was taken by police from his jail cell to the bank and surrendered to Olsson.

The two bank robbers and their four captives stayed together in closest proximity for almost six days and nights. From the start, the criminals had conducted negotiations with the police by shouting over the phone. During the first three days, the hostages made and received numerous phone calls to and from police and relatives. On his request, Olsson was connected with the Swedish prime minister. The robber demanded a large ransom payment, a getaway car, as well as the use of an airplane to leave the country. He underscored his threats by choking one of the captives, whose frightened gasps were clearly audible over the phone.

The next day, hostage Kristin took the initiative and phoned the Swedish chief executive. In a long conversation taped and broadcast to the public, she indicated her disappointment with his cautious attitude: "I think you're sitting there playing checkers with our lives. I fully trust Clark and the robber. I'm not desperate; they haven't done a thing to us. On the contrary, they have been very nice. But you know, Olaf, what I'm scared of is that the police will attack and cause us to die." Later Kristin stated: "I'm not in the slightest afraid of him," and then "I want to come out with these two guys—I want to go with the robber and no one will accuse you or anyone else, I have said so on the radio today, the whole Swedish people knows that we want to go with Clark and the robber." She continued: "This may sound stupid, but I want to go with the two, because I trust them," then "I know they would let us go as long as the police don't chase us." The prime minister would not give the permission requested and continued to argue with Kristin. The chief executive's persistent refusal to go along with her suggestion made her angry. With a sarcastic "thanks for the help," Kristin hung up on him.[2]

Repeated surrender requests by the police were turned down by the robbers with obscenities. Shots were fired by the criminals. When the police tried to carry out their plans to pour gas into the bank vault, Olsson had nooses tied around the four hostages' necks so that they would be hanged if the gas caused them to slump into unconsciousness.[3]

Intensive negotiations went on for several days. Three hundred and fifty thousand dollars in Swedish paper currency was dropped down to the terrorists, after Olsson agreed to let the police inspect the hostages. The police commissioner found everybody relaxed and cheerful; one convict in a friendly gesture had his arms around the shoulders of two women. The hostages made no request, except to be permitted to leave with the robbers.

Then, the police decided to get tough. They rationed and then altogether stopped the food supply and, by closing the door of a wall, confined the group to a small area, glaringly lit from above. After more than four days of negotiations, police drilled holes into the ceiling and walls, according to a suggestion presumably made by the New York Police Department. Olsson took potshots at the officers who were drilling and wounded one of them. Water streamed through the drilled holes, and the room was plunged into darkness for hours at a time. The police relented after a while because of threats to the hostages' lives.

Twenty-four hours later gas was poured down noiselessly from aerosol cans. Despite elaborate planning, the fumes were not strong enough to cause unconsciousness, but the hostages were unable to obey Olsson's order to put the nooses on again. Everyone was lying on the floor gasping and choking, when finally the robber shouted his surrender.

Gas-masked police demanded that the hostages come out first, but all of them refused. Kristin insisted that the two robbers precede the hostages, otherwise the criminals might be gunned down. The startled police complied. The group, first the trembling hostages, then the gunmen, walked out together, embraced and kissed each other, shook hands and cheerfully bid each other goodbye (Kristin: "We'll see each other again."[4]) before the criminals were arrested, handcuffed, and led off to jail. Even on the ride to the psychiatric hospital to which the hostages were taken for observation, the women begged for understanding of their captors: "Don't be too hard on them," Kristin and Elizabeth pleaded with the chief of the Stockholm criminal police, Gunnar Aaström.[5]

The slow progress of the bank drama, which was reported hourly on Swedish radio and television, greatly stimulated the public's fantasies. Rumors were rampant and numerous. "Inside" reports were published about sadistic excesses and sexual orgies in the bank.

After their arrest the robbers were promptly charged with rape and other sexual misconduct. But the hostages insisted that their captors had behaved like gentlemen. Perhaps, the authorities suspected, one of the women had been "under severe stress for several days and what she says now may not reflect the truth, or what she might feel a few weeks from now."[6] But the hostages did not change their stories, even after traces of human semen were found on the carpet of the room in which they were held captive. Later, on the prosecution's insistence, one of the hostages clarified that Olsson indeed had asked her for permission to caress her. He had touched her with her clothes on, then became excited, whereupon the hostage had refused to further participate. She suggested instead that he might find another way to satisfy himself. He did.

Right after his arrest Olsson regretted that he had been incapable of exploiting his advantage to the fullest: "I was too soft, I should have shot one of the hostages."[7] Later on he confirmed psychiatrist Dr. Nils Bejerot's suggestions that the girls appeared to have succumbed to the criminals' charms, and that the criminals had been unable to commit murder, as they had intended, due to the developing bond of mutual friendship.[8]

Olsson was given ten years of prison for robbery and hostage-taking. Clark, who was serving a six-and-a-half-year sentence for former offenses, succeeded in having his conviction for his participation in this episode overturned by the appeals court. He argued that the police had compelled him to abandon his cell and to become Olsson's accomplice. Did he freely chose to participate in the criminal venture? Was he guilty if he was compelled to start with, but then participated willingly and actively for the sake of survival, for personal gain, or just because he happened to be there?

HOSTAGES' REACTIONS Some journalists were astonished that "the hostages seemed to harbor little ill will towards their captors."[9] Under the ironic caption "Darling Gangsters," a European newspaper[10] commented on the deplorable state of a society (i.e., Swedish society corrupted by decades of welfare state, high taxes, and softness towards criminals) in which hostages taken by force and subjected to dire threats on their lives, not only showed sympathy for their captors, but criticized the law-and-order attitude of the authorities. (One hostage vigorously protested that newspapers had called the incident a "drama" and had denounced the captors as vicious criminals, while according to the hostage, they had been polite, struggling human beings.)

The police authorities also found the hostages' attitude incomprehensible: "After what they had been through in the vault, it is hard to understand the reaction," said Detective Inspector Kurt Krantz.[11]

Dr. Lennart Ljonggren, physician in charge, commented that the hostages, on admission to the hospital, "remained in the first stage of reaction to catastrophe, characterized by overwhelming fright, fear of death, chaos and the elimination of all normal laws."[12] Dr. Bejerot added: "The hostages were in a state of shock in which they rejected reality to put off facing the terror that struck them." But days, weeks, and even months after their plight was over, the hostages, talking freely about their harrowing experience, did not change their minds. They insisted that the criminals only did what they had to under the circumstances, that putting nooses around their necks was more a "demonstration" than indication of any intention to kill. Kristin said to the doctors at the hospital: "They never harmed us, I was more afraid the police would do something, so we would be killed."[13]

In various ways, all the hostages (including the man) said the same: The robbers had not always been kind, but they were humane, tender, and had made them feel secure. The hostages often wondered why the police had not been as considerate as the criminals. Even after it was all over, they wondered whether there was anything wrong with them, because they could not get themselves to hate their captors. They persisted in thinking of the police as the enemy and of the criminals as those to whom they owed their lives.

After an adequate period of observation, the hostages were discharged and declared perfectly normal from a psychiatric point of view. Kristin and Elizabeth returned to their parents, Brigitta to her children and husband. The psychiatrist commented on the pressures of a common emergency and explained the hostages' gratitude toward their captors as a mechanism characteristic of a survival situation connected with what psychoanalysis calls identification with the aggressor.

Undoubtedly, the psychiatrists were correct. The situation in a cage when survival is at stake creates strong feelings of belonging in a group held together by a common danger that is sooner or later attributed to a common enemy: the outgroup (the police and rescuers in general). Initial calculated acquiescence turns into willing submission and the enjoyment of dependency, accompanied by an attribution of charismatic omnipotence to the group leader.

Yet there was more at work here than the mutual identification between aggressor and victim which consisted of strong, libidinally charged ingroup feelings combined with aggression projected onto the outgroup.

Criminals such as Olsson and Clark have little to recommend them to active, well-bred, good-looking, young working women and men. Indeed, none of the hostages was particularly attracted to the convicts in an overt sexual manner, and none of them was love-starved or sufficiently frustrated to savor the excitement of this coerced adventure as a pleasurable experience. The victims were not impressed by their captors' intellect, glamour, or daring. They just felt sorry for them.

The robber had told them of his own childhood, his wasted life in prison. He had talked about the senselessness and injustice of the criminal justice system and had aroused the hostages' pity when he spoke about his "fear of having to return to prison again."[14] Poor devil, what he needed was brotherly understanding, sisterly love, motherly care. Without exception, that is how the hostages felt. They all wanted to protect the two unfortunates who had threatened them and almost taken their lives. They cared for and wanted to take care of the poor devils. They could do no more, but they felt compelled to do no less.

Other Poor-Devil Incidents

There have been numerous events before and after Stockholm that on careful scrutiny permit no interpretation other than the poor-devil syndrome.

After skyjackings, passengers and hostesses often have nothing but kind things to say about their captors. Two airline hostesses are known to have returned weapons to skyjackers because they felt sorry for the poor devils, who had been "so nice" and who, in the women's opinions, should be trusted and helped. One U.S. airline hostess regularly visits "her" skyjacker in prison. She wants to wait for and marry him after he gets out of prison some ten to twelve years from now.

In 1971, two professional criminals held up a bank situated on one of the busiest streets in the middle of Munich, Germany, in plain daylight. They took seventeen hostages and demanded a large ransom payment and safe passage out of Germany. In the ultimate confrontation after ten hours of negotiations, a hostage and one of the criminals were killed as they entered the getaway car. His accomplice was overwhelmed by police before he could harm any of the remaining hostages.

At the trial, an attractive young woman who was one of the bank customers held hostage testified that she never felt threatened by the defendant and that she pitied him. She wanted to do everything she could to help him. The judge sternly reminded her that this man had been directly responsible for killing two people, one of them a totally innocent young girl, and that the convict, a hardened criminal, had frightened, intimidated, and threatened numerous hostages, including herself, for many hours. The witness would not be swayed. She stated that she knew all that but nevertheless would stay in touch with the defendant and wait for him until he had served his jail sentence. Possibly, she thought, she would marry him.

In 1971, Sir Geoffrey Jackson, British ambassador to Uruguay, was kidnapped by the Tupamaros and kept in the "People's Prison" for nine months. He was guarded by shifts of three hooded revolutionaries who occasionally pistol-whipped and mistreated him. Because of tight handcuffs, his hands were paralyzed for months. In his book *Surviving the Long Night*[15] Sir Geoffrey describes his daily life with the terrorists in great detail. As time went on, he advised them about the distribution of food, redesigned their hoods, and talked and argued with them. In retrospect, he wonders whether the ferocity and the dramatic bluntness that he disliked in his captors were created by their unfortunate situation in life rather than by defects in their personalities.

After five days of siege, Dutch police staged a three-pronged surprise assault on the prison chapel in Scheveningen, where two imprisoned Arab convicts and two Dutch criminals were holding fifteen hostages, among them women and children. Rushing in with a fusillade of shots into the ceiling, the riot squad immediately overwhelmed three of the convicts, but the fourth managed to hide among the hostages. It took several minutes of panic before the last terrorist, the Algerian Mohammed Koudache, could be picked out from the group of hostages surrounding him. After their nearly miraculous rescue, one hostage explained that, strange as it may sound, they had grown to like their captors, who had been good to them. They hadn't wanted to hand Koudache over to the police.

The most dramatic instance of developing strong feelings for kidnappers and everything they stand for is, of course, the case of Patty Hearst (see Chapter 7). Long before there was any indication that this strange coerced conversion would take place, I warned the Hearsts of the possibility that Patty would begin to think fondly of her captors. Undoubtedly a genuine victim when she was dragged from her Berkeley apartment, Patty apparently was first coerced and then voluntarily identified with her brutal captors, whom she saw, according to her statements on the tapes, not at all as aggressors, but as victims of a brutal system. She became a gang member in good standing, viewing at least for a while, the police, her family, and her former associates as the real aggressors, who victimized her as well as her captors.

Victim Solidarization

For terrorists, victims are primarily a means to an end. They are used instrumentally to bring about certain effects. For the most part, a victim's fate matters to a terrorist only to the extent that it is relevant to the terror objects (the victim's family, friends, employers, governments). Terrorists can hope to achieve their ends only as long as the victims are alive (or believed to be alive) and unharmed.

The victims' friends, relatives, and governments share this overwhelming interest in the life and welfare of the victims, although for vastly different reasons. The victims serve as protective shields and bargaining tools and thus involuntarily guarantee a temporary alliance with the antagonists that forms the basis for ne-

gotiations and bargaining. The helpless pawns thus
represent the common link between terrorists and their
objects. There is no good reason to mistreat victims as
long as they behave, and in fact, they are rarely subjected by crusading terrorists to any sadistic surplus
torture or other "irrational" deprivation beyond "necessary" threats and psychological pressures.

Physical proximity and exclusive interdependence
between captors and captives promote budding emotions of belonging. Antagonists forcibly thrown together turn into co-victims and easily find the common
enemy that victimizes them both. They are in the
same boat, and a "we" feeling is established on the basis of the shared experience and the common danger.
The kidnapper's threats and actions create a grotesque
new group with a short-range common purpose. The
"we" feeling of the group is all the stronger the longer
the caged situation lasts and the greater the expectation of imminent common death. Fear caused by the
emergency situation is blamed on those who, in order
to cope with the emergency, have become the immediate, concrete danger. From the prisoners' perspective,
it is "us" (captives and captors) against "them" (relatives, police, and government).

For the victim, the kidnapping has all the frightening and some of the attractive features of an exciting event. Ordinary routines and habits are interrupted,
and all the small, repetitive considerations of a hum-
drum existence are replaced by the one overwhelming worry about survival in the next few hours or days.
The realistic fear of impending death is one of life's
most extreme situations, in which the deep-seated,
repressed, and denied emotions of existential anxiety
and transcendental concern are freed and mobilized.
Many victims discover or rediscover God (there are no
atheists in foxholes or in hijacked airplanes or kidnapper's hideouts). Many experience a never-before-
felt closeness to relatives and friends, and they console
themselves with fantasies about how their folks will be
alarmed and worried.

Some captives undergo infantile regression to a

state of apathy, depression, and utter dependency in order to cope with a situation that indeed has rendered them totally impotent and under the complete control of omnipotent figures. They may have to conceal intense futile rage, pervasive anxiety, or extreme despair. Yet, some may also experience a kind of cataclysmic relief because what they had anticipated in their fears has finally happened.

A few may envy and secretly glorify the brute force that has subjugated them. The attraction of the brutal caveman, unrestricted by the rules of civilized conduct, is a feared and desired eroticized fantasy, shared by many women and men who are forced to give up their powers of decision making ("Do with me whatever you want"). Total surrender is not always devoid of relief and even pleasure. It means a return to an early childhood situation; one can yield completely without guilt because one has no choice, no responsibility.

After the initial shock, many victims try to overcome their feelings of helplessness by indulging in notions of role reversal. The gap between the victim's enforced passivity and the captor's forceful activity is bridged, understandably enough, by consoling fantasies that "this cannot last long" and that there will be a day soon when they will be liberated and then can do to their captors what now is being done to them.

After prolonged exposure to omnipotent control, many victims take on characteristics of the aggressors by whom they have been coerced and to whom they have had to submit. Liberated, the victim carries within himself traces of the former oppressor, like festering sores. The remembrance of repressed previous suffering will be repeated in reverse in the transitions from detested passivity to desired activity. In this "identification with the aggressor," the attacker's aggressiveness proves contagious and is imitated, repeated, and internalized by the victim, who becomes like the aggressor.

But other, subtle processes may also be set in motion. As the aggressor at times develops interest in his victims as human beings along with feelings of tenderness, pity, and concern for them, they in turn may unexpectedly identify with him as a co-victim. The submission that began as a reasonable and appropriate means for coping with duress is perpetuated by nonrational, largely unconscious introjection (internalization of external events) and projection (externalization of inner conflicts), identification, role changes and reversals, and inner adaptations. The kidnappers could have killed me, the victim reasons, or tortured me or starved me. But they haven't done any of these things. The absence of death or cruel punishment is interpreted as reward, and wishful thinking fortifies the belief that the kidnappers are reliable, restrained, possibly even chivalrous. Budding gratitude mixes with emerging hope. Since the worst hasn't happened yet, maybe it never will. I may be spared after all, thanks to their being fair-minded and simply misguided.

Terrorists may talk to their hostages a great deal about their own mental and physical suffering, about how they and their families were oppressed, abused, and exploited (the justifying self-pity is always the same). The victims begin to feel with them and for them. They start to "understand" their captors. The attackers are seen as desperate, confused, deprived individuals, victims themselves, who by circumstances rather than by evil intent have been forced to employ force against others. They come to feel that the terrorists are entitled to their protection and care, possibly even their help and support. The former devils have become poor devils.

At least as powerful and much more frequent than erotic fantasies of rape and pleasurable total submission are feelings of protectiveness for the poor devils who have suffered so much and in their desperation cannot help themselves any other way.

The abject helplessness of the victim is projected onto the aggressor, who in a larger context is also seen as a comrade and victim in the experience of this newly found solidarity. The turn from passivity to activity is achieved by the desire (and the fantasy) to help and

care for those human beings who had suffering inflicted on them before they were compelled to inflict
it on others. Such a response can be called victim
solidarization.

In our society, identification with the aggressor is
considered perfectly normal and adjusted to reality,
that is, reality syntonic (consistent with a reality shaped
or mutilated and determined by violence). You are
blameless if you can place all the blame on an original
aggressor with whom you had to identify. Identification with the aggressor provides the perfect justification and excuse for your own violence.

Unconscious identification with the aggressor is
consciously encouraged, promoted, and even enforced
by those with vested interests in violence. To produce
combat effectiveness, military officers treat trainees the
way they want the trainees to treat the enemy. The most
basic of all training aims at the transfiguration of the
personality by identification with the instructing officer,
who acts as aggressor, so that the soldier himself can
become a dependable aggressor against the dehumanized opponent (gook, kraut, Jap, or whatever stereotyped label he may wear). The potential aggressor who
lives in all of us becomes the actual one by being
forcibly exposed to calculated aggression. The trainee
is being conditioned for obedience, ruthlessness, and
insensitivity to mourning, sympathy, and human closeness. The mass media help by advertising and glamor-
izing the toughness cult and the mystique of violent
masculinity.

The antifeeling, antigrief, antiguilt education is not
confined to the military establishment and its admirers
and imitators. Conformist acceptance of violent reality
calls for tolerating ongoing intense, widespread, and
unnecessary human suffering with a minimum of guilt
and grief. Hardening and the acquisition of toughness
are mandatory reality adaptations; insensitivity and indifference become survival virtues. Identification with
the aggressor has been the initiation rite into and the
entrance fee demanded by cultures of violent indifference and indifferent violence. It is the process by which

the hidden terrorist in all of us becomes manifest. The victim, given the opportunity, will always become the victimizer. Violence breeds violence.

Although the poor-devil phenomenon is an adaptation to a situation of extreme terror, it should not be dismissed as merely pathological. It deserves careful consideration for what it suggests or expresses about the possibilities of human response in a world that considers violence normal and even healthy. It is not only depraved collaborationists, outright masochists, and love-starved females who develop, sometimes after considerable emotional struggle with themselves, those strange twinges of sympathy and empathy with their attackers. Yet these feelings of solidarity are considered unusual and irrational in contrast with the more frequent, hence allegedly more normal and rational emotions of vengeful hatred and pitiless retaliation. Violent aggressors bristling with self-righteous justification are prevented by the initial conditions and aftereffects of their aggression from getting closer to their victims. Very few aggressors (some Germans, some participants in the Hiroshima raids, some Vietnam veterans) identified with their victims sufficiently to understand and to make restitution. But by recognizing and identifying with the victim dimension of the aggressor, the victims could initiate and further human solidarity based on the universality of human suffering. Emotions do not just distort; they also motivate and clarify. Concrete action, based on this emotional understanding of the other, not as aggressor, but as co-victim, may constitute one of the few remaining hopes of mankind.

6

Rape of the Mind

Things have a price and are interchangeable; human beings do not and are not because they are believed to possess unique intrinsic value. Ideas, accomplishments, and works are deprived of their human character when they are merely traded like commodities on the marketplace. By the same token, men and women are dehumanized when they are treated like merchandise to be bargained with and exchanged.

The coerced dehumanization so popular among terrorists today represents a novel perversion in the repertory of human aggression against its own kind. New technological and psychological sophistication has raised the ambitions and possibilities of modern kidnappers. From kidnapping for extortion and blackmail, they have advanced to kidnapping for redistribution of wealth and change of social conditions, and finally to kidnapping for educational purposes. The ideological indoctrination is allegedly performed for the benefit of the victim, who is forced to convert "freely," to demonstrate not just consent but conviction. Coercion, having obscured its brutal origins, is then at its most triumphant when the victims are compelled to experience submission as a voluntary decision. This is rape of the mind.

Thought Reform

Simple educational techniques, based on sophisticated psychological theory, are readily available to effect genuine conversion. Practically anyone trained in dehumanization can teach dehumanization. Profound changes can be brought about through a variety of coercive maneuvers disguised as liberating, uplifting, and therapeutic.

Old-fashioned indoctrination and intimidation procedures produce obedient compliance as long as the pressure lasts. Crude torture may still break the spirit and the body. But modern thought manipulation (called thought reform or reeducation) succeeds in systematically implanting new and durable inner convictions that are experienced as all the more voluntary, self-initiated, and spontaneous the more they have been coerced.

True believers have always considered the misguided heathens and heretics to be steeped in error and possessed by evil; they must be purged, with or without their consent. Their brains, filled with false ideas, must be cleansed of all dirty material to prepare the way for the message of salvation. That salvation is accomplished if possession by false consciousness is acknowledged and totally reversed through confession, self-accusation, insight, recantation, and the acquisition of a new self.

The end result of this educational enterprise is the individual's coerced belief that he thinks and does voluntarily what he has been forced to think and do. Extreme coercion may result in the manipulative experience of voluntariness with all traces of coercion or manipulation erased. Through the increasingly popular device of label swindle, slavery is re-experienced and renamed freedom.

In totalitarian countries the forcibly subjugated citizens are treated as hostages and become victims whether or not initial coercion was followed by seemingly voluntary acceptance. Kidnapping quickly establishes a miniature, "perfect" totalitarian society, and terrorism creates the terror situation of absolute domination.

Kidnappers and totalitarian rulers, temporarily secure in their hideouts or palaces, want not just to do away with the old spirit but to create a new one. They want not only to rule but to educate; they want to get rid of their victims or else turn them around and win them as converts.

Infantile Helplessness

Human beings are born helpless and, in contrast to most animals, require total care and total control for an extended period of time.

In all cultures, at all times, the growing infant is confronted with a preexisting cultural system of rules and habits. Regulations, goal definitions, and values are interpreted and represented by parents, teachers, and other powerful persons. In the obligatory process of socialization, the surrounding culture educates (acculturates) the infant by using rewards and punishments, by realistically and morally validating the cultural assumptions, and by offering reference persons for imitation and identification. In the beginning, the educational process is compulsory and compelling, no matter how benign its intent. The child is totally exposed and surrendered to his environment because of his biological weakness and lack of experience. The infant cannot yet decide for itself; even if everything is done for its benefit, it must be forced in its own interest to express and to behave itself in keeping with what the surrounding culture deems right and appropriate.

Cultural value systems differ widely from each other, but what they all share is the belief that their system is superior to that of others (or at least not inferior) and that the external world is really exactly the way their particular culture sees and interprets it. From this ethnocentric conviction derives the educational obligation to imbue (i.e., imprint, impress, condition, train) the children with the attitudes, thoughts, and patterns of action defined by the culture as right and proper so that they will be able to function happily and effectively. At first the seemingly uncomprehending, unruly, and inconsistent child will have to be compelled to do what is good and right for it by external pressures.

However, the aim of education is not just compliance with external rules, supervised and enforced by external authority, but the imparting of the conviction that these rules and prescriptions are right and should be followed on one's own volition. The educators explaining the meaning of certain regulations will hold themselves up as examples and products of cultural compliance; they will promise the child that he will become as powerful and beloved as they are if he only believes and does what they believe and do. Children imitate their parents' behavior, not because they have tested the moral or utilitarian value of the parents' views, but because they believe in, fear, and love their all-powerful parents.

Total Institutions

Early child rearing is a benevolent but total institution, one that selects and manipulates rewards and punishments, stimuli, and response possibilities. The controllers of this situation have the ability to preselect all incoming stimuli and to offer only a limited number of available interpretations. They have the capacity to select and direct a person's responses by encouraging some and deterring other forms of thought and behavior.

Totalitarian societies, prisons, and kidnapping situations are also total institutions, usually malignant from the victim's point of view. In these instances, the dependent infantile state has been forcibly reestablished by coerced infantilization. Totalitarian regimes capitalize on childhood dependency and on the tendency to seek an escape from adult responsibility in order to make malignant domination appear to be benign tutelage. The sudden imposition of a total institution by capture, imprisonment, or kidnapping is a fearsome occurrence. But in spite of its horror, it frequently also gratifies overt and covert dependency needs. Forced infantilization is not so much a repetition as it is an innovation because it is the fully developed adult who is coerced into regression to this childhood state. Consciously and unconsciously, dictators and kidnappers (and, for that matter, anybody powerful enough to attempt thought control) draw on the experience of educators and therapists to exploit tendencies to seek escape from freedom. They make the most of their victims' childhood memories, feelings, and longings.

Strategies for Mind Change

The systematic application of three overall strategies, all based on the establishment and maintenance of a total institution, make modern conversion techniques novel in that they produce not merely consent but inner conviction. The strategies are: coerced complete involvement of the total personality; channeling all efforts into psychological self-scrutiny and personality change; and use of bogus peer groups who appear to be allies but in fact are representatives of authority.

For total commitment to occur, the victim's full personality has to be engaged in systematically imposed, concentrated efforts from which there is no escape. Automatic compliance and intellectual engagement are not enough; the victim must not withhold anything. The performing soul doctor insists that for the good of the reformee nothing be left out or held back in the free give of the subject's total personality.

"Brainwashing" is an inadequate term for these endeavors. Not even "brain impressing" will do because it is not just the brain but also the heart, all the sense organs, and the guts (particularly the guts) that have to become totally involved in the reform effort. The individual must not be granted the luxury of any privacy or the privilege of any secrets. He is instructed that he can become truly himself only if nothing belongs to him alone any longer.

Consistently and emphatically, the individual has to be taught the basic psychological lesson that he alone is to blame for his trouble. Even if he has done nothing specifically wrong, the hangups of the past are the results of his own misinformed, misguided, distorted, tradition-bound, wrong way of thinking and feeling. But he can help himself by his willingness to accept wholeheartedly the help of those who have the proper outlook and attitude.

The total institution has decided that the individual needs help and prescribes the type and intensity of education, reeducation, or therapy required. The individual, however, is deceived about the true state of affairs. He is given the illusion that what, in fact, has been ordered for him and imposed on him has been what he personally desired. His obedience to overwhelming authority is to be experienced by him as if it is the fulfillment of his own wishes. The total institution has totally succeeded only when the individual feels that he wants and is responsible for what has been imposed on him from above.

Just as coercion is concealed by the label of free choice, submission is experienced as a struggle of and for personal identity. In these endeavors, the victim is assisted not only by the authority figures acting as teachers but also by peer groups composed of co-prisoners and other previously indoctrinated victims. These friends and helpers have either gone through a similar educational process or have never required any such reeducation because their original education equipped them with the correct view.

In the captive situation, the victim is constantly exposed to the pressures of a carefully selected and thoroughly ideologically instructed group that only appears to be a group of peers and auxiliary therapists but is in fact acting as the agent of authority.

This bogus peer group is charged with the responsibility of shaping the newcomer's self-image, which is to become his psychic reality according to their preconceived design. By helping him discover and enhance "his" reality, true reality is evaded and concealed. But this new reality is not at all "his," and he is free neither to search for anything resembling his self nor to experience anything as real other than what his captors have so designated.

Complete authoritarian control from above, and often from far beyond, is accomplished and at the same time blurred by the deliberate use of betrayed betrayers who appear to be colleagues and comrades but are, in fact, stool pigeons and the extended muscle of the representatives of authority.

This personal relationship with the group members that, with or without sexual overtones, may be sufficient to induce the subject's cooperation by the inherent compulsive power of suggestion and by distortion of the subject's awareness so that this distortion may appear to be consciousness-expanding enlightenment. The total context is altered by making psychological breakdown appear to be the precondition for acquiring mental health, to declare renunciation of former ties as therapeutic catharsis, and to hail every kind of despicable behavior (ratting, lying, betrayal, false accusations) as heroic deed and expression of new loyalty. The completely conditioned, mass-manufactured illusion of freedom and dignity will then be defended as the highest accomplishment and the most precious possession of the autonomous personality.

Techniques of Mind Change

The vast modern repertoire for thought reform contains many fragments of recognized psychological theories. It borrows heavily from behavior theories, conditioning (classical, instrumental, and operant), psychoanalysis, and group therapy. The psychiatric methods used to restore sufferers from mental illness to health are used in reverse to create a state of mind equivalent to and indistinguishable from mental illness. Utter terror systematically produces man-made insanity, almost always in the service of a sacred cause.

The grand strategies of total involvement of personality, coercion of motivation, and use of a bogus group are carried out by techniques that aim to weaken and sever former ties, establish new ties and associations with and in the present environment, internalize the newly acquired insights and bonds, and reinforce the new beliefs and activate the new personality by group experience and participation.

SENSORY DEPRIVATION   Incessant exposure to intensive pounding and/or complete isolation (or an alternation of the two) are immeasurably more effective in breaking a person and making him more susceptible to outer influences than the cruelest physical tortures. Human beings cannot tolerate the prolonged absence of sensory stimuli without experiencing extreme frustration and utter confusion culminating in psychotic episodes.

Changing external stimuli guarantee the stability of the inner equilibrium. If the outer environment does not provide such stimulation in sufficient measure, it will be self-manufactured by fantasies and illusions and finally by delusions and hallucinations. When the individual is cut off from accustomed sources of emotional and sensory support and deprived of familiar sights, sounds, and experiences, fantasies merge with memories and imagination with actuality. Everything becomes uncertain and blurred. The victim-subject cannot distinguish any longer between his own beliefs and reality. His confusion and fear obliterate any safe differentiation between what exists, what is suggested to him, and what he himself believes. He can no longer trust anybody or anything, least of all himself, because his former frames of reference are not only unavailable but become increasingly unbelievable, even unimaginable. This loss of confidence in the fidelity of one's own perceptions and conclusions destroys all self-esteem, self-reliance, and the basic trust in the integrity of one's own personality. Deliberately created confusion and the systematic application of unexpected shocks and contradictory stimuli make for total loss of orientation and self-confidence.

In this manufactured state of anxiety and agitation, resistance to indoctrination is lowered. After days, weeks, or months of isolation, almost anyone is willing to say or do whatever is required to escape the hell of being alone with his own fearful expectations and fantasies. Variety is, not the spice, but the essence of life; the imposition of sensory deprivation is the most exquisite form of psychoterror and mind torture.

BRAIN IMPRESSING   Terror (i.e., maximum fear produced by intimidation) is a high-tension and drive state that increases the need to respond. The disruption and loss of former structure create a need for the new structure offered by social cues from the new environment. The cleansing and rinsing phase (or, rather, the destroying of personal identity disingenuously named brainwashing) results in alienation, anomie, absence of social relatedness, depression, and withdrawal until and unless new ties are formed. Opportunities for acquiring such new bonds are offered in abundance. The masters and their agents seem anxious to show the newcomers genuine affection. As often as not, the victims eagerly accept their new friends for the simple reason that they are there. The switching of allegiance is not always perceived as such. Often an individual's perceptions and memories have been so distorted that his behavior appears to him not only acceptable but consistent with his customary way of functioning.

The preliminary softening and crushing of old structures aim not just at attitudinal changes but also at dislodging the basic values to which attitudes are tied. Shifts in belief in a direction opposite to the subject's starting position are brought about by constant, repetitious, crudely simplified indoctrination or by the deliberate creation of total uncertainty, in which the subject is provided with few (if any) explicit verbal cues and is left to change his convictions seemingly independently.

Simplicity is the key to indoctrination. As long as the often-repeated messages can be clearly understood, any claim to truth or objectivity is secondary. Stress on existing shared values (decency, sincerity, benevolence) and on common goals increases the impact of indoctrination, which remains persuasive even when the intent is obvious. The content of the message is not as important as its credibility; therefore, all efforts are concentrated on representing the authority and its agents as omnipresent, omniscient, omnipotent, and totally irresistible. Through the workings of psychosocial defense mechanisms and through ingratiation, belief in the new authorities' competence increases their overall credibility and also their attractiveness.

Once total control is accepted soberly and without moral judgment as unchangeable destiny, various doublethink tricks and ingenious label swindles do the rest. Infantilization poses as maturity; the result of coercion becomes spontaneity; total enslavement is called final liberation; compulsion is named therapy; and loss of individuality means becoming a real person.

BACK IN THE FAMILY New converts tend to see any absolute authority as increasingly benevolent, understanding, and sincerely interested in their welfare. For a while, everything seems to work for the masters; even their inexperience may be advantageous to them. Blundering sometimes increases trustworthiness and stresses the sincerity of the authority that is not suspected of impersonal technological efficiency.

Total change is more comfortable and hence more frequent than gradual reconciliation of believed differences in resolving cognitive dissonances between traditionally held old and imperatively demanded new attitudes. If submission is inevitable, one might just as well get it over with quickly. The strongest inducement for submission is the lure of a return to a genuine family situation, guaranteeing full acceptance and complete security. The new community from which terror emanates is also, like the family, an agency of love. Disciplinary measures are experienced, not as techniques of domination, but as necessary demands conveying interest and concern. Under the protection of all-powerful parental figures, all the brothers and sisters mutually love and aid each other in spite of minor squabbles. Individual freedom, powerless in the face of these coercive circumstances, is willingly relinquished in favor of joining a new, powerful family unit. With parental omnipotence restored, the mind revives all memories and fantasies of past infantile bliss.

MONOPOLY OF INTERPRETATIONS   More important even than total control over information received by the victims is the exclusive monopoly over all permissible interpretations of that information. The captives get their news carefully selected and prepared for their digestion. They will also be given a pseudo choice between various possible meanings of this news. No matter which of the various interpretations is chosen, it will always be right because the "false," misleading alternatives will not even be offered for selection.

During the indoctrination process, periods of incessant pressure alternate with indeterminate periods of quiescence. In the beginning, great strictness is exercised, giving way to leniency after the turning point of budding compliance has been reached. Using another tactic practiced by many police forces to obtain confessions, roles are distributed. Some authorities or group members play the bad guys, who mercilessly pursue the prisoner until he does what is expected of him; others become the good guys, who are nice, understanding, and comforting, promising all kinds of benefits and privileges. Frequently, these role distributions are not separated, and everybody takes turns playing any required role. The strategically planned use of group dynamics becomes particularly effective when the role players do not playact but, rather, act on their conviction that they are helping the subject in the same way they themselves were helped.

The projective paranoid mechanism of singling out an enemy and then blaming everything evil on him is used and reinforced vigorously. Opposing ideas are personalized because real people can be hated more intensely than abstract ideas. It is the others, the former associates, who are to blame for everything—

the suffering of the world, the previous suffering of the terrorists, and the present suffering of the victims. The victims are cruelly blamed, but only to the extent that they are still part of the other, the enemy. In the opinion of the captors, the victims are guilty by association. Therefore, the victims should confess their guilt, criticize themselves, and be willing to undergo a complete change.

Self-criticism, turning against all former associations and rediscovering one's "real" self in direct opposition to everything one has been in the past paves the way to atonement. But opinion need not be altered directly. By changing the perception of object and objectives, new meanings emerge. The manipulating authorities can claim that the victim was manipulated by the enemy, that his former self was not a genuine person but a copy, possibly even a cover.

GROUP BELONGING   The group is the final and most important agent of change. Belonging to the group is both the proof and the goal of that change. Testimonials are more persuasive than lectures or preaching; persons or groups vouching for the illuminating and liberating effect of the conversion they have undergone are more likely to be believed than professional convincers or dispassionate theoreticians. But it is actions that speak louder than words, particularly one's own actions. Full membership in the strongly motivated group is granted only after the convert has proved his worth by submitting to arduous initiation rites and trials of his loyalty and endurance. If he can be induced to perform irreversible actions with and for the group, he will be firmly welded to the unit because his internal demands for consistency will compel him to talk and think as he has acted. Disowning his action would mean not only desertion of the group but also betrayal of his own integrity. Therefore, every group attempting to make converts is not satisfied with verbal declarations and tries to elicit actual participation in order to tie the new member to his new convictions by commitment through action.

In order to gain admission, prestige, and approval from the group, the convert has to engage in spectacular actions.

The dedicated group members, linked to each other by common danger, shared goals, and mutual guilt, become an idealized family that totally satisfies the members' needs for belonging. As long as any member remains totally committed to the group, he or she can be certain of the family's total trust, acceptance, and love. Indeed, this totality of acceptance, reflected in an inner state of bliss as a result of liberation from anxiety and guilt, is often subjectively experienced as rebirth. The old individual is dead and forgotten; a new man or woman, the representative and personification of the new group spirit, has been born.

Conscience in the Repair Shop

Various psychological theories explain the process of conscience formation and its internalization in different ways: as a result of conditioning, of Oedipal conflict developments, of imprinting or imitation, of mimesis and identification. All education aims at having the subject not just do what he is told but to want to do it. The parental wishes and prohibitions are supposed to become part of the child's new personality. The child internalizes the cultural norms by incorporating them into his personality organization; soon the introjected parental commands and demands will be experienced, not as compliance to external requirements, but as expressions of his innermost wishes. Even in the parents' absence the child will soon act and feel as he would if they were there because they actually *are* there—within him. They have become introjected objects within his own personality, which has been enriched by the inner agency, the superego, for his internal, independent guidance and evaluation. External compulsion has become superfluous when rule conformity is enforced by the inner voice of conscience. The superego has taken over the parental task of distinguishing between right and wrong and of watching over adherence to the right; it will reward proper and punish improper thoughts and behavior by guilt feelings and lack of self-esteem.

Internalization not only frees the individual from external pressure but makes him more independent of external supports; for the mature person, the superego is the most important source of approval, self-worth, and identity confirmation. Once internalized in the conscience, certain value systems that are no longer subject to rational scrutiny or to volitional change become the basis for habituated thoughts and feelings and for automatic patterns of action. No child has chosen his parents, his nation, his race, his religion, his language, or his culture; yet after he has successfully internalized the parental, cultural, and other values that at first were forced upon him, he will experience and from then on uncritically accept as absolute, indisputable, and right what has in fact been coincidental, arbitrary, and relative. That is why rational or irrational, divinely or satanically inspired value systems may have exactly the same convincing power for those who have received the proper mythological instruction. The development of such virtues as altruism, dedication, willingness to sacrifice, and self-sacrifice is less dependent on the content of the value system than of the degree of its internalization, which provides a unified, consistent, even though possibly irrational basis for understanding and action.

Just as it was once internalized, the superego can, under conditions resembling early infantile helplessness, be partly or completely externalized and projected again. When an individual is under duress, so-called charismatic leaders, bosses, executives, companies, and movements, as well as ideologies, religion, even science (Milgram's obedience experience experiments),* and

---

*In Yale Professor Stanley Milgram's obedience experiment, randomly selected New Haven residents were persuaded to apply electric shocks of increasing severity to alleged participants of a test, who "had to be punished" when they forgot certain memory items. The Milgram experiment, repeated in other countries and in other settings with essentially the same results, proved that the vast majority of

certainly dictators and kidnappers can become temporary or permanent substitutes for individual conscience. The individual may endow them with his superego functions and then temporarily or permanently obey, follow, and be judged by them as if they are his own conscience. Externalization of the superego relieves anxiety and responsibility, and as long as the external repository of the superego function (God, leader, beloved, group) can be satisfied, the individual feels at peace with himself and the world, contented, committed, approved, and loved.

In the reeducation process of compulsory thought reform, former established internalizations are first dislodged from their anchorage in the personality by denunciation of the sources and the content of the former introjected values. The former superego is weakened, confused, shaken, undermined, and cut off from its supplies, until it is projected and externalized. Then persons and symbols are offered to serve as recipients of superego externalization to act in lieu of and on behalf of the individual conscience. Yet this is only a transitional phase; the externalized superego has to be reintrojected because only such internalization establishes the semblance of voluntariness and independence that guarantees proper thought control and action. Indeed, it is the purpose of the whole reeducational enterprise to have the old internalized superego replaced by a new one, preferably more securely and permanently internalized and integrated into the new personality structure. The terroristic thought controllers compel the individual to divest himself of his most precious and intimate personal possession and to surrender his superego to them; they force him to send his conscience to the repair shop run by his masters.

---

normal adults in civilized countries will be capable of torture and possibly of killing unknown innocents who have never done any harm to them. This brutal aggression will be performed without much hesitation or guilt if it appears legitimized or compelled by convincing authority, even if such authority is as nonviolent as the prestige of a scientific experiment.

They, the supreme craftsmen and experts in the manufacture of a clean and easy conscience, will fix it up as if it were a denture or a defective watch. The forcibly borrowed superego, renovated and polished, will be returned for introjection with a lifetime guarantee of smooth functioning and reliable service.

There is no mystery to the production of honest conviction and good conscience, nothing requiring miracle drugs, hypnosis, charisma, or ultrasophisticated, arcane methods. Given sufficient time, sufficient indoctrinated fanaticism, and total control of the environment, conversion efforts will invariably succeed with a variety of people, regardless of their age, sex, race, nationality, or personality makeup. There is something for everybody in the vast repertory of thought control that mimics and mocks but also successfully imitates and employs well-known educational and therapeutic techniques.

For thought control and thought reform, the establishment and maintenance of total institution is absolutely essential. The astonishing results of defining and redefining freedom and dignity can be accomplished through total control over informational input, over all interpretation possibilities, over guided responses, and over the regulation of reward and punishment. The defense of human dignity and freedom has to consist of the prevention and correction of those conditions under which dignity becomes a fraudulent label and freedom another name for coerced yet voluntarily accepted submission.

Successful Conversion

Marc Hillel, a French Jew, and his French wife, Clarissa Henry, who is of English Protestant stock, recently published the sensational results of their research, also shown in the color documentary *Of Pure Blood,* a story about Nazi leader Heinrich Himmler, who initiated "the Fountain of Life enterprise for the selective breeding of a super-race."[1] This program encouraged promiscuous sexual relations between selected "racially superior" German women and equally superior SS men. The children stemming from these unions were lavishly cared for in beautiful surroundings. But, as was not discovered until much later, many foreign children from occupied countries were also taken from their parents to be raised in Fountain of Life camps. As always, justification came easy. Himmler commented: "How can we be so cruel as to leave a potential genius with our natural enemies?"

An old Polish woman, mother of a child who had been forcibly taken away from her by the Germans thirty-two years before, desired nothing more than to resume contact with her daughter but was notified by the daughter's lawyer that the young woman "considers herself German and has no desire to remember the past."[2] No doubt hundreds or thousands of such kidnappings were committed. Very few have become known because the victims of such brutal coercion are prevented by that very same coercion from recognizing that they are victims. Obviously, this tragic effect does not mitigate but rather accentuates the severity of the crime perpetuated. The crime is rape of the mind.

All kinds of large and small thought-manipulating crimes are committed daily. Label swindle provides inoffensive new names for the offensive practices: teaching discipline, implanting belief, briefing, indoctrination. In California, a large organization "saves" eighteen- to twenty-year-old mystics who have fallen under the spell of religious sects that hold beliefs contrary to those of their parents. The organization's techniques include forcible abduction and a period of enforced purification called deprogramming.

A totally dependent status makes minors and those who can be reduced or coerced into the state of a helpless minor subject to programming, without their consent and against their will, presumably for their own benefit. More often than is comfortably assumed, crimes are committed against dependents in the name of education. Children are battered and sexually exploited; soldiers are trained beyond the point of exhaustion; citizens of dictatorial regimes are coerced into puritanical abstinence and discipline, all for their own good. Battered children often want to return to their parents or develop strong emotional ties to raping relatives; soldiers often glorify the school of hard knocks through which they became "real" men; citizens of a totalitarian dictatorship often praise the regime that denies them their rights. This is not an excuse for but just adds to the tragedy of child beating, rape, oppression, and deprivation of liberty.

Rape Prevention

Normal human beings should be protected against unwanted programming. In fact, every attempt to coerce them in any such manner should be considered a criminal offense, even if it is allegedly or actually undertaken for their benefit. In a free society, the forcible denial of free decision in matters of political and religious preference, exertion of rights and sexual choice, or the coerced imposition of such decisions should definitely be prohibited by specific sanctions of criminal law.

Rape of the mind, without regard to the sex of the victim, represents just as violent an intrusion into the most private and sacred sphere of personality functioning as physical rape does by force or threat of force. The victim of mind rape is just as much at the total mercy of a brutal seducer as any victim of physical rape. The adverse results of coerced psychological procedures may be as traumatic, pervasive, and permanent as any physical violation. The difficulties of legally separating this offense from other types of permissible, everyday conduct (such as education, suggestion, pressure, and seduction) are not, as a matter of principle, any greater than those involved in the delineation of rape from aggressive physical conduct in general. Rape of the mind should be a crime.

The prosecution would have to prove that somebody was forcibly and against his will physically removed from his environment; cut off from accustomed sources of information and emotional support; deprived of any access to independent counsel, advice, or information outside the range of his or her abductors; and subjected to crude or subtle forcible techniques to change his or her mind. The integrity of an independent and free mind deserves as much protection as the integrity of the body. The coerced, complete physical control over a human being (except by persons specifically entitled to such supervisory control, such as parents, teachers, law enforcement authorities, and physicians) employed to bring about changes of opinions, convictions, and attitudes either deliberately or as an accidental benefit of such enforced complete control should have the same legal significance as penetration has in rape cases. Rape of the mind should be an actionable offense (possibly in addition to kidnapping), regardless of the age and sex of the victim. (His or her particular infirmity or helplessness may be an aggravating circumstance similar to the provisions regarding contributing to the delinquency of a minor or statutory rape.) Subsequent consent to the illegal rape of the mind would at best be a mitigating (rather than an exculpating) circumstance, but at times it would also be considered an aggravating circumstance because voluntariness subsequent to rape of the mind may be the result of extreme and particularly cruel coercion.

The rapid development of so-called mind-altering techniques (mind attacks) that can be expected to work quickly and effectively against the will of a person make legal protection of the mind's freedom of choice desirable, even mandatory. In view of the overwhelming technological and psychological tools at the disposal of hidden and overt persuaders, the individual is incapable of defending his very individuality by himself because his will can be perverted and channeled without his consent and contrary to his desires. Society's defenses therefore have to start earlier; protective barriers have to be erected against establishing a coerced situation in which thought reform can be effectively attempted and carried out. Rape of the mind should be made a criminal offense to be prevented or punished by sanctions of the criminal code.

7

The Hearst Case

I had expected the call. On February 14, 1974, Charles Gould, publisher of the *San Francisco Examiner,* phoned my Beverly Hills office and invited me on behalf of the Hearst family to consult with them at the earliest possible moment. I left for San Francisco the same evening.

Patty Hearst's strange kidnapping on February 4, 1974, had made banner headlines all over the world. Assassination of highly placed persons, extreme violence against groups and individuals, criminal kidnappings for ransom, jail breaks, prison revolts, skyjackings, mayhem, arson, and murder in the service of a high ideal had become commonplace enough in contemporary America, but this was different. A lovely young woman bearing a famous name had been brutally dragged away by a mysterious army that seemed to demand nothing for themselves but everything for the people, in whose name they claimed to act. Ostensibly they followed the example of Middle Eastern or South American Robin Hood terrorists, who had used hostages, preferably the innocent, to obtain release or other benefits for their oppressed brothers and sisters.

No matter how many such events had occurred

in other countries, they had never really penetrated American public consciousness because nothing of the kind had happened on U.S. soil. Now the American people were not just horrified and shocked; they were totally confounded by the bizarre circumstances of the kidnapping, the bizarre legal and military language employed by the kidnappers, and the bizarre content of their demands. Who were these people ganged together in the self-styled Symbionese Liberation Army who had claimed credit for the incomprehensible murder of a black school superintendent several months before? What did they really want? Were they urban guerrillas fighting for political ends? Were they common criminals? Or were they crazy? Nobody seemed to know the answer.

In spite of frantic efforts, law enforcement agencies could not get one good lead on the culprits. Political scientists and pundits could not agree on whether to classify the SLA as revolutionary, counterrevolutionary, or the figment of a sick imagination. The tortured Hearst family, whose appeals and goodwill gestures had remained unacknowledged, did not know what to do next. Because none of the ordinary moves had yielded any results, the time would soon be ripe for the experts of the mysterious and irrational: the clairvoyants, the soothsayers, the astrologers, the psychics, and last and least, the psychologists and psychiatrists.

John Peterson of the *National Observer,* who had interviewed me within days of the Hearst kidnapping, wondered why someone like me had not been called into the case from the beginning. In their anxiety and confusion, the Hearst family (and, for that matter, the law enforcement agencies) appeared in dire need of professional guidance. If there ever was a case in which the admittedly controversial principles that talking is better than shooting and negotiations are better than confrontations should be tested, this was it. Peterson suggested having me retained as adviser and consultant. I agreed on the conditions that my services be freely solicited by the parties concerned, that I would have adequate access to available information, and that nothing would be demanded of me that would be incompatible with professional ethics.

Arriving at the Hearst mansion around midnight, I gingerly stepped over a mass of tangled radio and television cables partly blocking the entranceway. I met the Hearst family in the large living room: Mr. and Mrs. Hearst, their next older daughter and her husband, Willie Hearst III, Patty's fiancé Steven Weed, Arthur Lester, a number of FBI men, several family friends, and a Dutch psychic who sat in an adjoining room concentrating deeply on a picture of Patty and one of her brown leather shoes. Talks with the family members and with Weed continued until the wee hours of the morning. We resumed again the next day and night and the following day.

My friendly arguments with the psychic, which the family members kept alive by deliberately provocative questions, afforded what little comic relief there was in the anxious vigil. The psychic, recommended by a hard-nosed police officer, talked about his successes in previous cases. He was very optimistic about the early return of Patty, with whose life-force he was in almost constant touch through alpha waves. He knew he could locate her soon. She was in a place near water, he said; he could hear drips. Almost everybody wanted to believe him, but his explanations of how he arrived at his results sounded so convoluted and obscurely superscientific that they undermined the hope he intended to convey.

By the time I got there, Randolph Hearst had already agreed to the food giveaway program as a goodwill gesture. There was much discussion about what and how much should be offered, when and how the effort should be organized. Our main immediate concern was, not how to conduct negotiations, but how to get them under way in the first place. Obviously, strong, unusual, and possibly pathological motivations played a large part in the SLA's conduct. While I attempted to guess some of these psychological motives, I advised against provoking the kidnappers by proposing that a psychiatrist negotiate with them, let alone offer to help or cure them.

Understandably enough, feelings of indignation, rage, and helplessness ran high and were expressed in strong language. On sober examination of the total situation, everybody (privately, even the law enforcement officers) agreed: The SLA had what we wanted —namely, Patty—in their complete control. We had little choice. If we wanted her back unharmed, we had to work through them. We had to buy time and their goodwill and make the most of the one concern we definitely shared with the kidnappers. As Randolph Hearst expressed it, "I think the one thing we have in common is that the SLA and I don't want to see my daughter killed."

I continued to consult with the Hearsts by phone for the next several weeks as we waited for word from Patty's captors. Randolph Hearst not only permitted but urged me to talk publicly about Patty and the family's attitude. He wanted it known that the family availed itself of whatever services existed for guidance and counsel. He did not suggest that the SLA or Patty needed psychiatric help; rather, he sought advice so that he himself might understand. I did the best I could, which was not much. I am hardly consoled by the hindsight recognition that under the circumstances very little could have been done.

In retrospect, it seems evident that all our deliberations and decisions had only a very slight influence, if any, on the developments that took such tragic turns, precisely because no real negotiations were ever possible with the SLA in hiding. All negotiating skills are useless if there is nobody to negotiate with. Our first effort had to be directed towards bringing about a negotiation situation, yet we had nothing to offer that would induce them to contact an intermediary or to materialize temporarily out of the thin air into which they seemed to have dissolved to tell us what they really wanted. We had nothing to give them that would make the suspicious fugitives believe in our sincerity, at least, for the purpose and for the duration of negotiations. Of course, we did not know at the time how helpless we were; singly and together; we used whatever wisdom, experience, and intuitiveness we possessed to prevent the worst, although not everybody always agreed on what constituted the worst.

For purposes of establishing negotiations, I suggested ignoring the undoubtedly present elements of crazy and criminal terrorism in the composition of the group and the motivation of the members' personality makeup. They should, I thought, not be treated as kooks, bums, or dingbats. Rather, they should be accepted as the crusading terrorists they represented themselves as being, in the hope of inducing them to behave in accordance with their flattering self-description. "Hacker thought we should, as much as possible, treat the SLA at face value, even to the point of incorporating their rhetoric in our replies."[1] They should be held to the terms of the Geneva convention to which they had appealed; they should be reminded that in terms of their own ideology, no single individual or family, no matter how powerful, wealthy, or influential, can be expected to be omnipotent. According to Marxist beliefs, even the pillars and supporters of the capitalist system are at the same time also its prisoners. A warfaring party could impose stiff conditions, but to ask for the impossible was sadistic, criminal torture.

Therefore, they should be told in some way or another that it was unreasonable and counterrevolutionary to make demands that were abstract, global, and hence impossible for any individual or family to fulfill. A specific date for the beginning of negotiations should be set in exchange for the Hearsts' renewed goodwill gesture. "Hacker also thought we should demand a specific date for the beginning of 'release negotiations' in return." These and many more suggestions along the same lines were designed to convince them that the Hearsts were honest and serious in their attempt to have Patty returned unharmed and that they had no intention of double-crossing them.

Looking ahead, I thought out loud about the possibility of the strange solidarization effect between captors and captives that had been observed in similar cases and about how to prepare for this implausible and yet not infrequent contingency. "Then, after discussing similar cases, Dr. Hacker made two very important observations, which stuck in my mind but which I didn't think were applicable to Patty: that prisoners, particularly kidnapping victims, often develop sympathies with their captors and that like prisoners of war, kidnapping victims return to people who have come to resent them, making readjustment difficult for both sides."[2]

Turning Point

On my next weekend visit to Hillsborough, several members of the Hearst family were quite cool to me. On March 4, 1974, *Newsweek* had written that

> the corporation's new offer, making any further payments contingent on Patricia's release, moves the negotiations into a new phase—one endorsed as strategically sound by Dr. Frederick Hacker, who specializes in the study of political terrorism and has been counseling the Hearsts in their ordeal. Hacker also theorized that the cheerfulness of Patricia's voice on the second tape might indicate that she is reacting to her danger by adopting her captors' viewpoint. This is not that surprising, Hacker said; in some skyjacking cases, stewardesses have established a quasi-love relationship with the hijackers and later were reluctant to testify against them.*

Did I really think that my reference to airplane hostesses and other crime victims who have been openly sympathetic to their captors and torturers was appropriate to Patty's case?

*In *The Strange Case of Patty Hearst*, John and Francine Pascal quote Steven Weed as saying that he "remembers that a psychiatrist gave him and the Hearsts some advice in the first week of the kidnap. The psychiatrist told them that they would have to prepare themselves for Patty's identification with her captors. Later we realized that it would have been truly amazing if it hadn't happened under the circumstances."

   In the midst of our arguing, news about the receipt of a new tape arrived. The cassette was rushed to the Hillsborough home and we all listened together as Patty began by hoping that "the voice of their guns express the words of freedom" and by ending "It is in the spirit of Tania that I say 'PATRIA O MUERTE VENCEREMOS.' "[3] The tape of April 3 had confirmed my hunch. The loving daughter began to upbraid her parents, announced having "embraced" the name Tania, and openly sided with her kidnappers. The Cassandra prediction, anticipating the unthinkable and yet possibly inevitable, had come true.

   The strange process of conversion, so utterly incomprehensible and disturbing to all those who believe in the eternal neat separation between good and evil, between right and wrong, had started. The young innocent, whose well-being had been the concern of millions, changed within a few weeks into one of America's most wanted criminals. The dangerous villain Tania became the target of as many bitter curses as sweet Patty had been the subject of devout prayers.

Victim Choice

Trying to make sense out of the seemingly senseless incidents of history, it is hard to accept that something so extraordinary should happen to a person so average in spite of her wealth and afterall so ordinary as Patty. But happen it did, testifying to the indiscriminate ruthlessness of the terrorists, who cunningly selected their target with careful, long-range planning. Patty was accessible; her full name and address had just recently been listed in a student newspaper. She was, in fact, an ideal or natural victim choice. In retrospect, it almost seems the choice could have been figured out in advance. Not surprisingly, Patty Hearst's name was found listed along with several others earmarked as victims in the SLA papers left in Nancy Ling Perry's burned-down Oakland apartment on January 10. Somewhat more surprisingly, this information, which could have been used for protective security measures, was either never communicated to the FBI or ignored.

It was precisely her disinterest and noninvolvement in radical politics that made her an appropriate choice for her terrorists, who wanted to capture a shining symbol of the poisoned and poisonous capitalist system. But most important of all, Patty was a Hearst. She carried the name of a family that is part of American folklore, a symbol of enormous wealth and its ostentatious display and also of the irresistible power of the mass media.

Donald DeFreeze, who adopted the war name Cinque after a rebellious slave leader of the seventeenth century, may not have known that Patty's great-grandfather, the colorful George Hearst, was the only member of the California state legislature to cast his vote against the adoption of the Thirteenth Amendment, abolishing slavery, in 1865. Cinque probably did not even know that his own historical namesake had later on become a slave trader himself. But what he and the other SLA members undoubtedly knew was that the legendary Hearsts represented the mythical newspaper fortune and empire, and still wielded magical (i.e., mass media) power. Patty's grandfather, the controversial, ruthlessly innovative William Randolph Hearst, had taught the nation and the world that attention-getting news about surprising, scandalous, or spectacular events could be made to pay off handsomely in money and in political influence. That publicity success can be achieved by dramatically embellished reports about either actual spectacular events or events made spectacular by exaggeration or even by the free play of inventive fantasy is the essence of the Hearst legend.

The media princess was a prize catch. Her possession guaranteed that the terrorists' print-in-full requirements would be carried out with utmost accuracy, thereby elevating a small, anonymous, insignificant group to the status of a strong, internationally known, and feared army. By capturing Patty, the kidnappers also captured an audience of millions who, with insatiable appetites, swallowed the facts and conjectures fed to them by the media. Picking Patty was a winner for those who, without her, would not only have been certain but, worst of all, unknown losers.

Disunity of Command

Charles Gould, on first inviting me to the Hearst home, remarked that the situation there was "schizophrenic." Of course, only individuals can be mentally ill; situations or nations cannot be (although they may act "crazy") and therefore cannot be treated in the same manner as individual patients. What Mr. Gould meant was that there was total confusion and disorganization; pushes and pulls in all kinds of directions; people, groups, and all kinds of interests trying to cooperate, yet managing to counteract and work against each other, creating binds, double and triple binds, and every other conceivable confusion. There were, except late at night and early in the morning, dozens of people milling around—FBI agents, representatives of the state police, members of the Hearst organization, television people, advisers, well-wishers, friends of the family, friends of the girls, friends of the friends—talking to one another, huddling in little groups, exchanging whatever scanty information was available, discussing, planning, plotting. There were two telephones ringing almost constantly, and people were forever coming in and going out with messages for everybody from everybody. Mr. Gould was unfortunately wrong in thinking that I could reduce the confusion; as one more person, I probably added to it.

During the day the mansion was surrounded by television reporters and cameramen with their equipment, waiting for the news that came sparingly. They were inquisitive, trying to grill any newcomer. They asked persistent and often indiscrete questions, but there was no obligation to answer them.

FBI agents were in constant attendance at the house, monitoring television coverage and writing and receiving messages. Practically every evening there was an informal conference involving Randolph Hearst, Willie Hearst, Patty's brother-in-law, Charles Bates, local head of the FBI conducting the investigation; and assorted other participants, including myself on two occasions. If there was anybody in overall charge, I was not aware of it. The channels of communication also remained unclear and unspecified; it seemed that everybody said whatever he heard or thought to anybody he could get to listen. Obviously there were innumerable rumors, hints, and suspicions to be checked out, yet no one knew to whom to address such requests. Understandably, everybody's mood was subdued. There was a cordial atmosphere in the air, everybody trying to be helpful and cooperative but nobody seeming to know how. At these meetings, information, theories, and conjectures were exchanged with considerable openness and informality, but one was never sure that the conference partners were telling all they knew or, for that matter, whether they should.

Steven Weed and others complained that the FBI would not give out relevant information, but we hoped that Charles Bates knew more than he said he did. He was most reassuring, hinting that the FBI knew a great deal about the SLA, particularly its women members, and that surely it could not be too long before they were caught. He said publicly that he expected Patty to return for her twentieth birthday (February 20, 1974).

From all appearances it seemed that there were three distinct authorities planning and acting independently, sometimes at cross-purposes and always without previous consultation with each other, at least to my knowledge: the FBI, the state police, and the Hearsts. The Hearst group, including myself, often speculated about what the FBI could do in this or that hypothetical case. Local FBI and state police representatives frequently claimed to be unable to make decisions with regard to an assumed future situation, and they referred to consultations with higher-ups. Randolph Hearst communicated by phone with some of these officials, but everybody, at least the three major groups, seemed to be doing his own thing. Prior to Patty's announced conversion and her criminal involvement in the bank robbery, law enforcement authorities seemed to permit and even encourage the Hearsts to use all means at their disposal for contacts, negotiations, and compromises, without committing themselves in advance to any course of action except to carry out their lawful assignments. This stance, however friendly, cooperative, and sympathetic, clearly doomed the Hearsts' attempts to failure.

After making the promise of the $2 million food giveaway program, our primary aim was, first, to establish contact with the kidnappers and, second, to find out what they considered of sufficient value as exchange for Patty.

In her first taped message, Patty had tied her own fate to the fates of Russell Little and Joseph Remiro, the two members of the SLA who were in custody, charged with the murder of black school superintendent Marcus Foster. They were, according to her statement, as innocent as she herself, "simply members of the group and had not done anything themselves to warrant their arrest." We all agreed that Hearst should offer to pay for the two men's legal counsel, whom they were free to select. This might be a beginning, indicating his good faith once more, but it certainly would not be enough. I suggested that the Hearsts hire an attorney believed to be acceptable to the SLA to act as go-between; the professional relationship between the attorney and his clients would be legally protected, so that the SLA could trust him, at least for purposes of negotiation. The idea was quickly dropped; it just would not work. Nobody was in a position or had any inclination to guarantee that an attorney, if anybody could be persuaded to undertake such a dangerous mission, would not be followed by law enforcement officers in the expectation that the lawyer would lead them to the SLA.

After the first goodwill gesture with no strings attached had failed to accomplish any of its purposes, and after Patty had announced her conversion, the

promise of another $4 million provided but not con-
trolled by the Hearst Foundation to be distributed in
accordance with the wishes of the SLA on sole condition of Patty's safe return seemed to make some sense
and was at least worth a try. The original SLA suggestion for a totally impractical $400 to $600 million
giveaway program did not bode well for the success of
any reasonable compromise.

In the beginning, we thought (erroneously, as it
turned out) that the kidnappers, regardless of and in
addition to their political motivation, must be interested
in their own safety. Various possible plans were ven-
tilated and preparations were made. We conjectured
that in the style of crusading terrorists, the SLA might
at some point demand a getaway plane to seek asylum
in a South American or Arabian country. Under the
assumption that they would agree to any such bargain,
how could they be brought to the airport? Who could,
or would, grant any kind of immunity for crimes committed by American citizens, and under what circumstances? Nobody knew, or at least nobody would say
and commit himself. If the kidnappers had only been
foreign, everything would have been easier, the
chances for Patty much brighter.

In discussing such plans, the FBI's representatives
did not seem totally averse to the possibility of an un-
der-the-table deal, but they and we did not know what
the attitude of the state authorities would be, and certainly no law enforcement authority in this country
could openly and publicly make an announcement
promising immunity of any sort to dangerous criminals.
But if we could not make any arrangements inducing
them to communicate and were not in a position to
offer anything that conceivably could be of value to
them, what was the use of making plans about the
content of future bargains? We knew then we were defeated before we even started.

In some cases of kidnapping, the terrorists' lack
of any existing responsible command structure makes
negotiations difficult or impossible. In this instance, it

was the good guys, widely divergent in their views about appropriate methods, in their aims, and in their image-making interests, who had no consistent command structure. Possibly, even probably, nothing would have worked, but what is more crucial in hindsight and for possible future occasions is that nothing conceivable could have worked under the circumstances unless the kidnappers were not just criminal lunatics but also stupid and inept blunderers and fools. Crusading terrorists very rarely are, but conventional law enforcement treats them as if they were; that is the main reason why terrorism is the increasing danger it is.

The Hearsts were blamed for having agreed to the badly bungled food giveaway program in the first place. The attorney general of California wanted the introduction of bills prohibiting ransom payments, and California's governor made his famous "joke" that the food recipients should contract botulism. The then attorney general of the United States ordered the FBI to "go in there and get them," as if it were that simple. After all, Efrem Zimbalist, Jr., and his FBI crew do it on television every night. Not only has the lay public read too many thrillers in which the criminals are always caught, but they have seen too many television shows demonstrating the brilliant irresistibility of the FBI. Apparently, the FBI and other law enforcement people are also so enthralled by their mass media image that they believe reality follows the cinematogenic pattern; that is, the images created by movies.

Experience, even experience of failure, should teach something. What have we learned so far that we are also willing to act on? The need for a clearcut, generally known, and easily accessible communication and command structure through which information can be received and given and responsibilities can be assumed is universally agreed upon as a precondition for successful antiterrorist measures. At House committee hearings (see Chapter 10), FBI representatives testified that they had done a lot of research on terrorists and that there was no need for outside study-action teams, who, being unfamiliar with law enforcement methods, would only interfere with existing command structures and quick decision making. In Washington, Ambassador Lewis Hoffacker (special attendant to the secretary of state and coordinator for combating terrorism) and the FBI spokesmen said they had their own action teams, which included psychiatrists, sociologists, and other experts. Possibly, but at Hillsborough I did not see any and never heard of any such arrangements.

THE EXAMINATION THAT WAS NOT   More than a month after I began consulting with the Hearsts, a San Francisco reporter called to tell me that according to a probation report he had unearthed, one Dr. Frederick Hacker had been named as the psychiatrist who had examined and treated Donald DeFreeze and had recommended probation for him. How could I, he asked, act as the Hearsts' consultant when DeFreeze had been my patient? Had I at least divulged this fact to the Hearsts? I had absolutely no recollection of any such examination, but then the Hacker Clinic has a couple of thousand current patients every year, and I had in the late 1960s seen many court-referred defendants. I could easily have forgotten an examination of five and a half years before.

Although there was a reference in the probation report that Donald DeFreeze had been referred to me for psychiatric evaluation, the staff could locate no record in my files. I told the reporter that I could neither find nor remember anything. He did not believe me. All the secretaries searched frantically, turning over every page in the file cabinets. Finally, they came up with the information, located in a dead file. The mystery of the forgotten examination was clarified, but not without raising more weighty doubts about another mystery.

I had not remembered or recorded Donald De-

Freeze's examination for the simple reason that it never took place. My office had received the customary background material and Judge Neville Barrett's court order for a psychiatric examination on November 26, 1968. However, I had left for Europe four days before and did not return until December 13, as I reconstructed from my passport. Therefore, my secretary had, on receipt of the court order and the enclosed papers, duly reported my absence to the court clerk with the routine request for further instructions. Usually, a continuance is granted automatically under such circumstances. Anticipating this routine arrangement, my office set a new examination date (December 20, 1968); but at the beginning of December my office received notification by defense counsel that the matter was disposed of and that my services were no longer required, whereupon my secretary returned the court order and the enclosed papers. In order to double-check, I had written a note to the judge on December 20; but I never received a reply and promptly forgot about the matter, without ever having seen DeFreeze, known his name, or read any of his records.

Yet I would not let the matter rest there. In April 1974, I phoned Judge Barrett, who had issued the court order in 1968 and who was now sitting in Torrance, California. Because of the recent publicity about DeFreeze, he had refreshed his memory by looking through the court files, which also contained my original appointment, its cancellation, and my note to the court. The judge kindly offered to state the facts of the case in writing, which I did not think necessary after reading a supplemental probation report signed by the deputy probation officer, David B. Calhoun, Centinela Area Office, dated December 6, 1968.

In this report, the probation officer stated that although I was court appointed under the provisions of Section 730 of the Evidence Code, the diagnostic summary of the Reception Guidance Center at Chino, California, where Donald DeFreeze had been studied, had recommended that the defendant be committed to the California Department of Corrections. The report goes on:

> At the date of dictation, Dr. Hacker has not examined the defendant and is, in fact, in Europe and not due to return to Los Angeles until the 9th or 10th of December and probation officer will not be aware of Dr. Hacker's findings and recommendations until shortly before this matter is heard in court.

The probation officer "considered requesting a continuance to enable the inclusion of Dr. Hacker's examination" but decided to submit a recommendation without benefit of such information.

A continuance of one or two weeks, routinely granted under such conditions, would have made it possible to have my examination performed and my report rendered. Or else, why was another of the numerous psychiatrists on the court panel not appointed instead of me? And why was a private psychiatrist appointed at all after the defendant had spent three months in Chino for observation? Customarily, private psychiatrists examine defendants before such confinement in Chino but never, in my experience, afterward. What could a one- or two-hour examination unearth that three months of around-the-clock observation could not uncover?

The probation officer noted the recommendation submitted by the Reception Guidance Center in Chino:

> It does not appear that DeFreeze could be safely released under supervision to the community at the time. This is based primarily on the defendant's penchant to possess firearms, his escape from custody, as well as having some bombs in his possession, plus the apparent disorganization of his thought processes.[4]

Admitting that "releasing the defendant on probation with his past history of being involved with weapons and his often-mentioned mental confusion does represent something of a hazard," the probation officer interpreted the Guidance Center's remark that he should be placed in a facility offering psychiatric treatment as a "favorable prognosis should he become involved in a meaningful psychotherapeutic situation."[5]

Probation was reinstated on the condition that psychiatric treatment be provided within the community, but DeFreeze never consulted a psychiatrist. The Probation Department either did not take note of the defendant's failure to comply with the conditions of probation (that he was not to discontinue therapy unless authorized to do so by a probation officer or by the court) or at least never notified the court.

This sequence of events is extraordinary and its explanation puzzling: After three months' observation, the state's official evaluation center recommended prison for DeFreeze based on an abundance of evidence of pronounced and repeatedly demonstrated violence. This recommendation was over-turned and reversed by a nonmedical probation officer who, for unknown reasons, decided not to wait for one or two weeks in order to obtain the court-appointed psychiatrist's opinion or to seek a substitute examination.

Probation recommended by a private psychiatrist is sometimes denied by the probation officer and/or court, but I have never before or since seen the opposite, i.e., that a probation department or court would grant probation which medical authorities recommended against.

Rumors persist that Donald DeFreeze was an undercover agent or police spy employed to infiltrate radical black organizations. The police department and the district attorney's office deny any such connections. I only know that in view of his repeatedly demonstrated, consistent pattern of violent conduct and his frequent use of automatic weapons and explosives, the readiness of authorities, who are not exactly known for their leniency, to grant this obviously dangerous man probation over and over again is strange. During that period, my appointment as psychiatric consultant and its cancellation occurred. There was nothing illegal about it, but the procedures used were unprecedented in my experience. I have visited Vacaville and Soledad many times. It is extremely difficult even to get in, let alone get out. It is not my impression that either place is a location from which convicts can just walk away as DeFreeze did. The accumulation of these facts is suggestive, but I am not sure of what, because it is hard to imagine that any authority would have thought of using a man as unreliable, unstable, and explosive as Cinque for any of their purposes. I am not sure that it is very important to solve this riddle, but a riddle it remains.

General Field Marshal Cinque

On May 6, 1974, General Field Marshal Cinque of the Symbionese Liberation Army died in the holocaust of the televised SLA overkill shoot-out—a suicide. The coroner's report indicates that, "struck by two bullets, Cinque had killed himself by a shot through the temple to avoid the painful death by burning and choking like his comrades, or to escape the indignity and humiliation of falling into his enemy's hands."[6] Twenty-eight years before, another general field marshal, Hermann Göring, a former fighter pilot, drug addict, and terrorist, had taken his life by swallowing a cyanide pellet. He had not been able to avoid capture and trial by his enemies, who had sentenced him to death; but at the last moment he cheated them out of enjoying the ultimate triumph of their victory. Rather than permit them to execute him on their terms and in their way, he executed himself.

The two men have nothing more in common than their similar titles (and their love for such titles) and the common suicidal motives to stave off their certain execution by the enemy. Hermann Göring was the proud and boastful commander of the mightiest air force the world had known up to that time; his title and the field marshal's baton were conferred upon him "legitimately" by the Führer himself in a rousing cere-mony. Cinque commanded nothing, not even his na-tive English language; it is not at all certain that he was the leader of the dozen or so women and men who grandly called themselves a "liberation army." Had they known each other, Göring would have despised the sniveling, low-class black *Untermensch*. Cinque would have hated the pompous fat man who ostenta-tiously displayed his innumerable decorations on spe-cially designed parade uniforms and who plundered Europe of its art treasures in order to add them to his enormous, ostentatiously exhibited collections.

But Cinque might have liked and been liked by Charles Manson, who inspired, not an army, but a combative family of men and women to indiscriminate murder and wanton self-abandon. They are two of a kind, perilously teetering on the narrow edge between criminal insanity and insane criminality, both protective big brother figures, counterculture heroes, and martyrs endowed with magical charisma by the frustrated ex-pectation of their fanatic, identity-seeking followers. Both of them carefully selected the rich and famous as targets for maximum publicity, and both had their group members shed their pasts and adopt new "re-born" names. (Sadie McGlutz, alias Susan Atkins, par-ticipant in the ghastly Sharon Tate murders, changed her name to Coba to indicate the beginning of a new life in her new family. Said the murderess with charac-teristic candor, "In order for me to be completely free in my mind, I had to be able to completely forget the past."[7] Both guided and supervised grotesque, vio-lent initiation rituals. As if to prove that everything is possible when no holds are barred, they planned and executed the most implausible, bizarre scenarios, composed of genuine nightmares and melodramatic gimmicks. Forcing the mass media to transform their dangerously infantile, primitive, and brutal fantasies into legends for mass entertainment, these more than half-crazed outlaws promoted themselves to modern superstars of terror.

Crusading terrorists are customarily organized in

military or pseudomilitary fashion. Small groups with large ambitions often have only chiefs. Everybody gets a high-sounding, significant title to compensate for the group's actual insignificance. The fewer people they have to carry out their orders, the snappier their sharp commands are and the more pretentious the vocabulary of their legalistic-militaristic jargon is. Statements and pamphlets are all declarations or constitutions, every congregation of people becomes a federation or an army, to intimidate the enemy with the fiction of a mighty organization; every communication becomes an order or a command or a verdict, to justify even the most arbitrary decision. And, of course, every kidnapping is an arrest; every killing, an execution.

Children of all ages love to play soldiers. Their infantile ego needs bolstering through the show of martial strength. All the make-believe shouting and shooting and military carryings-on with command and obedience gestures make them feel like real big shots, like emperors, kings, or field marshals. Childish saber rattling, or rather Molotov-cocktail waving, turns from playful boastfulness into bloodshed when automatic weapons can be easily purchased and high explosives can be easily produced; when real big people, real police, and real armies can be frightened; and when real newspapers print and real television stations show the reckless game playing as terrorizing reality.

Playing soldiers is not that harmless anymore because television, the adults' best diversion and the kids' most reliable baby-sitter, has blurred any distinction between pretended and real violence. Fictional violence has been made to look just as real as the genuinely killing variety (if not a little more so). Shooting is no longer a harmless sport for hunters and marksmen; automatic weapons can transform even a loner or a gang of determined few into a formidable army, and most important of all, publicity seeking can become as explosive as any heat-seeking missile. Without ingrained authoritarian customs habituated from childhood on, without the free availability of disastrously destructive weapons, without the irresistible attraction of mass media fame, without the myth that the harmlessness of goodwill is an American reality rather than a hypocritical delusion, a pitiful gang of stir-wise convicts and radical intellectuals could never have become a terrifying army nor the wretched Cinque their awe-inspiring general field marshal.

They signed their half-literate manifestos *Venceremos* ("We shall overcome"). They never had a chance with their paranoid, megalomanic, deluded claims; but we, the good, decent, law-abiding people, titillated for months by the anxieties of the unfolding saga, did not win either, and we paid a high price for our big show. Our prisons, which spawned the SLA, are still the same; our societal values, including the myth of our harmlessness, have not been scrutinized and changed but are brutally defended everywhere with escalated counterforce. The SLA was outnumbered by Los Angeles's finest by 500 to 6; they were no foreign army, in fact, no army at all, but a bunch of admittedly heavily armed and fanatically determined desperadoes. According to the police reports, the same the world over and indistinguishable from the terrorists' justification "there was nothing left to do" but the overkill of no-search and destroy, which gave Cinque in death what he never could have in life: meaning, importance, dignity, and a hero's reputation.

CHARISMA In her last tape (June 6) Patty-Tania, mourning her dead friends, said of Cinque:

> Cin knew that to live was to shoot straight. Cinque was in a race with time, believing that every minute must be another step forward in the fight to save the children. He taught me virtually everything imaginable. He wasn't liberal with us; he'd kick our asses if you didn't hop over a fence fast enough or keep our asses down while practicing. Most importantly, he taught me how to show my love for the people.

His other SLA comrades and some former prison associates described him as kind but tough, immensely strong, determined, consistent, unmistakably emanating the charisma of revolutionary leadership. Is this the same fellow who cooked and brewed tea in Mizmoon's apartment, writing down the revolutionary slogans she dictated? Is this the same guy who, severely beaten as a child, followed an erratic, totally disorganized, and unsuccessful criminal career, with violence directed particularly against black women? Is this the same man who, groveling and submissive, made the following statements to the probation department in 1968?

> I was able to be shown my wrongs and problems and also learned how to stop it and do something about them, and as easy as these words may sound, believe me, it was hard and sometimes took many tears to face the truth. But with God's help I did, and really both found myself and changed my outlook on life. I put all of my hope and trust and faith in Christ and you know He didn't make me ashamed of Him nor did He fail me.[8]

It is the same fellow.

When biographies of the charismatic Adolf Hitler were written at the peak of his power, many associates from his earlier days, even those who had been in close contact with him for years, could hardly remember him or anything about him. He had been that insignificant and unremarkable. Yet he later became the archetype of the revolutionary liberator and charismatic evil genius. Does such inspiring charisma flow irresistibly from an extraordinary person, or is it just the blinding reflection of the blind needs of his followers?

The SLA

The public incineration of the SLA core members in Los Angeles, broadcast on national television, transformed six youngsters into charred bodies and transfigured them into martyrs. Their motivations remain mysterious; the SLA people defy any neat classification into crazy, criminal, or crusading terrorists. If they were crazy, were they unbalanced to start with, or did they become mentally unhinged as a result of inner pressure or their fugitive existence? Rumors persist that the devastating overkill effort might have been mobilized by the authorities to guard these mysteries by burning them along with their possessors.

A compass and a canteen were found on Cinque's body; he was wearing heavy pants, calf-high army boots, and three pairs of woolen socks—in southern California on a day when the temperature rose above 80 degrees. Had they planned to move into colder rural areas, where the compass, canteen, and heavy clothing would be appropriate? Or had Cinque so completely identified with the mountain fighter Che Guevara that he felt compelled to dress like his idol?

The SLA's origin and its main figures are well known by now. In 1968, a group of black convicts at Vacaville suggested the formation of an organization that could work on the special problems of black prisoners. The Black Cultural Association was accepted and recognized by the authorities as a self-help group, originally intended as a conduit for facilitating the prisoners' communication with the outside world. Teachers from nearby communities, among them Colston Westbrook, ran classes for the inmates on subjects ranging from Swahili and nation building to astrology. Cultural meetings, held on Friday nights and attended by several hundred outsiders, included speeches, poetry readings, plays, and debates, as well as a flag ceremony featuring the tricolor of the Republic of New Africa. Berkeley radicals, mostly women, relieved the prisoners' loneliness by frequent visits to Vacaville. At times, the convicts appeared to be overtaxed by so much attention; there was an average of about five women taking care of each BCA member. Westbrook explains that he was not too popular with the white women in the SLA because he frequently took lewd pictures and sexy black women into the prison. "If you want to dangle a carrot in front of the inmates to get them to learn and to come to meetings, you don't dangle communism, you dangle fine-looking chicks," he said.

Following their humanitarian impulses far more than political motives, the white Berkeley women, burdened by but also enjoying their social guilt and sexual identity diffusion, made their trips to the abandoned Vacaville prisoners with increasing frequency and enthusiasm. Gentle, poetically inclined Camilla Hall, a Lutheran minister's daughter who took her beloved cat with her in her fiery death; popular, outgoing, bright Patricia "Mizmoon" Soltysik; angelic Angela Atwood, who longed to find something in which she could believe totally and exclusively; Nancy Ling Perry, cheerleader of Nixon's alma mater Whittier College in Orange County, Barry Goldwater supporter turned drug user, topless blackjack dealer, and fruit juice vendor; and many others felt it their duty to give generously of themselves to those who had been given so little by society.

Absolute faithfulness to nonwhite men only and determined social mobility downward (as reckless as any social climbing) were the proudly displayed status symbols of the liberated white radicals. The women contributed the SLA's slogan, programs, and general rhetoric culled from secondary and tertiary sources on radical literature. But the preoccupation with contemporary themes such as prison reform, lesbianism, black struggle, and food programs seems to have left little room for the ideas of Marx, Lenin, or Mao. The pompous declarations of the SLA contained no particular philosophy and hardly any serious political thought, leftist or otherwise. What is worthless as political analysis or theory nevertheless works like magic as pure communication, testifying to the honesty of distress, the sincerity of desperation, and the depth of confusion.

Unified in thought, the budding SLA needed a deed that would strengthen its cohesion and demonstrate its importance to the outside world. The Oakland school system had approved a plan for the introduction of identity cards to curb the spread of drug use and trade among students. An SLA Court of the People found various school board members guilty of crimes against the people and the children. Unknown assailants killed Oakland School Superintendent Dr. Marcus Foster and severely wounded his deputy Robert Blackburn. In identical letters to newspapers and radio stations, the SLA claimed credit for the execution, which was carried out professionally enough, yet turned out to be a severe blunder. Dr. Foster had withdrawn the plan for the identity card system several weeks prior to his death; furthermore, he was known as a devoted, well-intentioned educator. And he was black, hardly an appropriate target for anonymous white executioners, made up as blacks, who loudly proclaimed that they were fighting for the liberation of blacks and other nonwhites from white racist oppression.

The SLA members learned from their early mistakes. The next direct actions, Patty's kidnapping and the Hibernia Bank holdup, were not only faultlessly executed but had been carefully planned in advance and demonstrated ingenious target selection. Reliably delivering tapes and other messages to metropolitan addresses, seemingly from nowhere, was also no small feat of skill and cunning by the SLA. Between seven and twelve people successfully evaded literally thousands of FBI and other security forces mobilized for the specific purpose of discovering them. The SLA members did not even feel compelled to keep a low profile. They popped up periodically in Berkeley or in San Francisco and at a sporting goods store in Los Angeles, disappearing without a trace after kidnapping, robbing, and engaging in some gratuitous shooting to attract attention and to intimidate.

Then, suddenly and for no recognizable reason, the undisputed masters of hit-and-disappear urban guerrilla tactics changed their mode of operation. Arriving in Los Angeles, Mizmoon, Nancy, Camilla, Angela, Willie Wolfe, and Cinque conducted themselves with such deliberate insouciance—displaying their weapons, offering large sums of money, sending neighborhood children for food and drinks—that their discovery within hours would have been a virtual certainty even if a parking ticket found in one of the getaway cars from the sporting goods store caper had not revealed their new, extremely unsafe location. Why did the same people who had done everything right suddenly do everything wrong? Had their cover been blown in the Bay Area? Had Los Angeles been an arbitrary choice? Did they not care any longer? Had they become confused and desperate? Had they suicidally chosen their own place of death as a last act of defiance? Or had they actually come to believe the grandiose claims of their own propaganda that they would not be betrayed by anybody in a black neighborhood? Every one of these explanations seems absurd, but there are no others.

In *Harper's* magazine (September 1974), Larry Farrell suggests that the SLA and the LAPD sought to accomplish each other's mission, that in exchange for providing an enemy image to the police's liking, which gave them the opportunity to show off their professional skills publicly, the police outdid themselves "in obliging the terrorists' Kamikaze intentions."

At the SLA's last stand, the strategy of total extermination employed against the Vietcong was used against the six barricaded terrorists, causing the police operation to take on all the aspects of a full-scale battle against a national enemy.

Defining the SLA as the enemy served to unify the security forces in the edifying belief that they served a higher national purpose than merely maintaining peace and fighting ordinary criminals. Their sacred mission became the total eradication of the opponent. Enraged and humiliated by their publicly revealed failure to capture the SLA, they compensated for their frustrations with a nationally televised combat victory. Even after the battle, television provided a law-and-order paradise; the police, as merciless in their justification as they had been in burning and killing, predictably accused the SLA of having started fighting first, implying that the police had acted only in self-defense. Granted, the SLA was heavily armed and expended thousands of rounds of ammunition. Miraculously, however, they did not hit anybody. Although they were known to be armed and dangerous, their misdeeds amounted less to a crime wave than to a wave of crime reporting. By no stretch of the imagination did they constitute a menace to national safety.

Before the SLA fired a single shot, tear gas grenades were thrown into the house on Fifty-fourth Street, which was tightly surrounded by 500 officers. There is little evidence to support the theory that the SLA's Molotov cocktails were ignited by the tear gas and started the fire; it is more likely that the blaze was caused by the fire bombs. Why were no increasingly insistent warnings given with sufficient time for the SLA to consider surrender? Why were no calls placed to the phone in the house, which was in good working order? And particularly, why were no more energetic rescue attempts undertaken? There is no cogent explanation at all.

The police report considers it a fact that "under no circumstances whatsoever" (underlined in the report) would the SLA members have surrendered alive. Using the alleged suicidal intentions of the SLA as an explanation for accommodating them accordingly, the police report emphatically states that the course of action chosen "most effectively balanced the values at stake." In an astonishing piece of retrospective prophecy, which is contradicted by all relevant experience in similar cases, the report informs us that "they were prepared to surrender only their lives, and did so. This would have been true had the confrontation lasted for days and weeks, rather than hours. It would have been true had not a single bullet been fired."

In view of the fact that there is no willingness on any side to use evidence for critical examination rather than in the service of justifying past actions, what good would it have done to find out more about the subtle motivations of the unfortunate six? The police report commended its officers for doing exactly what they had to do. In their opinion, absolutely nothing else would have been compatible with their responsibility to protect the community. Those who have always accused the "pigs" continue to do so, saying that they slaughtered innocent heroes. Damage suits for destroying property have been duly filed; allegations that police would have used different tactics if the incident had taken place in Bel Air or Beverly Hills rather than in the black ghetto have been duly rejected. And so the blame-calling and justification charade is repetitiously performed by a changing cast, forever pronouncing the same lines.

Carnage and Carnival

What does remain is the memory of the greatest carnage-turned-carnival television spectacular ever—bigger, better, and more dramatically decisive than President Kennedy's assassination or the Olympic terrorist incident in 1972. The mass media serve as propaganda agents, spokesmen, display windows, and main motivators for the forces of terrorism and terroristic antiterrorism. Millions of television viewers were invited, even compelled, on that night of May 17, 1974, to participate in the gigantic immolation. The tragedy of confrontation was turned into mass entertainment; and real death, into the supreme spectacle.

Events become socially effective and important through their mass-reproduced image. Often they take place only for the sake of the image; they are produced in order to be reproduced. The image is no longer only the reflection of reality; the image *is* reality, most likely the only one accessible to us. We have to rush home to see and hear what's really going on; the place in front of the television screen is the center of contemporary experience and the observation point of the universe, which is brought right into our living room for our edification, stimulation, and entertainment in neatly subdivided pieces. Distinctions between real and fictional violence are blurred; the fiery auto-da-fé in the real ghetto did not look much different from any similar scene staged in a studio. Shown during prime time, it was also just about over in one hour, which is desirable timing for a crime program. But the knowledge that it was happening right then and there, in front of everyone's eyes and ears, added a new dimension to the experience, as well as intensifying the entertainment value. The youngsters in the burning house were, for the duration of the show, no longer isolated. Millions either identified with them or reacted indignantly against them; in their doom, they finally had involved the people of this nation. They had aroused the guilt feelings of those who, through adjustment and accommodation, had betrayed their youthful visions of a better world. They had strengthened the determination of those who believe in burning out evil in order for the good to survive. They had rekindled the passion for the realization of the American dream, forgotten and abandoned in the contemporary morass of confusion and disillusionment. They had terrorized the complacent into an indomitable crusading spirit—against crusaders.

Many were satisfied that the desperately violent terrorists ended as they had started: by bombs and fire and through the will of the people, coming from the muzzle of a gun. But some saw, in the inescapable disaster of the few fighting the many against insurmountable odds, a symbol of their own ruined world, engulfed by destructive flames. The ersatz Götterdämmerung in the shabby ghetto house was neither majestic nor inevitable; it was provoked by a sorry group of impulsive, confused, and fanatical terrorists who, by courtesy of impulsive antiterrorists and by the "showification" of their death, could for one historic moment achieve an otherwise undeserved relevance, precisely because of their confusion and desperation. Blinded by their self-produced identity and self-importance, they too had given up or thrown off their revolutionary mission, the realization of which depends on winning the hearts and minds of the people who are to be liberated. Tired of waiting, they had betrayed their dreams to the violence of instant direct action and to the comfortable petit bourgeois fallacy of positive thinking. Nancy Ling Perry said, "I've learned what one really believes in is what will come to pass."

Taking the high of their family feelings for the reality of an established community with the people, they confused their own revolutionary desires and their passion for revolution with the revolution. They died in the belief that to feel and to talk revolution is to achieve revolution.

Nothing remains but the memory of the greatest-ever television spectacle about carnage turned into carnival.

Terroristic Options

Terrorists deny the existence and relevance of freedom by forcibly depriving their subjects of freedom and transforming them into mere objects, often in the name of freedom. Believing themselves to be in possession of the sole truth and the only real inspiration, terrorists usurp the privilege to awaken and teach the cowardly, uncomprehending masses and to mold human nature into a cast of their own preference. They reeducate forcefully and forcibly, presumably always in the interest, even though often against the will of, the educational objects. They are convinced that they know better and that they are therefore entitled and even obligated to impose their will on the doubtful, the reluctant, or the resistant. They deny the normal adult the freedom to decide for himself what he considers to be good, useful, or important for him.

Everybody who, no matter how sincerely inspired by seemingly unselfish reasons, believes himself entitled and/or obligated to impose his views and conceptions forcibly on another adult human being, for his own or for the other's interests, is a terrorist of some sort.

Terroristic thinking and practices reduce individuals to the status of puppets, but they also deny individual freedom for exactly the opposite reasons. Terrorists also believe that the claim of individual freedom is but a cover and rationalization for decisions that have been made, not by, but for, the individual. They believe that you think and do what you are compelled to think and do by your racial, national, social, and sexual identities; you are a corporate liar or a facist pig, not because you have done anything individually, but because you belong (not necessarily by your own choice) to a group that is presumably responsible for the commitment or toleration of atrocious crimes. You are an insect because you have been exposed to establishment insects, and by not fighting them at the risk of your own life, you have become the beneficiary and accomplice of a tainted system. Guilt by belonging is added to guilt by association. The mere fact of your being white or black, old or young, Wasp or Jew makes you involved and guilty. The fact or fiction of belonging is assumed to pervert the individual's inner processes to such an extent that what he actually thinks and does is not important any longer. It is as if every member belonging to an inimical identity has been so completely brainwashed by his collective racial, social, or sexual unconscious that his own actions and reactions can be safely disregarded.

Every person who, no matter how sincerely or for whatever unselfish reason, believes that he can judge, evaluate, and treat another adult human being on the basis of his associations or his belonging to a certain group is a terrorist of some sort.

Terrorists impose on the human being the sole choice between being either a social marionette or a biological (racial and sexual) automaton. They will try to make sure that the option for an individual's limited and conditioned but possible freedom will soon not be available any longer. With Patty Hearst, they succeeded. In the extreme situation of total control over their victim, they managed to convert establishment-tainted Patty into the "clean" revolutionary Tania, who celebrated suffered coercion as the birth of her liberated, genuine self.

Easygoing Patty Hearst, having turned into the bitter revolutionary Tania, disdainfully declared in one of her later tapes that the idea of her having been brainwashed "is ridiculous to the point of being beyond belief." To the contrary, she claims that Steven Weed, who had made the brainwashing suggestion, "is the one who sounds brainwashed. I can't believe those weary words he uttered were from his heart. They were a mixture of FBI rhetoric and Randy's simplicity." The brainwashed, far from wanting to be pitied or rescued, accuses the would-be liberator of being himself enslaved and brainwashed; the victim of force celebrates the results of brute force as true liberation.

Initiation Rites

Patty's and her captors' tapes spell out the dramatic story of a prolonged initiation rite, of how the one-time victim became an applicant to membership, then a recruit, and eventually a full-fledged soldier of the SLA. On the first tape, Patty was audibly nervous and hesitant, but she claimed that "they" were not frightening her unnecessarily and that her life seemed more threatened by her rescuers than by her captors. On the second tape, she emphasized that she was all right, that she was treated well or at least no worse than a prisoner of war. She pointed out that the SLA, her parents, Steven (whom she recommended to her parents' care), and she herself had a common interest, namely, her safe return. A slight note of criticism appeared in her lines: "People should stop acting like I'm dead. . . . Mom should get out of her black dress, that doesn't help at all" (February 16).

The typical manifestations of the poor-devil phenomenon became evident: realistic acceptance of the given situation created by the kidnappers, beginning establishment of common bonds, expression of a common interest, feeling threatened (together with the kidnappers) by the police, and understanding of the captors' motives.

The third tape left no more room for doubt. She accused her parents of lying and hypocrisy, stating, "I have chosen to stay and fight" (April 3). On the next tape (April 18), she boastfully reported the exact amount taken from the Sunset Branch of the Hibernia Bank in San Francisco, rejected the hypothesis that she was coerced into participating in the bank robbery or was brainwashed, and included her fiancé in the insults so far directed only at her parents. Characteristically, she attributes disturbance (intimidating, brainwashing) to those who consider her disturbed (intimidated, brainwashed). In the last tape (June 6), her expressions were even more shrill and more vulgar.

Patty became as self-assured and insultingly condescending as any fanatically indoctrinated person, indoctrinating fanatically. She assumed the name Tania, given to her in remembrance of Che Guevara's comrade and girl friend (probably a Russian spy) who committed suicide. She was also given and had fully adopted her captors' vulgar military vocabulary. Like all good soldiers, she had to prove her toughness by using rough expressions. Bourgeois mentality is a "putrid disease"; all enemies, including her family, are "pigs and fascist insects"; bourgeois values, attitudes, and goals are "fucked up" (June 6 tape). The military idiom does not attempt to explain anything. It does not tell very much, but what it tells is clear and simple. Language in uniform, even in the garb of the SLA, reduces communication to commands and invectives.

Kidnapped, frightened Patty at first was terrorized into compliance with her captors' demands, for sheer survival. Then, "understanding" developed, as so often the accompaniment and fringe benefit of terror. She displayed signs of the poor-devil syndrome, seeing her aggressors also as victims who deserved empathy and sympathy rather than censure and blame. Isolated, cut off from all former ties, under a constant barrage of guilt-raising pressures, she was coerced into wanting to belong. In ever harsher tones, she began denouncing the enemy, that is everybody to whom she formerly belonged and everything that she formerly was: her family, her fiancé, her life-style, her values, her unawareness. In typical fashion, she proved her emerging solidarity with her kidnappers, who, as her education program progressed, became her beloved teachers, models, friends, and comrades. She adopted a new war name, not to conceal her identity, but to insult and intimidate the enemy and to give notice of the depth and permanence of her new commitment.

The suicidal self-abandon of participation in high-risk, spectacular group enterprises magically sealed the covenant of her new belonging in the baptism of fire. This indissoluble bond was reinforced rather than weakened by mourning for her dead comrades. Patty-Tania passed through all the stages of the initiation ritual. She now truly belonged to the decimated, terroristic army-family that gave her special attention and warm feelings of closeness. New kinds of love and tenderness forced upon her made her reach a new, climactic emotional high through the promise of unconditional mutual loyalty.

Anticlimax

In an episode full of unresolved ambiguities and mysteries that the subsequent trial compounded rather than clarified, there is at least one clearcut fact: Patty was a genuine kidnap victim. Nobody can reasonably question any longer that violence was inflicted on a hapless and helpless victim when ruthless intruders dragged the screaming, half-naked, young woman out of her bedroom after having slugged and kicked her fiancé. Nothing points to the often suspected, frequently asserted complicity of either Patty Hearst, or for that matter, Steven Weed, with the attackers. The popular conspiracy theory found no support in factual evidence; the bullets and cyanide traces discovered in the Berkeley apartment (as reported by the press and confirmed by the FBI several months after the event) were there because the kidnappers had dropped them when, upon leaving, they fired numerous shots in the apartment and on the street. The kidnappers had taken the contents of Patty's purse and Steve's wallet; that is why they had her identification and her father's credit cards in their possession. Of course, there was a conspiracy by the SLA, but neither Patty's fiancé, nor Patty had any part in it. Certainly, what occurred on February 4, 1974, was happening to Patty Hearst, it was none of her doing. In spite of the guilty verdict, it is certain that what occurred thereafter would not have occurred if it had not been for this first crucial event. All the subsequent actions of Patty Hearst were decisively influenced and "caused" by what was happening to her on that fateful day of kidnapping and many days thereafter.

After Patty's conversion had become known through the widely published tapes, large segments of the public and the press engaged in two distorting simplification attempts in order not to have to come to terms with the strange phenomenon of coerced conversion which, unsettling, disturbing, and frightening as it may be, nevertheless exists as an incontestable fact. The first such attempt was to deny its genuine nature; indeed, if Patty had owed previous allegiances to the kidnappers or participated in a conspiracy to abduct her, all the complications of having to account for her change of mind would be avoided. Second, if she were dead, it could be expected that with the disappearance of the subject having been turned into an object of thought-reform, the puzzling issue of coercively manufactured free will could also be more easily repressed, denied, forgotten, and buried.

With the capture of the very much alive, "self-employed urban guerrilla" which Patty named as her profession at her arrest, the problem of whether and how much blame to assign to physically and psychologically coerced conduct re-emerged as nagging moral dilemma.

From the very beginning, I was asked no question more frequently than: Can Patty conceivably still be alive? Patty was said to have been murdered right away, her voice having been faked by an imposter. On at least two dozen occasions, Patty was reported as having been killed by her captors, having been murdered by rival groups, or having committed suicide. Ill-concealed behind anxious worry was the strong wish for her death. In the beginning the public's unacknowledged death wish was associated with fantasies of unrestrained revenge against the SLA. The concern for her life seemed to protect her kidnappers. If she were dead, law enforcement authorities, believed to be omniscient, according to their public image, could go in, get the kidnappers without squeamishness about the methods employed, and restore a tarnished reputation for efficiency and toughness. Obviously, they would have done just that anyway if they had only known where to go.

The FBI and police, led on a not-so-merry chase by Tania, who was not even hiding but unexpectedly popping up here and there, only to disappear again, expressed concern that "if she isn't found, we'll have to face the possibility that she may have been murdered by DeFreeze and his group before they were killed." That would have solved the case neatly, but unpredictable Tania's voice on another tape after her comrades' death proved she was very much alive and still capable of mocking, baiting, and humiliating her pursuers.

The desire to terminate the intolerable tension of having to helplessly wait for new developments increased the public's death wish. A child returning from an unaccounted absence that has created intense parental fears is often punished in retaliation for the parent's anxiety. After her announced conversion, rage and disappointment pushed all other emotions away. If Patty was one of the SLA, then she should suffer their amply deserved fate better now than later. Patty, who inspired the concern and prayers of all the good people of America, had created a great deal of anxiety in everybody, even as an innocent victim. By her conversion she had let down all the decent folks back home; the spoiled little brat was not worth all that trouble after all.

For everyone who sympathized with Patty and the grueling physical and thought tortures she was subjected to as divulged at her trial, there was at least another one who asked sarcastically why so much fuss was made about a rebellious rich kid turned bank robber. Justice is hard to obtain for the very poor and the (ostentatiously) very rich. But when, sometime after the trial, emaciated and run-down Patty was reported not just to suffer from tormenting, heart-rending psychological trouble, but from something palpably physical, a collapsed lung, public opinion once more veered toward a more charitable view. Identification with the victim temporarily replaced the retaliatory urge. Hadn't the poor girl suffered enough?

Patty Hearst, alive after all, is a constant reminder of an as yet totally unsolved thought puzzle: What are the logical, psychological, legal, moral consequences of the clearly manifest possibility that, nowadays, not only behavior and belief systems can be steered and changed by external force, but that free will, the very core of the personality, can be manufactured by coercion?

Five hundred ninety-one days had passed between Patty's totally involuntary kidnapping by the SLA and Tania's totally involuntary capture by the FBI. On September 18, 1975, law enforcement agents arrested a dangerous fugitive from justice who had participated in a number of crimes. On being taken into custody, the defiant female confirmed by her statements, her clenched-fist gestures, and her subsequent chat with a friend, that except for physical identity she had nothing in common with the old Patty. The interview with the daughter of the president of the bank which she had robbed was surreptitiously recorded and introduced as evidence in the trial. The friend testified that Patty indeed seemed "very different, dazed and disoriented"; expressing unhappiness about her arrest in vulgar language and describing her political convictions as "revolutionary feminism." She was, as yet, Tania, the rebellious SLA member.

When she cooperated with the SLA on her later tapes, when she participated in the assault on the Hibernia Bank, when she "reflexlike" used her automatic gun in front of Mel's Sporting Goods Store, when she loved Cujo and mourned her dead friends, when she criss-crossed the country and skillfully hid from the authorities, and when she finally was arrested, she was Tania. The riddle remains how Patty became Tania (and how Tania became Patty again; or did she?).

Only in totalitarian countries is being charged with a crime equivalent to being convicted and sentenced for the offense. Democratic societies, in contrast, are proud of a judicial system that rests on the presumption of innocence (and for that matter of sanity) until proof of guilt. The penal code, reference 20, the California Penal Code, provides that "to constitute crime, there must be unity of act and intent. In every crime or public offense, there must exist the union or joint operation of act and intent or criminal negligence." In other words, for a crime to be committed, the legally defined prohibited deed must coincide with a state of mind (intent, negligence, etc.) that is compatible with attributing individual guilt for the deed. We dare not punish when we cannot assign blame. Children below a certain age are incapable of committing a crime because they are presumed to lack the required reasoning power. Certain classes of the mentally ill do not possess "the sound mind and discretion" to be held accountable for an offense.

The ironclad legal (and moral) requirement that intent (or negligence) must be determined independently before a forbidden act can be declared a crime and the culprit punished as criminal, is often neglected for expedience's sake or considered a mere manoeuver of the defense.

But civilized law always has required, long before modern psychiatry made its significant contributions, that inquiry into the reasons and motives of why somebody has done something is legally as relevant and essential as the determination of exactly what he has done. Committing a premeditated murder and killing an attacker to protect an innocent child are both homicides, distinguished "only" by the reasons and motives for the act which makes one homicide a heinous crime and the other a praiseworthy, heroic deed. Prosecuting zeal in its eagerness to blame and convict often disregards such legal niceties, i.e., the Constitution, guaranteeing the freedom of us all. The highest law enforcement officer in the land, then Attorney General William Saxby, called the fugitive Patty Hearst "nothing but a common criminal" before and without a trial; but then his predecessors in high office have also sometimes been unorthodox in applying the letter and the spirit of the law they were sworn to uphold.

If a person at the time of alleged criminal conduct "as the result of mental disease or defect lacks substantial capacity either to appreciate the wrongfulness of his conduct or to conform his conduct to the requirements of law," this person is insane and not guilty by reason of insanity. This is the essence of the so-called Wade Rule adopted by the Ninth Federal District including California to replace the M'Naghten Rule, still valid law in the California State courts, which demands that a person can be exculpated for insanity only if "at the time of committing the act the party accused was labouring under such a defect of reason, from disease of the mind, as not to know the nature and quality of the act he was doing, or as not to know that what he was doing was wrong."[9] The new Wade test permits a not guilty verdict if the person knew his act was wrong but couldn't act accordingly. The Wade Rule goes on to state that preference was given intentionally to the term "wrongfulness" in place of "criminality" "in order to exclude from the criminal responsible category those who, knowing an act to be criminal, committed it because of a delusion that the act was morally justified."[10] In other words, the court enunciating this rule did not want to find anybody guilty who, even if knowing that other people and the law consider his actions as criminal nevertheless performed it on the basis of his delusional belief that it was morally justified and right.

Bank robbery is a federal crime because the federal government guarantees bank deposits; therefore, Patty Hearst was tried in Federal Court for her participation in the Hibernia Bank robbery. Her enforced loyalty obligation to the SLA could have represented a delusion or the equivalent to a delusional belief. Her new allegiance, violently imposed upon her, must have made her think that her violent "act was morally justified" which could have meant a verdict of not guilty by reason of insanity. The Wade Rule would have been applicable to the determination of her case if she, or rather her attorneys, had availed themselves of this defense. They did not. Possibly they thought that the

pity and sympathy they could arouse in the jurors
would be sufficient for an acquittal regardless of legal
requirements that the jurors might ignore; possibly they
had such supreme confidence in their courtroom skills
that they saw no need to aim for anything except
straight acquittal rather than afterwards have to deal
with a psychiatric hospital into whose custody a defendant found not guilty by reason of insanity is placed.
The defense won many legal skirmishes and most battles except the last one—and lost the case.

The defense had relied on the theory that Patty
acted under duress in fear of her life (as if somebody
held a gun or a knife at her); but Judge Carter was
duty bound to instruct the jury: "Duress or coercion
may provide a legal excuse for the crime charged
against her, but the compulsion must be present and
immediate . . . a well-founded fear of death or bodily
injury with no possible escape from the compulsion."[11]
Anticipating this inevitable instruction, Patty was compelled to claim that she was incarcerated under horrible
conditions, physically abused and raped, but also that
she subsequently lived under constant threats in immediate fear of her captors whom she despised. In order to prove coercion in a legally valid manner, she had
to deny any affectionate feeling for any SLA member
ever, including her love for Cujo, which she had declared on her tapes. She could not explain why she always carried the stone relic in the shape of a monkey's
face, while another part of the trinket that had been
given to her by Cujo as a token of their relationship
was found on her lover's charred body. When the court
permitted the prosecution to ask about her activities
after the bank robbery, the duress theory collapsed.
If the questions could not be avoided, the answers had
to be. She had to take the Fifth Amendment against
self-incrimination forty-two times in order not to have
to confirm what appeared obvious anyway. Of course,
there could not have been a sustained immediate threat
to her life, for every minute of her more than nineteen months of hiding; she had innumerable opportuni-

ties to surrender, to contact her family, to just walk away if—if she had been herself.

Clearly the theories regarding duress and physical coercion on the one hand and persuasive coercion on the other hand are contradictory and mutually exclusive in some respects. To compel desired behavior, a person either can be intimidated and physically coerced all the time, or else a person may have been persuaded and indoctrinated (by extreme coercion, for instance) so that any further intimidation and further physical coercion has become superfluous, because the person feels that he wants to do what, in fact, he has been made to do. Both theories cannot be valid at the same time, precisely because successful coercive persuasion (thought-reform, popularly, if erroneously, called brainwashing) makes physical coercion and immediate intimidation, which are the essence of duress, unnecessary. In any case, the jurors could not accept the intrinsic contradictions and apparently doubted the credibility of Patty's presentation. Ignoring the brutal kidnapping and its aftermath, they found her guilty as charged.

In contrast to ordinary witnesses who are required to tell their observations but not to make any inferences from what they have seen or heard, expert witnesses are permitted and even required to draw conclusions from their observations within the area of their expertness. Just because the ultimate decision about guilt or innocence is reserved for the "fact-finders," i.e., the judge and/or the jury, the use of expert witnesses to explain complicated matters beyond the experience of the "fact-finders" is a logical and inevitable consequence of a system of justice which leaves the decision about any matter of importance not to the experts, but to the lay community representatives instructed by an impartial judge.

Human judgment is fallible; but it is assumed that by permitting each side of a controversy to present as much evidence to support their versions of the truth, a jury of peers guided by the legal rules as interpreted by the judge and helped by clarification through experts, will arrive at as true a verdict as possible. Necessarily, this adversary system compels expert witnesses who are called to the witness stand by either party of the legal conflict to take sides. Not the experts' argumentativeness or greed or hankering for advocacy are the reasons for their having to side with one or the other party, but the rules of the legal system under which they have to work and testify. Experts often disagree, not in spite but because of their superior knowledge about certain matters. Economic experts disagree about the best way of fighting inflation, atomic scientists disagree about the existence of a clean bomb, surgeons disagree about whether a certain operation is necessary or not, Supreme Court judges disagree about crucial legal issues, psychiatrists disagree about whether a certain condition amounts to legal insanity. Since our system of justice demands a speedy and public trial for any offense, psychiatrists (and Appelate Court and Supreme Court judges) disagree in public and often join in the battle of experts considered by some as indication of lacking expertness or lacking development of a science that is expected to give simple answers rather than to explain the complexities of the human mind. The determination of motives and "states of mind" of another person at a certain time in the past is extremely difficult, particularly for the conscientious expert who knows about all the possibilities of conscious and unconscious distortion and forgetting. It does not take an expert to know that human feelings and actions are often inconsistent, confusing, and accessible to many interpretations all of which may be partly true; yet in the courtroom, clear-cut either-or statements—was she (conscious, willing, intimidated) or wasn't she—are deemed to be more effective, yet complicated reflections of complicated, ambiguous, and vacillating human feelings and actions certainly come closer to "the truth." Psychological truth is not always plausible and hardly ever pleasant and simple. Therefore, like the messenger of old times bringing bad news, psychiatrists are made responsible for what they only try to report. Only too often does a trial designed to determine the validity of the charge or the defendant's credibility turn into a trial of the motivations, personality, and credibility of the expert witness. The defense psychiatrists with professional credentials superior to those of the prosecution were not able to convince the jury in the Hearst case, probably also because their "brainwashing" hypothesis conflicted with the main thrust of the defense's efforts relying on the theory of duress. The all-important psychological (and moral and legal) issue of whether guilt can be assigned and punishment administered when a person's seemingly voluntary conduct has been imposed upon and compelled by overwhelming forces beyond the person's control, was only raised inferentially and certainly not decided.

After Patty Hearst had simply been found guilty as if the cruel kidnapping had never happened to her, she had to face the same sentence as any other common bank robber. Yet the judge postponed imposing a definite sentence and referred Patty for further psychiatric study. The much maligned and often ridiculed medical experts are expected to make recommendations about how much time, if any, Patty "deserved" to spend in prison, as if there were any "scientific" yardsticks to medically determine length of sentence; psychiatrists are to assume a responsibility which the judge does not want to take, at least not alone. The legal system rarely permits psychiatrists to adequately help suffering human beings accused of criminal conduct; even more rarely are psychiatrists given an opportunity to educate the public about complicated psychological issues. But they may always be used as societal scapegoats, as targets for aggression created by uncertainty and complexity. They will reliably serve when responsibility is to be assigned for unpleasant decisions which society demands and yet does not want to make.

The law presumes that every normal adult is able to exert a free choice in his actions and is therefore responsible for the consequences of his acts. Yet it must also be acknowledged that human decisions can be influenced and manipulated sometimes to such an extent that freedom of choice is totally eliminated.

If there were no convincing hard facts to prove that behavior, attitudes, beliefs indeed can be influenced and changed by external stimuli and pressures, there would be no hidden and overt persuaders in billion dollar businesses, no political campaigns investing large sums of money and extending intensive efforts for "selling" a candidate, no bitter struggles over control of mass media and education. Of course, this type of influence is not coercive because in pluralistic societies, it is nonexclusive, noncompulsory, and competitive. Free will depends on the ability and possibility to choose between various alternatives. If no alternatives are available, there cannot be any free decision. For this very obvious reason, some societies like ours make carefully guarded provisions to guarantee freedom of speech, freedom of movement, freedom of competition, in order to make sure that people are exposed to various influences and can express as many various viewpoints as they wish. Totally dependent people, prisoners, kidnap victims and all those who, without possibility of escape, have to submit to a total institution that grants no option but one, cannot have any free will even if they profess or believe to do voluntarily what they are compelled to do. Everybody knows that; totalitarian societies act on that knowledge with considerable success: Complete physical control provides the conditions for psychological manipulation which cannot only determine behavior, loyalties, and perception, but may produce the subjectively sincere feeling of complete voluntariness as a result of utter coercion. The denial of free choice may be experienced as free choice. The highest accomplishment of skillful, at first coercive programming of another person's mind is that later on forceful methods, violent threats, and constant supervision are not necessary any longer because the person will have incorporated the programmers' demands to such an extent as to have become unaware that they are somebody else's and will have formed the conviction that the imposed-upon values and perceptions are expressions of one's own free will. At the Patty Hearst trial, this issue was not raised in that manner, but if it had been, the jurors called upon to reconcile this conflict might have asked themselves and each other an interesting question. Why had they, the jurors, to be sequestered and cut off from the outside world during the course of the trial at considerable cost to the government and even more considerable inconvenience to themselves if not for the fear that the influence of media reports or of relatives may pervert their independent judgment? Why was it then so farfetched to grant the possibility of coerced thought control under conditions of most extreme intimidation?

Patty was kidnapped, subsequently kept in complete isolation subject only to the intensive, physical, and emotional pressures of her captors who exerted total control over her. Everything that followed occurred in the sequence of these events, none of them Patty's doings or by any stretch of imagination the result of her choice or free will. For the determination of her responsibility, criminal or otherwise, it is not even relevant whether or not the scenes of cruel torture, violent rape, and humiliating abuse occurred exactly as Patty, threatened and intimidated by the other side, described them in dramatic detail. Nor is it particularly relevant, although very interesting, to speculate whether that is all that occurred. It is at least possible that not only physical intimidation, rapist assaults and kinky sex, but developing feelings of sympathy for her captors, which for obvious reasons, Patty did not talk about in the courtroom, played a part in the conversion process. Nor can the question of whether the SLA planned the kidnapping with an "education" conversion purpose in mind, ever be answered unequivocally. It was probably only after her capture that the kidnappers decided to transform the original victim into a convert, recruit, and comrade in arms, thus achieving an enormous propaganda victory.

After hearing the first tapes, I believed and still believe now, that the assumption of Patty's coerced change of mind as a result of concerted mind attack is the only version compatible with all known facts and contradicted by none.

It has been said that the time was too short for a complete conversion and that the SLA people were not experienced brainwashers. But neither of these arguments is convincing. Total control over a victim for several weeks in a situation of extreme shared danger is sufficient time, and no professional training is required, only ruthlessness and single-minded determination.

Nobody can doubt that after her involuntary capture and confinement by the SLA, the Berkeley kidnap victim was not the same any longer. The person that emerged after the SLA had worked her over was not Patty any more regardless of what Patty was or may have been before. Once successfully subjected to coercive persuasion, the unfortunate victim becomes more susceptible to coercive persuasion in a different, often the opposite direction. Programmed people can be de-programmed and re-programmed with amazing ease; the victims will rarely know how unfortunate they are because every presently held view will be considered by them as the truth, nothing but the truth arrived at by free decision: that is precisely what makes them unfortunate victims. We all are potential victims; given the "right" condition of physical coercion for psychological manipulation, it can happen to most of us and after a certain length of time, possibly to all of us.

On her tapes, Patty emphasized that she had "chosen to stay and fight."[12] She stated: "I would like to begin this statement by informing the public that I wrote what I am about to say. It's what I feel. I have never been forced to say anything on any tape. Nor have I been brainwashed, drugged, tortured, hypnotized or in any way confused. As George Jackson wrote, 'It's me, the way I want it, the way I see it.' "[13] Now we know what we then suspected, that she was maximally coerced and that her emphatic denial of any coercion was, in fact, proof of such coercion. At pres-

ent, Patty, who is reported to have promised cooperation with the authorities, claims that she freely decided
to denounce her SLA captors as formerly, under the
control of the kidnappers, she had "freely" denounced
her parents, her fiancé, her friends, and everything they
stood for. Freedom imposed for no matter what good
and right reasons is no freedom at all. Free will is not
an abstract notion but a concrete manifestation of human possibilities and the highest accomplishment of
the human potential, but free will claimed, when in
fact it has been imposed, coerced, and compelled is a
distorted caricature marking the human being's most
abject humiliation and shame.

We know about Patty Hearst before her kidnapping, we know that the person feeling herself to be and
acting as Tania wasn't the same any longer. What and
who is Patty now? What is her genuine identity, her
real she? We don't know, any more than we know if
she'll ever be able to liberate herself from overwhelming
pressures to search in freedom for her true self. Victimized, she is condemned to follow the victim's painful path for a long time to come, possibly until the end
of her ruined life. More than ever she deserves our
understanding and charity rather than our wrath and
condemnation.

PART III

The Challenge

8

Confrontations
and Negotiations

Terrorists everywhere have the immense practical advantage of surprise. They can choose the time and place of their attack. They act; the attacked can only react. Except under stringent conditions of outright war, when you shoot first and ask questions later, there is no absolute protection against determined terrorism, in Europe, South America, the United States, the Middle East, or anywhere else. The proud boast that hardline approaches eradicate terrorism, at least in a certain area, is contradicted by the record of what actually happens.

Terrorism—called by a variety of names (fight for liberty, vigilantism, anarchism, urban guerrilla movements, and so on)—has been no stranger to the American scene. In 1787, Thomas Jefferson wrote: "The tree of liberty must be refreshed from time to time with the blood of patriots and tyrants; it is its natural manure." During the War of Independence, the Sons of Liberty led the ultimately successful fight against the British Stamp Act in 1765 by a series of terroristic attacks. Vigilante movements attempted to uphold the law at the frontiers, using "flogging, expul-

sion, or killing"[1] as punishment and also as a warning
to the potentially disorderly. The Ku Klux Klan,
founded in Nashville, Tennessee, in 1867, committed
thousands of acts of clandestine and overt terrorism,
mostly against blacks, but also against Catholics, Jews,
and disagreeing Protestants, to promote the aims of
white supremacy and the fundamentalist values of the
Bible Belt. Klan violence ebbs and flows; it decreased
around the turn of the century, was revived in the
1920s, declined again, and has been on the upswing
once more since the 1960s. Although factions within
the labor movement and antilabor suppression measures sometimes resorted to outbreaks of violence, terrorism was never a continuing policy to achieve labor's
goals. U.S. anarchists also rarely engaged in terroristic
violence, in contrast to their European counterparts,
particularly the Russians, but there were several outbreaks attributed to anarchists. The most spectacular
was a series of mysterious bombings in 1919, during
the so-called Red scare. Then Attorney General Alex-
ander Palmer responded with a large-scale terror campaign during which thousands were arrested. (Very
few were ultimately convicted.) Nevertheless, the
bombings continued; in September 1920, forty were
killed and three hundred injured by an explosion in
Wall Street.

Various race riots in the mid-1960s, particularly
the Watts rebellion in the hot summer of 1965, marked
a shift in strategy from nonviolent social change to
violence for furthering black rights. Black power was
advocated by the Black Muslims, who called for a
separate sovereign black state, and by the Black
Panther organization, originally founded in 1966 by
Huey Newton and Bobby Seale for black self-protection against brutality. A variety of bombings and killings were committed by the Black Panthers (and many
more attributed to them), who are believed to be responsible for much of the general escalation of violence
and fear of violence during the late 1960s. Puerto
Ricans in the United States and in Puerto Rico demanded self-determination and sovereignty. The Chi-

cano Liberation Front took credit for a few dozen bombings of buildings, banks, and schools. Following the example of black violence, Bernadine Dohrn, a leader of the predominantly white leftist Weathermen, declared a state of war in May 1970, the beginning of revolutionary violence. The Weathermen, originally a faction of Students for a Democratic Society, became an ultraradical group advocating and engaging in all kinds of violence. Several bombings and other terroristic acts have been attributed on the Left to the Northwest Liberation Front, the New World's Liberation Front, the Red Guerilla Family, the Black Guerilla Family, the Sandino National Liberation Front, and the George Jackson Brigade, and on the Right to the revived activities of the Ku Klux Klan, the National Socialist Liberation Front, Alpha '66, Cuban Power, and the Jewish Defense League. The JDL is officially opposed to terrorism, but some of its members have been convicted of bombings, beatings, and one sniper attack. The maximally publicized terroristic spree of the SLA remains memorable as a significant stunt, but so far, terrorism from below has been neither very popular nor very successful in the United States.

Crusading terrorists are courageous—if ruthless disregard of human life, including one's own, can be called courage. That certain individuals and groups are discouraged neither by high risks nor by counterviolence is part of the problem that is compounded by the antiterrorists' staunchly maintained belief that deterrence will work.

Not every loss of life as a result of terrorism can be attributed to fate or to bad luck; ambivalence, miscalculation, and simple blundering are also decisive factors determining the outcome of historical events.

Tough measures without accompanying social and political changes were, in terms of their stated purpose, unsuccessful in South America, in Ireland, and in the Middle East. As the Canadian example shows, a combination of firmness in enforcing democratically agreed-upon rules with simultaneous readiness to make reasonable compromises and to avoid the pitfalls of conflict polarization and escalation pays off. Like generals, terrorists wither away when, after conflict is defused and deglamorized, there is no longer any need for their spectacular services. In England, terrorism imported from Ireland has escalated because Britain has not yet found a feasible way to extricate itself from an imperial heritage that has many connotations of former colonial terror. The United States has been remarkably free of political terrorism because the American institutions for the resolution of conflict and redress of grievances, available to everyone, have been believed to be working by and large in a satisfactory manner.

All this may have changed recently; the mood of the country as expressed in the ascendancy of law-and-order sentiment and in the popularity of certain politicians suggests that some modified terror from above (of course called something different) with a high-sounding patriotic label is no longer an option beyond the pale of imagination. An increase in all kinds of terrorism in the United States is therefore quite probable.

Israel has widely advertised its no-negotiations tough-line policy since the hostage trade in 1968, when eighteen Arabs were released from Israeli prisons in exchange for twelve Israeli hostages after an El Al hijacking to Africa. Sometime later the same year, seventy-one Arabs (some of whom are known to have become terrorist recidivists) were given their freedom in order to obtain the release of Israeli passengers on an aircraft destined for Tel Aviv but commandeered to Damascus. From then on, Israel has refused to engage in any negotiations with terrorists.

Overlooking the frightening aspects of the export and the internationalization of terrorism, the Israelis pointed out that since they had taken an uncompromising stand, terrorist attacks took place everywhere except in Israel and against El Al planes.

The United States and many other nations were deeply impressed; the terrorists were not. They knew that if they could raise the stakes high enough, the terror objects would have to negotiate, if not capitulate. Contrary to a widespread belief that yielding encourages future terrorism, it is the publicly announced unyielding approach that stimulates terrorists to choose their targets and victims in such a way that the terror objects cannot afford to refuse the terrorists' offers. Of course, no civilized nation can "wage war over the bodies of innocent children,"[2] and of course, every country would be forced to negotiate if its government leaders, its cities (through atomic threat), or large numbers of its citizens were seriously jeopardized by terrorist threats. Why does this kind of recognition have to wait until after the avoidable loss of human lives that might have been saved if the characteristics of crusading terrorism had been acknowledged? Since 1974, terrorism inside Israel has again become commonplace, yet toughness as a policy recommendation has lost none of its popular appeal.

Deal in Thailand

The investiture of the twenty-year-old Thai crown prince on December 28, 1972, was celebrated with pomp and circumstance in Bangkok. Therefore, two gentlemen, smartly dressed in tails, had no trouble passing the Thai guards and entering the Israeli embassy. After gaining entrance, they dropped their masquerade, overwhelmed the guards, and assisted two Black September comrades in climbing over the wall. They drew their guns and made hostages of six Israeli officials, including a visiting Israeli ambassador, demanding as usual the immediate release of thirty-six Palestinian terrorists in Israeli jails. If their demand was not met, they would blow up the embassy and kill the hostages. Thai authorities started negotiations immediately. They appealed to the terrorists' sense of honor by urging them not to take advantage of a national celebration. The Egyptian ambassador guaranteed the terrorists that the Thai authorities would not double-cross them and would keep their promises. Negotiations continued for nineteen hours; then the terrorists relented, agreeing to the release of the hostages if they were granted free exit. There were many tense moments on the way to and at the airport. The terrorists guarded their hostages with drawn weapons until the last moment because they were afraid of being tricked as the terrorists had been in Munich. The Thais expressed their appreciation of the terrorists' respect for the high holiday; the hostages were released unharmed; and the terrorists left for Cairo accompanied by two Thai officials and the Egyptian ambassador.

The first Israeli secretary praised the attitude of the Thai authorities that had saved their lives. Israel was satisfied with Thailand's successful action. The suspicions of the terrorists had been unfounded because the Thais did not even think of any double-cross.

The Thai example was not widely followed. Self-righteous impatience, national pride, and curiously archaic concepts of courage often have greater influence on decision making (or drift into violence because it comes naturally) than concern for the preservation of human lives. Many blamed the Thais for cowardice and lack of spine, although Black September had proved once more that in spite of rigid security measures, terrorists can strike whenever and wherever they choose. The generosity of the Arab terrorists was attacked by radical extremists of their own group; they, too, were accused of cowardice and spinelessness. In several newspapers in the West and in Israel, the terrorists were not just criticized, but, worst of all, pitied and ridiculed.

No Deal in Khartoum

In February 1973, a Libyan passenger plane was shot down by Israeli fighter planes over the Suez. World opinion turned against the somewhat apologetic Israelis, who had warned the civilian pilot and repeatedly asked him to land. Presumably, Israeli authorities had received reports that an Arab plane filled with bombs intended to perform a kamikaze attack on Israeli installations.

Israeli Prime Minister Golda Meir was on her annual visit to the United States. Subdued by having to admit at least partial culpability for the death of over 100 people in the Libyan plane, the Israeli government seemed in an unusually conciliatory mood; peace threatened once more. A couple of weeks later, world opinion once again turned against the Arabs.

On the Saudi Arabian national holiday on March 1, 1973, eight heavily armed guerrilla fighters from Black September crashed a good-bye party for American diplomat George C. Moore at the Saudi Arabian embassy in Khartoum, Sudan. Various diplomats managed to escape; others were released after they identified themselves as representatives of Arab or Eastern bloc states. The four children of the Saudi Arabian ambassador were also permitted to leave the building, but he, his wife, George Moore, the new U.S. ambassador Cleo A. Noel (who had just arrived), the Jordanian ambassador, and the Cairo-born Belgian representative were detained as hostages.

The terrorists soon dropped their original demands for the release of some German revolutionaries and Sirhan Sirhan, assassin of Senator Robert Kennedy, but they insisted that other prisoners in Jordanian and Israeli jails be given their freedom. On the radio, the fedayeen had listened to President Nixon's press conference, in which he stated that the United States would do everything in its power to save the hostages but would not yield to blackmail. An American "non-negotiator" with strict orders not to concede anything to the terrorists was on the way from Washington. Soon afterward, the terrorists received the code words "Cold River" (name of a Palestinian refugee camp in northern Lebanon that had been attacked by the Israelis the week before). This coded message confirmed what they had known since listening to Nixon's message: no deal.

The terrorists advised the two Americans and the Belgian that they would be executed within the hour and permitted them to make their last wills. The American ambassador thanked his Saudi Arabian host for the dinner invitation. The leader of the terrorists declared that all his men would consider it their honorable duty to participate in the execution; a few minutes later, the diplomats were killed by forty shots. Soon afterward, the terrorists surrendered to the Sudanese police. An anonymous spokesman for Black September declared that the bloody events of Khartoum had restored Black September's face, which had been lost at Bangkok, where the fedayeen had not carried out their mission to the end. The execution was to serve as a lesson to take Arab threats seriously.

War on Children

In 1973, terrorism temporarily came to a halt when large-scale fighting broke out in the Middle East. War absorbs and swallows up terrorism; the irregulars carry on by becoming regular soldiers and carry out their dangerous missions under a different label. Modern wars are rarely declared in advance. They rarely end with armistices; rather, they linger on in continued, if somewhat diminished, hostilities that may go on for months or years after the conclusion of solemn agreements to terminate them. On April 12, 1974, during such a period of the Middle East's customary "hot peace," characterized by the exchange of anticipatory protective and vengeful retaliation, a suicide squad of three Arab terrorists penetrated the Israeli border settlement of Qiryat Shemona. Children were hurled from a building, women were slaughtered, and a total of eighteen Israelis and the three attackers were killed. The subsequent, particularly intense Israeli reprisal raids into Lebanon were condemned by the United Nations in a resolution that did not even mention the preceding massacre. To bitter Israelis, it seemed that the world organization placed more value on Lebanese bricks and stones than it did on Israeli lives.

On May 14, 1974, three Arabs belonging to the Popular Democratic Front for the Liberation of Palestine (PDFLP), a fringe group considered moderate in the guerrilla movement, crossed the northern Israeli frontier, which, Israelis freely admitted, cannot be hermetically sealed against penetration, and attacked the sleeping Israeli town of Ma'alot. The terrorists had tried to stop a truck in which several Arab women were returning from work. Not succeeding, they opened fire, killing one woman. Four hours later, the invaders had reached Ma'alot, home of 3,500 Jews, mainly impoverished immigrants from North Africa. Pretending to be the police, they forced entrance into an apartment building, killing two members of the Yosef Cohen family and severely injuring two others. One child escaped unharmed because he had hidden and did not utter a sound; he was a deaf-mute.

Neighbors sounded the alarm, but incomprehensibly there were no troops or effective police forces in town; the police officer in a neighboring city attributed the cry for help to hysteria and ignored it. The terrorists proceeded unhindered and, as the subsequent Israeli investigation report to the Prime Minister on June 18, 1974, said, "in an entirely fortuitous manner" to a school situated on an elevated site. After shooting the janitor, they stormed into the school dormitories; kicked, clubbed, and herded together the sleepy, frightened children; and announced their demands to Israeli units (who had arrived in the meantime) in handwritten notes. They asked for the release of twenty terrorists imprisoned in Israel and for safe passage for themselves and their liberated comrades to Damascus, Syria.

Shouting and waving, the terrorists tried to impress the Israelis with their determination to kill the hostages if their conditions were not met by 6:00 P.M. but agreed to have the Romanian and French ambassadors transmit a code word to them indicating the safe arrival of their comrades in Damascus. The Israeli government met in emergency session, reversed its traditional policy, and agreed to yield. The Romanian and French foreign ministries were in constant touch with the terrorist commanders and their ambassadors, but no code word arrived. In spite of the desperate pleading of the children through the terrorists' portable loudspeaker, the Israeli government decided in the afternoon that there was no longer sufficient time to fulfill the terrorists' demands. Therefore, the Army's recommendation was accepted, and an attack was launched half an hour before the lapse of the deadline. One terrorist was shot as he ran to detonate an explosive; the two others sprayed the children with machine gun fire before they themselves were cut down. Twenty-nine people died at Ma'alot, including twenty-one children and the three terrorists.

Crusading terrorists are usually more familiar with the ruses and devices used in former incidents than the antiterrorism fighters are. At Ma'alot, the PDFLP spokesman had warned the Israeli government not to resort to games or tricks. He was ignored; the lessons of Munich and Khartoum, Bangkok and Vienna (see Chapter 9) were ignored; and incredibly enough, the messages of the terrorists were also ignored. Why? Because, according to the official Israeli report, "the chief of staff and the minister of defense did not ascribe any importance to the letters [of the terrorists]." Yet the Arab invaders had specifically written that if their demands for prisoner release and free exit were fulfilled, the children would be released unharmed in Israel. The Israeli government had rejected, as it must, having the children transported to Damascus or to any Arab country; but the terrorists' letters, never read by the government, had promised their release.

The record does not show that the government consulted any experts other than the security and army authorities. These highly competent professionals suggested what comes naturally in their profession: the military option.

The only explanation for this is psychological. Could it be that, deep down, some government officials or security officers did not want any conclusion other than a violent confrontation with the hated enemy, in spite of their officially expressed concern for the victims?

The terrorists did not trust the Israelis (the official Israeli report to the Prime Minister, June 18,

1974: "The terrorists view Israeli announcements with an absolute lack of confidence"). The Israelis did not trust the terrorists. In the absence of any existing mediation or escrow machinery, the terrorists suggested ad hoc that the Israelis accept the Romanian and French ambassadors as trustees for bargaining. For many hours the trustees and everybody else waited for the agreed-upon code word, which, according to the written demands of the terrorists and the clear logic of the situation, was to be given only after the terrorists' imprisoned Palestinian comrades had arrived in Damascus. The code word never came. After many hours had passed, the government reluctantly acceded to the Israeli army's suggestion to shoot it out because by then it was too late to fulfill the demands prior to the deadline.

The Israelis knew that the prisoners were still in Israel, so what was everybody waiting for? Holding out for the password that could not conceivably arrive was so obviously futile that suspicion arises that the futility was either the result of incredible negligence or intended in order to justify the subsequent violence on the grounds that no other alternative remained.

In view of the jeopardy to over eighty schoolchildren, the Israeli government had officially deviated from its staunchly maintained tough policy, which nevertheless prevailed at the end. Did the negotiations fail through hard luck or were they meant to fail? Nobody will ever know, any more than anybody will know how many of the twenty-one children killed and the sixty others wounded were hit by the bullets of their attackers or of their rescuers.

Limited Success at The Hague

On September 14, 1974, three Japanese Red Army terrorists shot their way into the French embassy in The Hague to effect the liberation of their comrade Yutaka Furuya arrested in Paris for using false papers and counterfeit money. They took the French ambassador and ten other people hostage. The police immediately surrounded the building and placed sharp-shooters on the neighboring roofs. The Dutch government met in emergency session, and the prime minister personally took charge of the complicated triangular negotiations. The Dutch government maintained constant contact with the disagreeing hawk and dove factions within the French government, which had acceded to the terrorists' demands for the surrender of Furuya but refused to make any other concessions.

When negotiations with the terrorists bogged down, the Dutch government had messages written in large Japanese characters on a paper roll spread out on the street below the embassy. The negotiations were resumed. Furuya, first reported reluctant to be surrendered, was flown from a Paris jail to Amsterdam airport and remained there for days, heavily guarded by French security officers. The ransom demand for $1 million was turned down by the French government, which also did not want to further endanger French lives by providing a French crew for flying the terrorists out of the Netherlands. Using the services of a large staff of experts from various fields, the Dutch government became convinced that some concessions had to be made in order to save the hostages. They whittled down the ransom demand to $300,000 and provided a getaway airplane. The flight officer of a volunteer Dutch crew visited the terrorists in the beleaguered French embassy to discuss the details of their exit and of the flight plan. After this visit, two women hostages were released, and the French ambassador was permitted to show himself briefly at a window to indicate that he and the other hostages were still alive. After more than one hundred hours of imprisonment, six hostages, among them the French ambassador, left the embassy guarded by their captors, who were wearing black hoods and white gloves, holding guns at their backs. A bus brought them to Amsterdam airport.

Three hostages who were ill had been left at the embassy. Exactly according to the agreed-upon plan, the terrorists boarded the airplane with their hostages and then released five hostages in exchange for Furuya, who had joined them in the Boeing 707. Thereupon they released their last hostage, the French ambassador, who, because of his dignified position, had been excused from putting up his hand in the surrender gesture. Minutes later, the plane was off, but the danger to the crew, who by necessity had become substitute hostages, was not over yet. Flight engineer Bernard Knight wrote in his logbook: "We cannot get anybody to accept these people. They are in a state of suicide at this time. This is a little worrying us."[3] Eventually they were permitted to refuel in Aden, then went north to Jordan, and ultimately landed in Damascus.

The Dutch prime minister expressed his "satisfaction and relief" in announcing the successful conclusion of the operation. He added, "We are very satisfied. Total success would have been the liberation of the hostages and the capture of the terrorists, but under the circumstances the making of concessions within certain limits can be considered a success." The French minister of the interior, prime minister, and president expressed their gratitude and appreciation, the president stressing the firmness and dignity with which the negotiations had been conducted by the Netherlands government.

After it was all over, the Dutch prime minister admitted that there had been certain divergences of opinion over tactics. The initial decision of the French government had been quick and inevitable. With the lives of their ambassador and ten other hostages, many of them French, at stake, they had hardly any choice but to exchange a terrorist who had not been involved in any violent crime within France. But as often happens in cases of this sort, the yielding in principle was to be toughened up (i.e., sweetened for those conceding) by making the conditions of yielding as hard and as uncompromising as possible. The toughness with regard to details serves as a compensatory face-saving device, as an excuse for or (as in the Ma'alot incident) as a reversal of the "soft" decision made under duress.

One faction of the French government, flatly refusing to pay any ransom or to provide a French crew, had urged the Dutch to be more firm and after that remained silent and uncommunicative for several days.

Patiently and tenaciously, the Dutch government continued to negotiate with all parties concerned on its own responsibility, encouraged by another faction of the French government that reimbursed the Dutch for the ransom money, which was returned untouched by the terrorists anyway. The Dutch remained firm in turning down last-minute changes demanded by the terrorists. With every passing hour, the danger to the hostages' lives became a little less grave; the group feelings developing under conditions of close confinement also worked to inhibit unrestrained aggression against the captives. Eventually, the flexible approach, considered reasonable because it was not committed to any preconceived position, paid off. Following the example of Bangkok, the terrorists had been firmly advised that in case they harmed any hostages, all deals would be off; following the example of Vienna (see Chapter 9), the Dutch recognized that something of importance to the terrorists had to be granted to them in exchange for the hostages. In the end, because there was no insistence that one side would win completely, nobody lost. In particular, nobody lost what is irreplaceable: his own or any other life.

The Dutch government, using all available skill and information to keep the negotiations with the terrorists going, had asked a Dutch expert on Japan, Professor DeVos, to interview Furuya, heavily guarded by French security at Amsterdam airport. Communicating freely, Furuya criticized his comrades at The Hague for not carrying out their mission vigorously enough; DeVos found him an "amiable fanatic." According to reliable sources, the French guards had orders to kill Furuya if the terrorists carried out their threat and murdered even one of their hostages. There had been some discussion of whether Furuya's death should then be reported as having resulted from deliberate execution or from having occurred during an attempt to escape. A poll taken during the event by a French newspaper indicated public opinion was about evenly divided between soft and tough approaches. Only a small plurality wanted the embassy stormed regardless of consequences, but an overwhelming majority was in favor of killing Furuya if any harm was done to any French hostage. The newspaper followed up its inquiry by more precise questions, although the affair had come to an end by that time. Those readers who had been in favor of Furuya's compensatory execution were asked what they thought would have happened to the other hostages at the French embassy after the liquidation of Furuya. The readers were stunned. They didn't know; they hadn't thought of that.

The use of counterhostages to deter terrorism has often been discussed and sometimes been tried. It had been suggested, for instance, that terrorists should be told that for each hostage hurt, one, three, or ten of their comrades held in jails all over the world would be executed. Is it ever feasible or legitimate to copy terrorism in order to fight terrorism?

9

Contrasting Solutions

Munich Episode

MUNICH TRADITIONS   The Bavarian metropolis of Munich has a special relationship to modern terror and terrorism. In the Sternbräu beer hall of that city, which was later to become the capital of the National Socialist movement, Adolf Hitler, number seven in his party, launched his sensational rise to power in the early 1920s by advocating the use of unrestrained violence for the achievement of political ends.

In 1923, Hitler staged an amateurish coup. Armed with pistols, he and his henchmen forced their way into a political meeting held in another Munich beer hall. Hitler fired a shot at the ceiling and forced the Bavarian prime minister to offer his resignation. The next morning, the Führer and his motley crew, composed of old militarists and right-wing fanatics experienced in vigilante-type murders, marched on the monumental Feldherrnhalle (Commanders' Hall). Confronted by the German military, they gave up after the first round of shots was fired. It was precisely this ludicrous failure, however, that laid the cornerstone for the future success of both Hitler and national socialism. Decades later, Hitler would try to erase his ignominious "victim" experience by using the Feldherrnhalle for the execution of traitors.

FUNNY GUY   A subsequent trial gave Hitler the publicity he craved, and his "honorable" imprisonment permitted him to dictate *Mein Kampf* to his trusted lieutenant Rudolf Hess. Although his opponents thought of him as criminal, most Germans considered him a "nut," a deluded, inept, and laughable character, harmless in his delusions of grandeur and his childish putsch attempt. How could anybody take him seriously? People laughed about him and his party; he appeared in every sense of the word "funny." His infectious ideological zeal was ridiculed as a manifestation of mental disturbance or a cover-up for egotistical brutality. Hitler had for a short while acquired the deceptive image of ridiculous ineffectuality. (Incidentally, not only the romantic Theodor Herzl and the many braggard Arab sheiks but also crippled German Emperor Wilhelm, strutting Mussolini, ramrod de Gaulle, and heavily bearded Castro were considered funny until their opponents' laughter turned to anguished despair.)

The Germans, and for that matter the rest of the world, had grossly underestimated the Nazi threat. The Nazis' eventual ascent to power through rhetoric, propaganda, and terrorism would not have been possible, in spite of unemployment and massive support from German industrialists, if anti-Nazis had not gratuitously provided the shield of ridicule under which Hitler's deadly serious political intentions were hidden until it was too late. The crusader had been misdiagnosed as crazy, until suddenly Hitler as chief executive was no longer quaint or laughable. Irresistible charismatic appeal was attributed to the heretofore funny little Chaplinesque figure, who suddenly inspired fear and awe. The transition from terrorist gang leader to chancellor and head of state went smoothly. Hitler's terrorist lieutenants and followers became ministers, high security officials, and police chiefs. While ruthlessly eradicating all terrorism in Germany through extreme terror, they organized their own terroristic acts in Czechoslovakia, Poland, and Austria.

OLYMPIC SPIRIT   It was again in Munich in 1938 that Hitler, assisted by Mussolini, dictated to the prime ministers of England and France his terms for the carving up of Czechoslovakia, the prize for Chamberlain's "peace in our time" that was to end not quite a year later with the outbreak of the Second World War. Since then, Munich has become a symbol of cowardly submission to the threat of terror, which does not prevent but only postpones and escalates inevitable violence. In 1972, the city with the tarnished reputation played host to the Olympic Games, hoping to demonstrate that Munich and Germany as a whole had changed totally.

The Germans planned the Olympic Games, not as an exhibition of national might, as the 1936 Hitler Olympics had been, but as living proof that the strong, aggressive tensions of our world can be tamed and discharged in games. However, the calculated irony of a fate, carefully arranged by the terrorists, ordained that the peaceful alternative to violence should instead promote violence in its crudest and most brutal form. The hope of peace was exposed as a naïve illusion, a cruel self-deception. Violently the terrorists taught a world of stunned and helpless spectators their "truth": that nothing shapes reality like violence.

On September 5, 1972, terrorism set a new world record: Never before were so many held spellbound in fear and horror by so few. This time radio and television did not have to manufacture that true-to-life quality; the bloody show was actually happening. There was no escape, either for the perpetrators or for the hapless victims of exported terrorism, or for the viewers and listeners (the terrorists' main target), who sat glued to their seats in mounting tension. "Kill them," enraged sports fans often shout. In Munich, they did. The sports reporters, suddenly forced to double as political commentators, announced the results from the violation of the Olympic truce on up to the massacre at Fürstenfeldbruck Airfield. And American television devoted 1,017 minutes of live transmission to the new Olympic discipline: freestyle killing.

At dawn of that fateful day, eight Arab terrorists, wearing Olympic track suits and carrying heavy weapon cases disguised as sports equipment bags, climbed over the fence of the Olympic village in two groups. Entering the Olympic compound, they rang at the front door of the Israeli team's quarters. Wrestling coach Moshe Weinberg, assuming some team members were returning late, opened the door, then tried to block the Arabs' entrance. He was shot. As the terrorists forced their way in, another Israeli was mortally wounded, but five Israelis managed to reach safety through an emergency exit. The remaining nine athletes were tied up, herded into one room, and held hostage.

The Israeli quarters were immediately sealed off by a strong police cordon. A hastily summoned high-level crisis command met, and the radio and television crews moved to the scene. The show was on.

Negotiations for the release of the hostages and for the extension of ultimatums were conducted by the Munich police chief and various other high officials, who offered themselves as substitute hostages. The terrorists remained adamant. They insisted on being permitted to fly to an Arab country with their Israeli hostages in order to exchange them for fedayeen held in Israeli prisons.

All attempts to smuggle disguised police officers into or to lure the Arabs out of the fortresslike quarters failed. The terrorists were extremely well prepared. They never exposed themselves without one or two of the hostages, and they chose their own exit route after the German authorities had pretended to give in to their demands.

Eventually the eight Arabs, together with their hostages, entered buses that transported them to waiting helicopters piloted by German police. They were brought to the military airport of Fürstenfeldbruck, where a large Lufthansa plane presumably stood ready to take them out of the country. Arriving at the aiport, a couple of Arabs from each helicopter jumped out, leaving behind the Israeli hostages, the German pilots, and their comrades. According to agreement, two terrorists walked the approximately 100 yards from the helicopter to the plane. After a few minutes of inspection, they descended. The terrorists had ascertained that the aircraft, although its motors were running, had no crew.

German sharpshooters opened fire on the exposed Arabs, and the shots were returned. A German police officer at the airport tower was killed. Then, there was total silence for one hour, interrupted only by various voices on the police bullhorn demanding unconditional surrender. There was no answer. Around midnight, the order was given to storm the field and pick up the wounded and disabled and any remaining terrorists. Both helicopters opened fire, and minutes later, a hand grenade exploded under one helicopter, engulfing it in flames. Police, trying to extinguish the fire, found all the occupants killed. Three Arab terrorists, who had escaped into the darkness, were found and overpowered without difficulty.

ALL SAFE, ALL DEAD   Seventeen people—eleven Israelis, five Arab terrorists, and one German police officer —were dead. Yet shortly after midnight, the official spokesman for the German government had announced that the operation was considered to be a success. The editor in chief of one of the official German television networks had declared that the hostages were all alive. Audiences all over the world heaved sighs of relief and rejoiced. The Israeli government in Tel Aviv gaily responded to the prime minister's toast to life.

Probably some minor official had observed the German pilots escaping from the helicopters after the first exchange of shots and mistook them for Israeli hostages. The optimistic rumor spread like wildfire, wishful thinking apparently making confirmation superfluous.

Only a brief interval lapsed between the joyful

"all safe" and the horror of the subsequent "all dead," but it was long enough to satisfy the media's requirement for a happy ending. The right side has to win without significant casualties in order to further convince the already convinced that only counterviolence can effectively meet and eliminate violence.

The denial was anticlimactic, like the belated correction on the inside pages of a newspaper that supposedly negates a statement dramatically splashed across the front page in banner headlines. Millions of people had confirmed their belief in the effectiveness of legitimate violence, and they would not have their conviction shaken by the truth of this or any other tragedy.

Could the bloodbath at Munich have been averted? Predictably, everybody responsible emphatically said no, absolutely not. The Germans, outraged by the crude disturbance of their happy Olympic Games, claimed that they had no choice but to follow the tough line suggested by the Israelis and the Olympic committee. To permit the terrorists to leave with their hostages would have been incompatible with their obligation to protect their peaceful guests at all costs. Germany could not have consented to what then Federal Minister of the Interior Genscher called "transfer of the place of execution." The German authorities did not have the power to release the prisoners held by Israel, but they had offered unlimited amounts of money and their highest officials as substitute hostages. They had explored all possibilities of force and guile and had used all delaying tactics to postpone confrontation until nothing was left but to use force. It was dreadful but inevitable.

SYMBOL OF THE "JEWISH CONDITION"   For Israel the Munich attack was more than an abomination and an insult to all humanity; it was a symbol. Unsuspecting, peaceful Jewish athletes had been trapped and mercilessly killed by unscrupulous, death-dealing fanatics, just as the state of Israel is constantly attacked by its Arab neighbors, who are bent on total destruction and genocide. The events in Munich seemed to Israel an exemplary dramatization of the unchanging Jewish plight, leaving no doubt about who was to blame. It was the Jews, always the Jews, who, as in the biblical legend of the lamb and the wolf, were attacked and murdered—if they had not learned to defend themselves effectively.

The mortal, implacable enemy had not changed, but the Jews had. Young Israelis hate the memory of their docile parents and grandparents being led to the slaughterhouse without resistance, like dumb cattle. Thousands of years of Jewish martyrdom have taught the Israelis that kindness, understanding, mercy, and other humanitarian values are luxury items and ornamental virtues that the eternally oppressed and persecuted can ill afford. They have neither time nor taste for psychological hairsplitting and intellectualizing hesitation. Confronted daily with the possibility of extermination, they want to depend only on their own strength and vigilance. In the Olympic spirit, Germans and Israelis had relaxed this vigilance for one moment, and right away the murderers struck.

Proud Israel, wishing to be a nation like any other, was willing to sacrifice the lives of its citizens in the fight for national existence, but it was not ready to make deals with extortionist kidnappers and to barter with criminals for human lives. The Israeli decision makers felt that they and they alone knew the only way to deal with treacherous Arabs. So that the age-old Jewish tragedy of an innocent people slaughtered would not be reiterated for all eternity, they had to risk the slaughter of innocent Jewish individuals in the higher interest of their sacred cause. The hostages were thus abandoned to their certain fate. Their death was to symbolize the indomitable will of their country to survive. It was dreadful but inevitable.

THE ARAB CASE   Arab moderates deplored the shedding of blood, for which they held the Israelis and Germans responsible. The German police, they said, had broken their promises and were therefore fully to blame for the tragic outcome. Desperate people could not be faulted for acting desperately in a desperate situation. The imperialistic robber state of Israel had deprived the Arabs of their homes and rights by violence; therefore, only spectacular deeds of violence could draw attention to the enormous injustice perpetrated by the Jews and condoned by the world's indifference.

Activist Palestinians celebrated the Munich attack as a major contribution to national liberation, as a breakthrough to world attention, as a victory over Israel, and as incontrovertible proof of Arab courage and Palestinian determination. The Arab invaders had been commandos on a military mission of revenge for innumerable humiliations. They had courageously died for Arab unity, for Islam, and for socialism. Dr. George Habash considered the action completely successful. The three apprehended terrorists refused to give any information except their names. They stated that they were soldiers and were entitled to the protection granted to prisoners of war. Captured soldiers should not be treated like criminals, and furthermore, they were sure that they would soon be liberated by their comrades. Because the treacherous Germans, following Israeli instructions, had chosen the course of "deadly insanity" rather than yielding to the terrorists' demands, the outcome was predictable. What had happened had to happen. It was dreadful, but inevitable.

NATIONAL HEROES The corpses of the eleven assassinated Jewish athletes were returned to Israel. They were given heroes' funerals, their caskets wrapped in national flags, and there was national mourning. The corpses of the five Arab terrorists were returned to Tripoli. They were given heroes' funerals with their caskets wrapped in national flags, and there was national mourning. At a hero's funeral, the German police officer was buried in a casket wrapped in the German flag; again, there was national mourning.

Every country had its heroes. Victims and perpetrators had sacrificed themselves for very different causes, each believed by its adherents to be more sacred than any other.

THE NEXT LINK IN THE CHAIN On October 29, 1972, the long-expected Munich follow-up event occurred: Black September comrades of the three jailed Munich terrorists hijacked a Lufthansa Boeing 727 with thirteen passengers and seven crew members. Two passengers who had entered the plane in Beirut had forced their way into the cockpit, announcing that "Operation Munich" had begun. The hijackers demanded the immediate extradition of their fellow terrorists jailed in Germany, or else they would blow up the aircraft. In order to emphasize their threats, they placed plastic bombs at various locations in the plane.

This time German authorities complied hurriedly. The prisoners were rounded up from various jails and brought to Munich's airport to be surrendered to their comrades, but at the last moment the terrorists changed their minds. They flew over the city but hesitated to land there because remembering the Olympics, they felt that the Munich police were trigger happy. Instead, they ordered the Germans to fly their prisoners to Zagreb, Yugoslavia. They commandeered their hijacked plane back to Zagreb but delayed their landing until the German plane with their fellow fedayeen had arrived. Even though the captain told them truthfully that there was hardly any fuel left in the plane, they refused to permit the machine to land until they could clearly see their three comrades lined up on the landing field and the guards had withdrawn as requested. Allegedly the fuel would have lasted for only about thirty more seconds of flight.

The liberators received their comrades with hugs and kisses. After an immediate refueling, the plane left with its three new passengers and landed two hours later in Tripoli. After an enthusiastic welcome, the terrorists left for an unknown destination. The other passengers and crew were released, the Germans returning to Frankfurt on a special flight the next day. According to rumors that were neither confirmed nor denied, some of the Arab passengers on the hijacked plane are supposed to have been in cahoots with the terrorists and were ready to help them if their services had been needed. The idea of having relief terrorists available just in case they might become useful in an emergency is a notion full of unexplored possibilities.

The various national reactions were predictable. The Israelis bitterly accused and reprimanded the Germans, who claimed that they could not have acted differently. The whole Arab world was enthusiastic about the brilliant outcome of the escape; the Arab revenge for Munich had been completely successful. Libya's foreign minister asserted that Libya would support any and every future action of the Palestinians, who would, of course, be granted asylum in Libya.

The Munich affair was over, but only after the spiral of unrestrained aggression had gone higher and higher, accompanied by ever more justification and escalating acts of retaliatory terrorism.

Vienna Episode

CRISIS COUNSEL   The crisis counsel summoned to the Austrian Ministry of the Interior in Vienna, command and nerve center of all Austrian security forces, had been in session for just a short while when I joined the minister of the interior, the minister of justice, the Israeli ambassador to Austria, another psychiatrist, the head of the state police, and several other high-ranking security officials.

I had run, rather than walked, the short distance between my hotel and the ministry in answer to an urgent invitation by the Minister of the Interior. There had been some delay in reaching me; the venerably traditional Hotel Sacher protects its old guests at siesta time by a gauze curtain of inscrutable politeness that yields but does not give. It took quite a while before the phone operator reluctantly consented to have me disturbed by what the caller had represented as a national emergency.

The group was in a somber mood. In Czechoslovakia, two heavily armed young Arabs with Lebanese passports had boarded a passenger train which was carrying some Russian Jewish refugees. A few minutes prior to arriving at the first Austrian border station, they had inquired about the various passengers' destinations. The occupants of one compartment (an elderly couple, a young man, a young woman and her child) had stated that they were on their way to Israel. Just as the train was stopping at the station, the two Arabs brandished their automatic weapons, which they had carried under their coats, took the five passengers and an Austrian customs official hostage, descended from the train, demanded a vehicle for transportation, and started distributing leaflets. The crude manifesto, in rather poor English, with many typing mistakes, introduced the terrorists as "Eagles of the Palestinian Revolution" acting in the name of "Palestinian Martyrs." It stated: "We haven't done this mission because we are murderers by nature, but because of the crime of the Zionists" and ended with the declaration that they "refuse any project except liberating our whole land from the Zionists."[1]

A civilian, volunteering as mediator, had arranged for a small delivery van to be brought to them. In the initial confusion, the young woman and her child managed to escape by running away. After some incomprehensible delay, the Arabs forced the Austrian official to drive the car in the direction of Vienna, with the exact destination at first unknown.

After traveling approximately twenty-five miles, followed by a host of police cars, they managed to enter the landing area of the Vienna airport at Schwechat, which is on the way to the center of the city. Having been prevented from boarding a waiting passenger plane, they parked their car on the airfield. Both Arabs were equipped with modern machine guns, explosives wrapped in greaseproof paper, and egg-shaped fragmentation hand grenades with specially constructed detonating devices. At least one of the terrorists always held the safety pin of a grenade in his mouth in order to underscore their determination to blow themselves up, together with their hostages, if their demands were not met.

They distributed more leaflets and specified their demands. They wanted to take their hostages to an Arab country of their choice in order to exchange them for Palestinian brothers jailed in Israeli prisons. They also demanded a guarantee that all further transmigration of Soviet Jews through Austria to Israel would be stopped immediately.

The terrorists and their hostages arrived shortly before noon and reached the airport at 1:30. The director of national security started to negotiate with them at 2:00. The first ultimatum, requesting an aircraft and fulfillment of all their demands, was to run out within a few minutes. That was all the information the crisis counsel had at that moment.

Buying a delay had to be our immediate goal. The ultimatum was extended for several hours. (Later it was extended three more times.) We were relieved that the terrorists had been "reasonable," at least on this small but vitally important matter.

GENERAL SETTING   Austria is the easternmost European country of the free world. Its eastern part is completely surrounded by Communist nations: Czechoslovakia to the north and northeast, Hungary to the east, Yugoslavia to the southeast and south. After its defeat in the First World War, the mighty Austro-Hungarian Empire had disintegrated, and a number of new small national states had been formed according to the principle of national self-determination. The tiny German-speaking remnant of the empire with 7 million inhabitants, became the first Republic of Austria, lasting from 1918 until 1938, when German troops occupied the country and Adolf Hitler, a native Austrian, declared Austria to be the eastern province Ostmark, part of the German Reich. Although a considerable part of the Austrian population welcomed the German troops as liberating brothers rather than resisting them as a foreign army of occupation, the Allies during the Second World War pledged themselves to restoring Austrian independence, declaring Austria the first victim, rather than an ally, of German national socialism.

At the end of the war, various parts of the second Republic of Austria, roughly within the boundaries of the first republic, remained occupied by the victorious powers: the United States, the Soviet Union, Britain, and France. The heavily damaged capital of Vienna, with nearly 2 million inhabitants, was put under alternating four-power control.

In 1955, Austria achieved full sovereignty by signing a state treaty that provided for complete independence and the withdrawal of all foreign troops from its soil in exchange for a constitutionally anchored promise of everlasting neutrality. Austria remains the only European country from which occupying Russian armies withdrew voluntarily after the peaceful conclusion of an agreement. Yet Austria is unquestionably pro-Western. In spite of ten years of partial Russian occupation, the Communist party has never attracted more than 2 percent of the votes in free elections and has no representatives in the Austrian parliament. But every Austrian knows that the Iron Curtain is less than thirty-five miles from the center of Vienna (and less than twenty from the Vienna airport) and that the country is surrounded on all sides by Russian satellites.

Because the bulk of American power is more than 3,000 miles away, it would be folly for Austria to provoke the Communist giant. These facts of life were accentuated by the bloody Soviet repression of the Hungarian revolt in 1956 and the bloodless occupation of Czechoslovakia by Soviet troops in 1968. The Hungarian and Czechoslovakian examples have shown that foreign help is unavailable and ineffective. The country's independence has to rely, not on alliances (which are prohibited by the neutrality promise), but on skillful, flexible adaptation to reality.

A combination of Austria's geographic position and humanitarian tradition has resulted in the country sheltering 1,650,000 non-Austrian refugees between

1945 and 1973. Practically all the emigrants from the Soviet Union to Israel, who automatically lose their Soviet citizenship on leaving their country, have passed through Austria. Their number, hundreds in the late 1950s and early 1960s, increased to more than 1,000 yearly in the late 1960s. Entry of Soviet Jewish emigrants escalated in the 1970s to 13,082 in 1971, and 31,140 in 1972, and 20,031 through September 1973, when the incident at the Vienna airport occurred.

For many years the Austrian government had leased Archduke Otto's old renovated hunting castle, Schönau, in the vicinity of Vienna to the Jewish Agency as a transit refugee camp. Nearly all the Russian transmigrants arrived by train via Czechoslovakia. They were met at the Vienna terminal by the Austrian security authorities, who never knew in advance how many refugees would be on the train. Carefully guarded, the refugees were then brought to the nearby castle, where they were welcomed, fed, and permitted to rest and to stay for anywhere from several hours to several weeks. The El Al airplanes that flew them from Vienna to Tel Aviv were sometimes overcrowded, but at other times refugees waited for days until there were enough passengers to make the trip to Israel.

Schönau was heavily guarded by Austrian police, yet very few Austrians knew its location or present function. For obvious reasons a low profile was kept in regard to the refugees, who represented potential targets of terrorist attacks. But since the immigration of Russian Jews to Israel had become an issue in 1972, Schönau became a symbol for the world's Jewish communities. The site was visited by the Israeli prime minister and by Jewish charter groups from England and the United States.

In spite of the flawless functioning of transportation to and from Schönau and the excellent care given at the castle, the highest Austrian authorities had for quite a while been aware of the growing security risks connected with this operation. Numerous threats had been received; in January 1973, three heavily armed Arabs were arrested in a Vienna hotel when their

Israeli passports were discovered to be fake (they had
been issued on the highest Jewish holiday, Yom Kippur,
when all Jewish offices are closed). A week later,
three other Arabs were arrested in Italy and returned
to Austria. They had been in contact with the first
group, and detailed sketches and elaborate plans for an
attack on Schönau were found in their possession. Extra
precautionary measures were obviously indicated, but
in view of the particularly tense prewar mood between
Israel and the Arab states, effective action, except for
tightening of security regulations, had been postponed.

KIDNAPPERS' DEMANDS Our crisis staff was in constant telephone contact with the airport, where the direction of internal security and another high government official had kept the negotiations with the Arabs
going. The Arabs were quite willing to talk, at least
most of the time. They repeated their original demands.
The Eagles of the Palestinian Revolution apparently
were one of the innumerable radical groups loosely connected with, but not under the direct control of, Al
Fatah.

Before agreeing to a time extension, the terrorists
had warned the negotiators not to use any Munich
tactics or they would immediately blow themselves up
together with the hostages. The Olympic massacre
was heavily on their minds and on ours; everyone recognized the similarity between this situation and the
one in Munich. We wanted to avoid a similar outcome at all costs.

The Austrian ministers of justice and the interior,
acting on behalf of their government, immediately decided that under no circumstances could permission
be given for the hostages to fly out with their captors.
The government never wavered in its determination to
protect the hostages in Austria rather than leave them
to an uncertain fate to be negotiated by other countries.
However, this decision was not communicated to the
Arabs. Instead, it was represented to them, truthfully,
that more time was needed to contact various important
government officials and to make the necessary ar-

rangements. M. Patish, the Israeli ambassador, an elderly, highly educated, and informed man who had spent decades of his life on a kibbutz, wholeheartedly supported the Austrians' refusal to shift their responsibility to another country. The first to be called after the kidnapping was reported, he stressed that Israel would have acted differently in the same situation, but he added that such a situation could not have arisen in Israel because there they had successfully wiped out terrorism. He felt strongly that a firm line should be taken regardless of sacrifices. Any encouragement of the terrorists, even for the purpose of saving lives, would mean jeopardizing innumerable lives in the future.

From the room in which we all sat he communicated with Tel Aviv and Jerusalem at least a half-dozen times during these events. He had long conversations with Prime Minister Golda Meir and Vice Premier Yigal Allon. He conveyed the good wishes and appreciation of his government and expressed his private and official satisfaction with the stand taken so far, together with the hope that the Austrian government would not agree to any concessions.

In the meantime, nothing decisive was happening at the airport, which had been sealed off by police in battle dress. All air traffic had been stopped, and the host of reporters, photographers, and television crews arriving in droves by car and train from all parts of Europe were kept at a safe distance. According to plan, police vehicles had been placed around the airport to prevent the terrorists and their hostages from making a sudden dash. Sharpshooters were in position, hidden from the sight of the terrorists in order not to incite further escalation. The terrorists, who did not permit anybody to approach their vehicle on the left side, reiterated their demands and indicated frequently that there was no point in further negotiations. They refused to talk to an Arab police interpreter; they also did not wish any Arab officials, including the ambassadors, to mediate. They felt they could handle the situation by themselves.

We were not displeased with the deadlock, but the two Arabs were. They feared the approaching night, when they suspected they might be tricked and overwhelmed under cover of darkness. The security director gave them binding assurances that as long as they did not harm the hostages, nothing would happen to them.

We considered an assortment of alternatives. Various experts were consulted, and it was confirmed that no nerve gas could be pumped or sprayed into the car to paralyze but not kill its occupants. The idea of drugging food, coffee, or cigarettes was discussed and rejected as unfeasible because the Arabs had refused any offerings except from the staff of the Iraqi embassy. The automatic weapons, hand grenades, and other equipment in the terrorists' "suicide belts" appeared to be modern and in good working order. It was estimated that after the release of a pin, a grenade would explode within one to three seconds, most likely killing everybody in the car.

The terrorists freely discussed the possibility that they could be shot by police at close range, but they pointed out that the explosives in their pockets and strapped around their bodies would be released when they collapsed; therefore, their own death would mean the simultaneous death of the hostages. The plan of a direct attack seemed too risky and was turned down, at least for the time being.

We advised that neither a cabinet member nor the chancellor should directly negotiate with the terrorists, in order to avoid strengthening their feelings of self-importance and irresistibility. Suggestions were made to ignore the terrorists and let them stew in their own juices, denying them the attention they craved, but we also knew that they were no fools and probably would not believe our feigned indifference. What would we do if they started to injure or kill the hostages one by one? Could we persist in ignoring them? We suggested continuing negotiations to gain time. How seriously were the terrorists to be taken? Did they mean what they said? Were they really willing to put their lives on the line to fulfill their mission? The answers to these questions became of paramount importance. Therefore, another psychiatrist and I were given the so-far-unique opportunity not only to advise the authorities but to conduct an on-the-spot clinical interview with the terrorists in order to determine their real intentions, their state of mind, and their dangerousness. I jotted down some of the details of this interview right after it took place and used the notes to make our official report, which was later submitted to the Austrian parliament and published by the Federal Chancellery, Vienna, 1973.

My psychiatric colleague, Dr. Willibald Sluga, and I were invited to accompany two cabinet ministers to the airport. Minister of Justice Dr. Christian Broda, veteran socialist and senior cabinet member, is a brilliant theoretician and skillful practical politician. On this day, September 28, 1973, he and Dr. Sluga had attended a law enforcement conference in Carinthia. When they received the news of the attack, they had immediately returned to Vienna by army helicopter. Dr. Sluga was an ideal candidate for the crisis staff; he is a knowledgeable psychiatrist, an expert in dealing with offenders in a manner that inspires their confidence without costing him his therapeutic authority. He had achieved national prominence when as a result of his efforts three dangerous armed criminals who had staged a prison break with hostages surrendered after several days of negotiations without one shot having been fired. Minister of the Interior Otto Rösch was crucial in the present situation, the man with the ultimate authority and constitutional responsibility in all matters relating to national security. Sober, energetic, imperturbably reasonable, and refreshingly pragmatic, Rösch has the deserved reputation of an excellent administrator who never loses his cool; he exerts a calming effect by his mere presence.

On the way to the airport we rediscussed all possible options in detail. We knew that this time we had to face men of a very different caliber from those Dr. Sluga had dealt with on the occasion of the prison break. All feasible methods of trickery and guile had been considered and deemed inappropriate, but yielding to the terrorists' demands would be totally unacceptable for humanitarian and political reasons. Very little room remained for imagination and negotiations.

At the airport we received the reports and suggestions of about a dozen high-ranking security officers, negotiators, and observers. There had been no change in the Arabs' position. They refused to make any concessions and had not even allowed the hostages toilet privileges. They had extended the time again, reiterating that at the slightest suspicious movement on the part of the security forces they would immediately kill the hostages. Opinion among the law enforcement officers was divided. Some felt that we should take a chance and get it over with; others advocated continued negotiations. Everybody remained disciplined, waiting for government orders.

At this point, Dr. Sluga and I suggested that the developing relationship of trust between terrorists and Austrian negotiators should be used to keep the Arabs talking, to keep them occupied, and to keep them reassured. We emphasized the necessity for good coordination, warned against any spontaneous "courageous" action that could escalate the situation into confrontation, and avocated that persons trusted by the terrorists be added to the negotiation team. We did not think that we should take an active part in the negotiations ourselves. We did not want to lie, but if the Arabs found out that we were psychiatrists, they could conceivably be provoked into action to prove that they were revolutionary soldiers to be taken in dead seriousness, not emotionally disturbed cranks.

In the chancellery at the Ballhausplatz, Austrian Chancellor Dr. Bruno Kreisky received constant reports from the scene at the airport. A few steps away, at the Ministry of the Interior, where we had returned from the airport, the chancellor insisted that the local Arab ambassadors become involved. He asked them to visit the airport in order to determine what the terrorists were up to and what compromise, if any, they might accept. After these consultations, the emissaries were to confer with him before the emergency cabinet meeting called for that evening.

The Egyptian, Iraqi, and Lebanese ambassadors responded. At first they were not received too enthusiastically by the suspicious terrorists, but they obtained a further time extension until after the cabinet meeting. Dr. Kreisky repeatedly asked the ambassadors whether their governments would guarantee the safety of the hostages, but no such guarantee was given. As in Munich, the responsible government statesmen of the Arab countries either could not be contacted or would not commit themselves. Furthermore, it was questionable whether any Arab government at that time had control over the actions of the Palestinian terrorists.

Once more Dr. Kreisky categorically rejected the terrorists' demands, but he hinted that he might be willing to suggest to the Austrian government the closing of Camp Schönau in exchange for the unconditional immediate release of the hostages. The ambassadorial team left for renewed talks with the terrorists, and the meeting of cabinet ministers started at the chancellery.

The hours of waiting dragged on. We heard from the airport that the terrorists had talked to an Arab ambassador without eyewitnesses but that the conversation with Austrian officials had bogged down. The Austrians had run out of topics to discuss; they now chatted about the weather just to keep talk going, according to instructions. Around 10:00 P.M., the minister of justice called from the cabinet meeting to ask whether my colleague and I would be willing to take the risk of talking with the terrorists directly. The council of ministers had made certain tentative decisions about a counteroffer. They now wanted to know how dangerous the situation was at the moment, whether further negotiations were desirable, and what we could possibly contribute by personal intervention. My colleague and I did not hesitate; we were ready, even eager to participate. We raced to the airport in a police car.

CLINICAL INTERVIEW WITH TERRORISTS   Dr. Sluga and I had not developed any particular strategy except that we agreed to introduce ourselves as doctors and that, true to this role designation, we would steer away from discussing purely political topics. Because of my more fluent command of English, which the terrorists spoke, I would take the lead; then we would have to play it by ear.

Since its arrival, the hijacked delivery van had been parked at the same spot on the airstrip, all brightly lit by searchlights. Two high-ranking Austrian officials were standing close by at the right side of the car; several armed policemen remained some distance away.

Dr. Sluga and I slowly approached the vehicle. When we were about twenty feet away, Mahmoud Khaldi, the spokesman, who was sitting in the front seat, indignantly called out: "What do you want?" I replied: "We want to talk to you." We had continued our slow advance to about ten feet from the car.

KHALDI: Stop! Stop immediately! I don't want to talk to anybody.

We stopped.

KHALDI: Who are you, anyway?

DR. HACKER: We are doctors.

KHALDI: What kind of doctors?

DR. HACKER: Medical doctors. We want to talk to you.

KHALDI: What about?

DR. HACKER: About the people in the car and mostly about you.

KHALDI: I don't believe you. You are not doctors. What would doctors want? You are state police people. [Turning to the Austrian officials]: Who are they, both of them?

AUSTRIAN NEGOTIATORS: We don't know them.

KHALDI [repeating several times]: They are state police officials.

ONE AUSTRIAN: No, they are not. If they were, we would know them.

ANOTHER AUSTRIAN [in somewhat faulty English]: You must be tiresome with such many people.

KHALDI [ignoring him]: How can you show me that you are doctors?

DR. HACKER: We can't. You'll just have to believe us. You have talked to so many people up to now, why not give us a chance?

KHALDI [after some thought]: Well, if you are doctors, tell me how I am. Am I healthy?

DR. HACKER: If you let me examine you, I'll be happy to tell you. Just take your clothes off.

KHALDI [laughing]: I can't do that. But look at my eyes; maybe then you can tell something.

DR. HACKER: Okay, but for that I'll have to come much closer.

KHALDI: Okay, come on.

Followed by Dr. Sluga, I approached the terrorist. Khaldi, who had rolled down the window on the right side, had taken the pin of the hand grenade into his mouth, and opened his eyes widely. Soueidan, the second Arab, was sitting in the back of the car on the right side; he grinned and nodded in an amused fashion. His vigilance never relaxed. Playing with the submachine gun in his lap, he occasionally put the hand grenade to his mouth. Although he never participated in the conversation, he seemed to understand what was said, as indicated by his responsive nods, smiles, and facial expressions.

I leaned nonchalantly against the car door to look at Khaldi's eyes.

DR. HACKER: They're a little shiny, but they look all right to me.

KHALDI: I'm fine; I'm all right; there's nothing wrong with me. You can tell as a doctor.

DR. HACKER: Most people are all right if you just look at them. Sometimes, when one examines them or talks to them longer, one finds

out there is something wrong that one has not
seen at first.

KHALDI: There's nothing wrong with me.
You mean there is something wrong?

DR. HACKER: I don't know. We haven't
talked yet.

KHALDI: What do you want to talk about?
Why should you be interested in me?

DR. HACKER: We are interested in human
beings and interested in protecting human lives.
Your life is in danger because you and your comrades put the lives of the people in the car in
great danger. We want to help and want to know
from you how we can do that best.

KHALDI: I don't need any help. I don't
want any help. I don't want anything. I just want
justice.

DR. HACKER: Well, it isn't justice to kill
innocent people.

KHALDI: Yes, it is. The Zionist bandits
have taken our land. From the camp where I
grew up, I could see the village in which my
family used to live, but the Zionists forced them
to leave. Now they are all dead. The Zionists
killed them.

There followed an elaborate recitation of Zionist
atrocities, part of which was repeated several times
during the interview: "The Zionist are thieves and murderers. They are imperialist bandits. They want to get
bigger and bigger. They are killing people indiscriminately, but particularly women and children. The world
has done nothing to stop them. To the contrary, everybody sends arms to the Israelis to be used against un-
armed civilians," and so forth. Over and over again,
he repeated: "The Zionists are bad, all bad. They are
bandits and murderers."

DR. HACKER [interrupting the explosive flow
of propaganda]: Tell me about yourself.

KHALDI: I'm not important. I'm a soldier;
I'm a commando. There are thousands like me.
We are under orders. We are ready to die. We

don't mind dying for Palestine. My comrade and I, we know that this is probably the last day of our lives. We are ready anytime. We know that, and our general knows it.

DR. HACKER: Who is your general?

KHALDI: We have a general. We have been trained for many months. We have been preparing for this for many years. We are prepared for everything! We know very well that you people only want to keep us talking to tire us out, but we won't be tired. Never! We have taken pills; we can stay awake for ninety-four hours. You have seen that in my eyes. I don't want to talk anymore.

DR. SLUGA: What have you taken?

KHALDI: If you are doctors, you know very well what we have taken. We have taken hundreds of these pills. We have some more with us. We can stay awake for ninety-four hours or possibly even longer.

DR. SLUGA: What color did the pills have? How many have you taken?

KHALDI: You know yourself, very many—many. We have planned everything, over and over again. We have gone through courses and lectures and instructions. The general told us exactly what to say and what to do. We know that the Jews tricked and betrayed our people in the Sabena plane [allusion to the incident in which Israeli security personnel came on board disguised as mechanics, shot the terrorists, and killed one passenger], at Munich, and many other places. We know that you just wait for us to trust you or to get tired and fall asleep, but we won't. We can stay awake. We are ready to die, but everybody in this car will die with us. Just try and you'll see. We have our orders.

DR. HACKER: You know in what country you are now?

KHALDI: Of course I do; this is Austria. We have nothing against Austria, but Austria permits the Zionists to travel through their country, so that they join the Israel army and can kill thousands of our women and children.

DR. HACKER: But why do you want to fight

in this country for the freedom of your country?

KHALDI: I just explained why. The Jews don't tell the truth; they don't tell the world the truth. We have nothing against Jews; everybody could live peacefully in our state. But Zionists cannot rob all the land they want and then tell lies to the world about us. We are completely forgotten. We are being killed, and nobody knows it.

DR. HACKER: But now everybody knows that. You know your raid has been very successful. The whole world knows what you have done, and I think you would do your cause a great service if you just let it go at that. Release the hostages. You know that the government has guaranteed you both free exit. I promise you that they will keep that promise.

KHALDI: That's not enough. You don't know what they have done to us.

DR. HACKER: Who?

KHALDI: The Zionists. They have killed everybody. In one raid, they killed my mother, and in another raid, two weeks later, they killed both my sisters. We have to do something to stop that. Also, we are under our general's orders. Don't think that you can weaken us. If one of us weakens, the other one wouldn't and still would blow up everybody.

DR. HACKER: What sense would there be to that? I just told you that you have reached your goal. Everybody knows about your action and the suffering of your people. The whole world will hear about what you have done. Why not be generous?

KHALDI: Because nobody is generous with us. We have been begging to be heard for years. You don't know what it is, growing up in miserable camps and everybody just waiting to get out of there to fight those robbers that have taken your land.

There was another long barrage against the Zionists about the injustices Palestinians have to suffer.

DR. SLUGA: Can I ask you why you made this attack just now?

KHALDI: We have planned everything; everybody is prepared. There were some before us, and there will be many after us. Just try to trick us, and we'll be avenged by hundreds and thousands of our comrades. We are soldiers of a strong revolutionary army. We are volunteering to die for the cause. We are ready to die anytime. We'll probably die today.

DR. SLUGA: But you don't have to die if you are successful. That's the whole point. You are doing very well.

KHALDI: We have to carry out the orders of our general. You cannot cheat us or trick us or betray us. We have negotiated; we have talked; we are not monsters. But don't think that we will get tired; we can stay up for many more hours. We have talked enough. I don't want to talk anymore.

Throughout the interview, Khaldi had held the hand grenade in his left hand and the automatic gun in his right. He now put the hand grenade on his lap, took a cigarette from his pocket, and lit it.

DR. HACKER [reaching into his pocket]:   If you are going to smoke, I'll smoke too. I'm a pipe smoker.

KHALDI: Stop that, don't grab your gun.

DR. HACKER [taking out his pipe]:   You ought to know better than that. I told you I'm a doctor. I'm not going to double-cross you. I don't have a gun. I never had one and would not know how to handle it. I'm a doctor interested in preserving, not destroying human lives. Although you're not a doctor, I wish you had the same interest.

KHALDI: I'm not a doctor, but I love people, and I love peace. But the Zionists will not let us live in peace. They have to be killed first, before we and the whole world can live in peace.

DR. HACKER: Tell me about yourself.

KHALDI: What do you want to know?

DR. HACKER: Well, I want to know about you and your family.

KHALDI: I'm Palestinian. I told you my whole family was killed, all of them. No one is left. Now the whole country is my family. The army is my family.

DR. HACKER: Well, you must have done something before you joined the army.

KHALDI: Sure I did. I was born and grew up in a Palestinian camp in Lebanon, near Beirut.

DR. HACKER: Oh, I was in Beirut last year, and I saw some of the refugee camps. Which one were you in?

KHALDI: It doesn't matter. They're all the same; we're all the same. We're freedom fighters, not terrorists. Where we come from doesn't matter. Our family doesn't matter. Our names don't matter; we often change names. All that matters is the country, which has to be liberated.

DR. HACKER: You seem quite intelligent. Where did you get your education?

KHALDI: I went to school, lots of schools, and then to the university. I am a lawyer, but I haven't practiced as a lawyer. I graduated from law school.

DR. HACKER: Do you have any friends?

KHALDI: I have thousands of friends. They are all in the movement. They are all soldiers, and we all fight for the same thing.

DR. HACKER: Aren't you interested in girls?

KHALDI: Sure I'm interested in girls; I love girls. I used to take out girls a lot.

DR. HACKER: Not now?

KHALDI: Now there's no time for it. I love girls, and I want to get married and have children like everybody else, but only when the time comes. This cannot happen before our country is liberated. All the young people must use all their energy to free the country. That's the first thing. We are engaged and married to Palestine.

The elderly woman sitting next to Khaldi, who frequently slumped against his left shoulder, was becoming very restless. She had been moaning, groaning, and thrashing around for the past several minutes.

DR. HACKER: Look at this lady. She doesn't know what's going on. She is an old, helpless woman; she could be your mother. Why do you do that to her? She is innocent. Why not let her and the others go?

KHALDI: We have nothing against them personally, but they are Jews. They are going to join the Zionist army and will kill our brothers and our families.

DR. HACKER: Don't be silly. How can these people join any army? They probably just want to go to Israel to die in peace.

KHALDI: We are not against them, but we need them now. We have to fulfill our mission.

DR. HACKER: Don't you feel sorry for them?

KHALDI: No, I don't. Their people did not feel sorry for our people.

DR. HACKER: But they were not even in Israel at that time. You can't blame them. You have fulfilled your mission anyway. Why don't you let them go?

KHALDI: I might.

DR. HACKER: Why don't you let them go right now? I promise you nothing will happen to you. You will not be harmed or tricked in any way. You will be permitted to fly out tonight. You have reached your goal anyway. Do let them go.

KHALDI: I can't right now, maybe later. I am expecting a message from the Egyptian ambassador.

DR. HACKER: But you don't want to go back on your word. You just said that you might release the hostages.

KHALDI: Yes, I said so, and I mean it. But we'll have to see what happens first. We'll talk some more later. Don't think that all these people can make us sleepy. We can stay up for many more hours. Come back later to talk.

DR. HACKER: So you want us to come back and talk about the release of those people in the car?

KHALDI: Yes, come back. We'll talk.

DR. HACKER [tapping him on the shoulder]:
Okay, we'll come back. You see, it wasn't so bad
talking to us. Good-bye now.

KHALDI: No, it was not bad at all. Good-
bye.

Dr. Sluga and I returned to the sandwich wagon,
in which various officials had congregated after standing for long hours in the bitterly cold night. We reported our findings and made our recommendations on
the spot. The director of security immediately communicated our findings to the chancellery. In the analysis of our observations and after pointing out the alert-
ness and intelligence of the Arabs that perfectly suited
the personality profile of crusading terrorists, we said:

1. The two Arabs gave the impression that
they were prepared to go to any lengths. They
felt subject to the pressure, real or imagined, of
their superiors' commands and typified the professional terrorist personality, fanatical, well
trained and thoroughly prepared for this particular mission. Thoroughly indoctrinated with stereotyped propaganda, they clung firmly to their
paranoiac belief in their own power and their
ecstatically heightened fantasies of aggression directed against both themselves and others.

2. The terrorists' emotional state was fully in
keeping with the "realistic" situation which they
had brought about, and with their intellectual in-
trepretation of it: a spectacular, heroic deed,
fully "justified" by its ideological motivation, a
military, commando-type operation, obviously
well prepared and frequently rehearsed. In the
course of the psychiatrists' conversations with
the terrorists, it became clear that the Arabs took
an extremely exaggerated view of themselves as
the standard bearers of a sublime cause and that
they felt their mission authorised them to risk as
many lives as might seem necessary for the fulfillment of their "mission". The hostages were
regarded as members of a group which bore collective responsibility for the humiliating position

of the terrorists personally and the Arabs generally, although the terrorists bore the people they held no personal ill will.

3. Suspected influence of drugs (probably amphetamines, stimulant amines, etc.) which lead to an over-estimation of one's own value and, connected with an exaggerated belief in a particular idea, to risks being underestimated or disregarded. . . .

The probability that the terrorists had taken drugs was strengthened by the following observations:

a) The terrorists' own constantly repeated claims, for instance that they could stay awake indefinitely since they had taken tablets;

b) The terrorists' general pattern of behaviour, bright eyes, etc. (a closer examination was suggested but rejected by the Arabs for obvious reasons);

c) The symptoms of tiredness observed by security officials between 5.00 and 7.00 pm and followed by a state of hyper-vigilant tension;

d) Motoric unrest, exaggerated movements and a state of excitement becoming evident in conversation (strikingly clear, highly concentrated sense of awareness, a considerable degree of attentiveness combined with extreme excitability), constant repetition of self-assured statements, characteristic of the state of extreme emotional stimulation, resulting from drug ingestion.

We concluded that there was:

Obvious, undiminished danger attached to the situation in view of constant threats with loaded firearms and explosives. At any time, these factors could, by chance or as a result of an awkward movement, a misunderstanding or an unexpected reaction on the part of the hostages, have led to disaster. This danger was increased by:

a) The extremely confined space—unprecedented in such a case. Six people, unable to communicate verbally, spent more than

thirteen hours together in conditions of extreme discomfort with occasional periods of
noticeably increased tension;
b) The possibility, in fact the increasing
probability of unforeseen reactions on the
part of the hostages, in particular the elderly
woman, who showed signs of extreme mental
stress;
c) The unwavering determination of the
Arabs. This became increasingly evident and
was confirmed by all observers. For the reasons set out above, it was not to be expected that they would allow themselves to
be diverted from their original plan without
receiving some concession which they might
interpret as a success.

The two determined terrorists were perfectly capable of recognizing delaying tactics and constantly
threatened to bring the affair to a bloody conclusion.
This threat was underscored by the probable intake of
drugs that are known to lead to irrational, unpredictable reactions, particularly as the effect wears off.

Prolonging negotiations to avoid escalation and
direct confrontation are usually indicated in a situation
involving barricaded hostages. Delaying tactics pay off
only when dragged out as long as possible, maximiz-
ing the effects of fatigue and dedramatization. But in
this particular situation, we did not see any reasonable
possibility of tiring out the terrorists or breaking open
the cage in which they had confined themselves and
their hostages.

On the basis of our direct, "clinical" observations,
we came to the conclusion that with a degree of probability bordering on certainty the two terrorists represented an acute and increasing threat. We had been
told that the Austrian government had made a counteroffer. In order to protect the lives of all concerned,
it seemed advisable to bring the negotiations to as
swift a conclusion as possible.

COMPROMISE   We were asked to stay at the airport
to wait for further developments. Immediately prior to

our interview, which had lasted approximately thirty-five to forty minutes, the Arab ambassadors had resumed talks with the terrorists. After we left, they approached the car again and engaged in lively conversation, leaving occasionally to phone the chancellor. A little after midnight, the Austrian radio broadcast the news that a government announcement was to be expected momentarily. The director of security brought a portable radio to the car so that the terrorists could hear the chancellor's message, which was to be broadcast in German and English. The terrorists remained suspicious, and the radio receiver had to be moved around to produce fading, in order to prove that the message was not a tape recording. Eventually, they believed the assurances of the Arab ambassadors that it was indeed the chancellor's voice that they heard.

Dr. Kreisky gave a very short review of the events, stated that "permission could not be granted for them to leave the country by air along with the hostages, since the Austrian government was not prepared to risk the lives of the three Jewish citizens of the Soviet Union." He declared that

> the government has decided in future to discontinue the facilities which have hitherto been provided, such as accommodation in the camp at Schönau. These are the conditions on which the hostages who are at present still being held will be released and the two Arabs will leave Austria within a few hours.

After the broadcast the Arab ambassadors, now in a jubilant mood, still surrounded the car. They indicated that they had succeeded in persuading the terrorists to accept the Austrian government's counteroffer, but important details were still to be worked out because the terrorists feared that they might still be tricked and betrayed. Security chief Dr. Oswald Peterlunger felt that we should try to resume our interview. After all, the terrorists had said that they wanted to talk some more, and they had even hinted that they might be willing to release the hostages.

Once more, we approached the car, and Khaldi welcomed us with a bright smile.

KHALDI: Oh, there are the doctors again.

IRAQI AMBASSADOR: No, they are not doctors. I don't know their names, but they are the fellows that were sent here to see if you are crazy.

DR. HACKER: But, your excellency, we can prove to you that we are medical doctors. We'll be glad to show you our credentials and have them confirmed by anybody you choose.

IRAQI AMBASSADOR: Well, I don't really know. Maybe they just want to determine whether you have taken any drugs. I think I heard something like that on the radio.

We finally convinced the ambassador that we had spoken the truth, but we had to continue our conversation with Khaldi in his presence, and he was obviously still skeptical. In any case, the former mood of at least limited trust and easy camaraderie was never restored.

Together with the ambassadors, we withdrew to meet the minister of justice and the minister of the interior, who had returned to the airport to supervise the final arrangements. The Egyptian ambassador eagerly reported that everything was set: The terrorists had accepted the Austrian counteroffer and were now willing to leave in a small aircraft with an Austrian crew of sports pilots who had volunteered for that purpose. The Arabs insisted, however, that the hostages enter the airplane with them. They argued that in Munich, the German authorities had treacherously lured the terrorists into an empty plane and then started shooting; therefore, they had to take special precautions. Yet they promised to release the hostages immediately after finding everything in order inside the airplane. The two ministers hesitated. What would guarantee the release of the hostages once the terrorists were inside the aircraft? The Egyptian ambassador pointed out that the terrorists had shown themselves to be entirely trustworthy; there was no reason to doubt their word. In view of what had happened at other places, their suspiciousness was not unreasonable. Did the government want to jeopardize everything over a minor detail at the last moment? The decision had to be made on the spot. The terrorists, through their ambassadorial spokesman, indicated they would brook no further delay; there was not even time to consult with the chancellor by phone.

The two ministers, acting for the government as a whole, took Dr. Sluga and me aside. As we walked along the dark airfield, they asked for our opinion. Certainly I would have hated to see the whole thing spoiled when a successful conclusion seemed so imminent; yet once the hostages were inside the plane with their captors, we had nothing to bargain with. In view of the psychological structure and the total indoctrination of the terrorists it was at least possible that they might succumb to the lure of total triumph by flying out with the hostages after all. Then, they, who were afraid of being deceived and tricked, would have successfully duped us. For these reasons, I said that I strongly advised against accepting this condition, no matter what the consequences. Dr. Sluga concurred, and the ministers agreed immediately.

We returned to the waiting ambassadors, and the ministers told them some other plans would have to be worked out. The Egyptian ambassador was desolate; he thought the terrorists would be adamant in insisting that things be done their way. We quickly suggested various alternatives that would guard the terrorists against being deceived and yet fully protect the hostages. Skeptically, the Egyptian ambassador went to the car to submit the new counteroffer, which, after several minutes of conversation, was accepted.

Police cars that had been standing for hours in a circle to prevent an escape began to withdraw slowly in order to permit free access to the small aircraft waiting at a remote part of the airfield. But, just as the convoy, consisting of the commandeered car and three other vehicles carrying the ambassadors, Austrian officials, and Austrian police, started to move, one of the police cars, whose crew apparently had misunderstood the instructions, drove in the opposite direction, approaching the convoy and thus seemingly confirming the terrorists' worst suspicions. Waving and shouting, the minister of the interior ran onto the airfield to stop the car. The unaccustomed sight of the minister directing traffic caused the driver to stop just in time, and the convoy proceeded unimpeded, disappearing in the darkness. (The getaway plane could not be observed from where we stood.) Thirteen minutes after the convoy had left, we heard the roar of the aircraft engine and saw the plane lifting off the ground; at the same time we saw all three cars returning.

Moments later, all doubts were gone; every uncertainty was relieved. The hostages emerged from the first car. Dazed and bewildered, stiff from interminable hours of sitting in cramped positions with guns pointed at them, they could not comprehend that they were really safe now. They looked puzzled; then, suddenly, they broke into broad smiles and hugged all of us who were standing around. They mumbled and then began shouting the few German words they knew: *"Danke, liebe Leute"* ("Thank you, you nice people").

No one who was there will ever forget that moment. Everyone's eyes were wet, and nobody was ashamed of tears. We tried to assist, or rather, half carry the exhausted hostages to the emergency Red Cross station at the airport terminal. But before the waiting doctors and nurses could take over, pandemonium broke loose. The crowd of newsmen and radio and television reporters, who had been held back up to now, swooped down on us. In the hailstorm of questions in English, French, German, Yiddish, Hebrew, Italian, Arabic, and Spanish, nobody could understand what was being asked, let alone answer. The hostages, crushed by the onslaught of sympathetic, congratulating humanity, had to be rescued by the police. They were taken to the emergency station and later to a hospital for a good rest in peace and freedom.

HAPPY END? At the airfield everything had gone according to plan. The terrorists and their hostages had waited in the commandeered car driven by the Austrian hostage while the Arab ambassadors had inspected the airplane and reported that the machine was ready to start. But the terrorists had not been satisfied; they had insisted that the Austrian security director and another high official accompany them into the airplane to make sure that they would not be double-crossed at the last moment. In the presence of the pilots and the two substitute hostages, the equipment was carefully scrutinized before the Austrian officials were permitted to leave the plane. Saying good-bye, they quickly closed the door and gave the signal to start. A minute later the plane was in the air, and the cars bearing the hostages were on their way back to the terminal.

Gradually the turmoil subsided, and some semblance of order was restored at the airport building. The almost deserted passenger terminal was transformed into a large radio and television studio. Any hypothesis or observation, no matter how peripheral, had become newsworthy. Every participant in the affair had become an expert. The ministers gave dozens of interviews, and Austrian television teams lined up the six people (the two ministers, the two psychiatrists, and the two high officials who had offered themselves and finally had served as substitute hostages). In short statements, we expressed our satisfaction about the bloodless outcome and about saving the lives of the innocent hostages. The official spokesman for Austrian television proclaimed that this was a night in which humanity could celebrate a genuine triumph; reason had won out against brute force, setting a pattern that should be noted and imitated throughout the world.

Finally, after more than an hour of incessant interviewing, the ministers called a halt to the questioning and we drove back together to town. I must confess that we were happy and satisfied. But, of course, we had also been very lucky. It gave us pleasure to recall the long hours of helpless waiting and the many small incidents when not skill but luck had made all the difference. By and large, however, we had the feeling (quickly to be called an illusion by many) that we had done a good job. Everybody had had his share in the success, and cooperation had been perfect. The crowning achievement of rescuing the hostages from almost certain death would remain a touching memory in our minds forever.

A message on the radio of the official car abruptly interrupted our mood of euphoria and self-congratulation. We were notified that the Israeli ambassador had indignantly left the Ministry of the Interior after hearing the news of what had transpired at the airport. He had expressed bitter disappointment at the actions of the Austrian government and had left for his home, where he was packing. He intended to leave Vienna in protest the next morning to report to his government.

Somewhat subdued, we returned around 3:45 A.M. to our meeting room at the Ministry of the Interior, where a few officials were still awaiting our arrival. The minister of justice decided to call the Israeli ambassador to try to clear up whatever misunderstanding might exist. We only heard one end of the conversation, as Dr. Broda became more and more emphatic and finally quite excited. Had not the terrorists' demands been turned down? Was the saving of four human lives not worth the closing down of one facility that represented an indefensible security risk and could easily be replaced by another? Did it count for nothing that Austria had, almost alone among European nations, shouldered the heavy burden of refugee care and that it was willing to continue doing so? "You can't talk to us that way!" Dr. Broda shouted into the telephone, apparently in response to continuing recriminations. "Don't you think we deserve, if not thanks, at least a word of appreciation for our efforts, that, after all, resulted in saving the lives of three Jews soon to become Israeli citizens?" Apparently, the ambassador could not see it that way, and the phone call ended in perfunctory politeness. Suddenly, we noticed how dead tired we were, exhausted, but not sleepy. We thanked each other, and the minister of the interior dropped me off at my hotel on his way home.

AFTERMATH   The next morning, Saturday, all Austrian and many foreign newspapers reported the course of events in great detail. There had not been any time for editorial comments, but Austrian public opinion initially seemed fairly evenly divided along political lines. The progressive Social Democrats overwhelmingly approved the government's decision, but the followers of the conservative People's party were outspokenly critical, some of them indignant and outraged.

Angry and even vehement Jewish protest actions were reported from Washington, New York, Los Angeles, Chicago, London, and various Dutch and French cities. Israel denounced the Austrian actions as unpardonable and incomprehensible. The U.S. government expressed its dissatisfaction and censure in sharp tones. Newspapers in countries that one year later would give a terrorist chief a standing ovation at the United Nations topped each other in scolding Austria for its encouragement of terrorism, as if all experience had not proved that terrorist acts, handled nonviolently, are much less likely to be repeated than those settled by violence.

Considerable parts of the influential Jewish world opinion found Austria as a whole guilty of rampant anti-Semitism. Nations that could not conceive of electing a Jew as their chief executive blamed the Austrian chancellor of Jewish origin for his anti-Semitic attitude because he did not sacrifice three Jewish lives to demonstrate his pro-Jewish sentiment; and because he refused to break his word, they accused him of giving in to the terrorists. The very same Austrians who only several years ago had successfully brought the issue of the rights of the German-speaking population of southern Tyrol to the attention of the international organizations by bomb throwing now claimed disdainfully that no self-respecting state could afford to make concessions to terrorist violence.

After several days the barrage of foreign criticism quoted by the domestic opposition had caused a counterproductive impact, surprising only to the psychologically naïve. Tiny Austria, attacked and maligned for alleged spinelessness by much bigger states who on previous occasions had made much more far-reaching concessions to force, felt unjustly accused and victimized. The embattled chancellor's popularity rose in the opinion polls; more than 80 percent of the population fully approved of the government's handling of the case, more than twice as many as right after the incident had occurred.

Aggression by outgroups, experienced as unjust, unfair, and undeserved, makes for strong cohesiveness of the ingroup, stimulating outward-directed defensive aggressiveness against the inimical world. Even those Austrians who until then had never heard of any of the Austrian contributions to the solution of international refugee problems bitterly complained about being made the whipping boys for the explosion of bad conscience on the part of other countries; the Austrian sacrifices for refugees, particularly for Jewish refugees, were self-righteously exaggerated. In the groundswell of counterindignation, doubts were voiced about whether Austria should in the future be obligated to remain an attractive target for terrorists because of its care for refugees, thus jeopardizing the safety of its own citizens and endangering its very independence, all for the sake of Jews that other countries, even Israel, were willing to sacrifice without hesitation.

Rescued victims often become targets for the unconscious resentment or open wrath of the community that was compelled to sacrifice money or prestige on their behalf. The victims' unwanted contact with outlaws stamps them as outcasts, and they can redeem themselves only by gratitude and praise for their rescuers. The actual victims in Vienna certainly had shown their appreciation in unforgettably moving fashion, but the hostile comments from abroad were interpreted as rank injustice and ingratitude. The rage originally felt against the attacking terrorists for having forced the authorities to negotiate with them on an equal footing turned into resentment toward any past, present, or future victims. The escalation of anti-Austrian aggression and Austrian counteraggression was quickly aborted by the outbreak of the fourth Arab-Israeli war a week later; Middle Eastern terrorism temporarily came to an end for the duration and for some time afterward.

In a long critical review session at the Ministry of the Interior, everything that had happened was subjected to close scrutiny. There was ample and overt criticism with regard to some mistakes and some omissions but, in general, the excellent collaboration of all security forces was praised, taking into account the fact that in dealing with fanatical terrorists who are willing to die for their cause, security forces are inevitably one step behind.

One week after the event, on the second day of Jewish New Year, the outbreak of the Yom Kippur War found Israel unprepared. The Israelis, who had blamed the Austrian state police for letting two terrorists slip through their security precautions, had overlooked or misinterpreted the movement of 200,000 Arab troops. The raging battles on the Egyptian and Syrian fronts relegated the Vienna incident to insignificance, although there were still some who went so far as to claim that the Arabs' "success" at Vienna had provided the necessary encouragement for them to engage in war with Israel.

After the Yom Kippur War, Israeli official and private opinion changed markedly. The Austrian approach seemed more acceptable because the war had tragically dispelled the myth of Arab cowardice, lack of discipline, and lack of organization. In late October 1973, on the occasion of Austria's independence day celebration, the Israeli ambassador sat peacefully chatting in Schönbrunn Castle with Dr. Kreisky, Dr. Broda, Rösch, and myself. The airport incident had not been forgotten, but its meaning and significance had changed.

Comparisons

The bitter conflict of the strife-filled Middle East had been exported to peaceful Austria as it had been, over a year before, to Munich, Germany.

In the past Austrians have had their share of the

Nazi atrocities; many high and low Nazi officials had
been Austrian, and hundreds of thousands of Viennese
enthusiastically welcomed the conquering Austrian-
born Adolf Hitler to Austria, which for many decades
if not centuries had been the breeding ground of aggressive anti-Semitism. Although the Allies declared
Austria the first victim, rather than a participant in
Nazi aggression, most honest Austrians knew and
continue to know that this declaration, entirely just
with regard to Austria as an independent state, does
not accurately reflect the active participation in and
toleration of the Nazi regime by many Austrians. If
there is any validity to collective historical responsibility, then Austria must, together with Germany, bear
the burden of national shame and national guilt.

In Munich and in Vienna, hostages were taken
and threatened because they were Jewish. In both
places, Israel, in keeping with its warlike stance, advocated strong, uncompromising measures, regardless of
sacrifices. Yet the reactions of the authorities were entirely different. Vienna came after Munich, hence the
immediate readiness for honest negotiations with serious consideration of options other than force or guile.
At Munich, Germany could not offer anything that the
terrorists wanted; the Austrians, on the other hand,
were able to think of a concession within their power
that would satisfy the terrorists.

In Munich, the police psychologist was prevented
from becoming involved. Indulging a popular preju-
dice, the authorities felt that when the situation became
really serious there was no time for psychological advice. In Vienna, the psychiatrists participated in all deliberations and advised according to their professional
knowledge. On specific request, they carried out a clinical evaluation and actually assisted in the ongoing negotiations. It was assumed that professional training
and experience would make psychiatrists at least as
reliable observers and expert interviewers as the usual
cast of diplomats, ambassadors, and security and police
officials acting ad hoc at such events. The psychia-

trists made no decisions, but they laid the foundations for rational decision making.

We had expressed our conviction that these two young, intelligent, and dedicated Arabs, acting not as isolated individuals, but as representatives of powerful groups in the service of a sacred cause, were not likely to release their hostages unharmed unless and until some concessions were made. The terrorists would have to be given something valuable, that is, not something that we cherished or that we thought they should cherish, but something that they themselves thought valuable.

This was different from Munich, where in view of a totally mistaken, unprofessional, and partisan evaluation of "national character traits," it was believed the cowardly, braggart Arabs would surrender in the face of a show of strength.

From the start, the Austrian government refused the terrorists' bid to turn the incident into a morality play at the hostages' expense. The government did not enter the competition to see who was better at blind courage, as if it took any real courage to order hundreds of policemen to shoot two terrorists. In Vienna, there was the sober realization that neither the future of civilization nor the existence of Israel were at stake but that the lives of four specific individuals had to be protected, not at all cost, but if humanly possible.

The Nazi regime had produced the modern phenomenon of the desk criminal, the responsible official who never bloodied his hands but by his signature decreed the destruction of thousands of people. In Vienna, nobody wanted to become a desk hero at the expense of innocents.

In Munich, it was officially declared after the event that from the moment of their capture on, the hostages had to be considered 99 percent dead. We never made that assumption, perhaps because we had personal contact with the hostages. We knew them; we knew that they were terribly frightened and in great danger but very much alive. They depended on us to keep them alive. For several long hours, we held their lives in our hands and were charged by fate with the responsibility, not for abstract humanity, but for these concrete human beings.

The Vienna compromise did not spell the end of all Jewish transmigration as intended by the terrorists; on the contrary, the incident led to its continuance at an increased rate. With the closing of Schönau, the safety of the transmigrants had not been jeopardized, different accommodations were made available, transfer was speeded up. The Arabs scored a limited and, in the context of later events, not very meaningful propaganda success. In Vienna, the authorities did not feel that the terrorists' propaganda or prestige gain was necessarily Austria's loss; or at least they were certain that if it was a loss, it was amply compensated for by four lives saved.

PERSONALITIES   Yet it was probably the difference in personality structure of the main decision makers that would prove crucial for the different handling and outcome. The German chancellor at the time of the Munich attack, Willy Brandt, and the Austrian chancellor, Dr. Bruno Kreisky, had been political refugees in Scandinavia during and on account of the Nazi regime, Brandt in Norway, Kreisky in Sweden. Because they both had been victims of terror, they not only could readily identify with the feelings of abandonment and helplessness of the hostages but actually remember those feelings as part of their own experience. They both had been persecuted and forced out of their country because they were socialist opponents of the totalitarian regime, but Kreisky additionally was of Jewish origin, and as such was marked for all time as the unremitting foe of nazism. By no stretch of the imagination could he feel himself in any way responsible for the Nazi crimes that had endangered him and exterminated members of his family. Because of this fixed role, he could not conceivably sympathize with Nazis or with any totalitarian regime. Kreisky's credibility and his capacity for political maneuvering are based on his undisputable, unambiguous, and nonambivalent attitude toward brutal force. No admirer of glorified violence, he is neither attracted to, tempted by, nor intimidated by violent threats.

Undoubtedly the Germans were also completely sincere in their ardent desire to save the hostages of the captured Israeli Olympic team. The German chancellor, Willy Brandt, called the Munich events an unmitigated catastrophe. For Brandt, who had knelt down in front of a monument for assassinated Jews in Poland and thus had accepted German responsibility for the National Socialist crimes, the repetition of the killing of Jews whom the Germans were helpless to save was the worst of all possible contingencies. He and his government would willingly have done anything to prevent recalling the memory of the most ghastly period of German history; he and his government would have dared to risk everything, including their own lives, to save those Jewish guest athletes—that is, everything but oppose the Israeli line.

For all decent postwar Germans the Jews had become symbols of innocent victims subjected to merciless persecution and extermination by a brutal criminal regime. The National Socialists had perpetrated their evil deeds in provocative self-righteousness without any recognizable doubt or guilt. Millions of Germans had looked the other way, would neither hear nor see anything wrong, and Pollyanna-like, carried on business as usual so that the fate of the Jews would be none of their business. No progressive and enlightened German government could afford to be associated with decisions or omissions that would raise the suspicion that the Germans were again indifferent to and hence guilty of the killing of Jews in Germany.

Under these circumstances, the German government followed—had to follow—the spirit and the letter of Israeli wishes that were founded on supreme confidence in military strength and in the effectiveness of uncompromising toughness. "Final solution" (*Endlösung*) had been the coyly euphemistic German term for the extermination of millions of Jews in so-called concentration camps. In order to avoid any association with this horrifying genocide, a peaceful new Germany in Munich brought about the final solution for all the Jewish hostages.

Kreisky, his governmental team, and their advisers, veterans of civil war and nearly all of them jailed at one time or another for political offenses, did not underestimate the deadly serious threat of violence; they had often discussed the probability of terrorism being exported to Austria. Knowing the "hostage feeling" of having to depend for survival on help from outside, they had a very personal stake in preventing the irreversible loss of human lives that, but for a turn of fate, could have been their own. This desire to save and to help dominated all their methodical procedures, scientific explorations, and rational decisions.

BODY COUNT   At the Munich airport seventeen people died in the wake of the terrorist attack on Israeli athletes during the Olympic Games; then, in exchange for the German crew of a hijacked plane, the three captured Arab terrorists were released a few months later and went scot-free.

At the Vienna airport, no shot was fired, no lives were lost, no fundamental right was given away, nobody, Jewish or otherwise, was up to then or since denied the opportunity to avail himself of Austrian help to reach the country of his choice safely.

In war or in warlike states, national myths, abstract symbolic notions, and the acquisition or retention of territory are given priority over lives. But for peaceful, civilized, democratic nations, the value of the individual human life must be supreme.

In Austria the warlike blackmailing threat of the terrorists was met by the peaceable fulfillment of the obligation to protect threatened human lives first under almost all circumstances, and it caused no irremediable damage. Considering that no war lasts forever and that the hope of mankind, no matter how uncertain, lies in peace and its emphasis on the supreme value of human life, the example of Vienna should be studied as at least one model of how to meet violent blackmail without yielding to or imitating violence.

10

American Approaches

The general public and its responsible decision-making representatives cannot be expected to possess expert knowledge about all the complicated problems of contemporary society. Their thinking will be predetermined as much by current stereotypes as by unbiased knowledge. Stereotypes, and for that matter prejudices and prejudgments, save the time and trouble necessary for independent examination and decision. They are not necessarily completely wrong or untrue; more likely they are partial truths, partly expressing and partly distorting reality. Rigidified to conveniently simple formulas, stereotypes represent evaluations that carry implicit instructions for action expressed in plausible clichés. They are tentative attempts to bring order into the chaos produced by the incessant bombardment of conflicting information.

No contemporary topic of any importance escapes the fate of being prejudged, predigested, and filtered through ingrained polarized stereotypes that are determined by childhood experience and education, by nationality and social class, by political background and favorite attitudes. Stereotypes about terrorism can be roughly and conveniently divided into authoritarian-rightist-tough and permissive-leftist-soft approaches,

although this in itself represents a somewhat stereotypical simplification.

The definite ideas that nearly everybody seems to
have about terrorists cannot be ignored; they must be
taken seriously if only in order to change them. The
following chart lists the most commonly held views of
both sides:

Authoritarian	*Permissive*
Terrorists are nothing but criminals. Treat them like criminals.	Terrorists are misguided idealists. Don't punish and kill them; try to understand and treat them.
Terrorism is a security and law enforcement problem. Sociologists and psychologists only interfere and confuse the clear-cut issues. Keep them out.	Terrorism, like war, starts in the minds of men and is largely a psychological and sociological problem. Try to solve it by treatment and education.
Right is right, and wrong is wrong; the law is the law. Enforce the law regardless of sacrifices.	In a civilized society, the protection of human life takes precedence over everything else. Preserve life at nearly any cost.
The only effective way to meet force is by superior counterforce. Shoot first; ask questions later.	Violence is obsolete and primitive, and civilization will eventually make violence wither away and disappear. Set an example by demonstrative non-violence.
Concessions and compromises only encourage future terrorism. Give them an inch, and they'll take a mile. Yield once, and you'll always have to yield. Don't negotiate with terrorists.	Two wrongs don't make a right. Don't meet force with force; negotiate always.
The more severe the punishment, the greater its deterring effects. There is no	Punishment is always useless in the long run, but particularly so in regard to

terrorism under strict dictatorship. Raise the penalties.	terrorists, who are more attracted than deterred by punishment. Seek alternatives to punishment.
Terrorism is the harvest of modern permissiveness. Abandon leniency, and have no pity on those who have no pity on us.	Terrorism has always existed, stemming from desperation or expressing protest of the weak and disinherited. Because it cannot be eliminated, come to terms with it.
Promises given under duress are not binding. Don't keep them.	Credibility is your main tool for persuasion and education. Keep your promises under all circumstances.
Behavioral scientists exculpate and encourage terrorists by "understanding" and justifying them. Don't pay any attention to them.	Every form of human behavior has to be understood and appreciated on its own terms. Show empathy, rather than rendering judgments.
There has to be law and order. You have to draw the line somewhere; that's what we have laws for. If the authorities can't help you effectively, resort to self-help.	There are many possible orders and even more laws, not all of them enforced. Self-help is also a form of lawlessness. Try to improve the law by lawful means, rather than by taking the law into your own hands.

You can evaluate where you stand according to your preferences for one or the other viewpoint, but they are both partly erroneous. Violence will not simply go away, no matter what you may wish, and unresisted violence will shape reality. But there are ways to meet violence effectively other than by counterviolence.

Congressional Hearing

In 1974, the Committee on Internal Security of the United States House of Representatives conducted months of hearings to consider new legislation and suggestions for administrative changes to meet the challenge of modern terrorism. Asked about the possibilities of identifying potential terrorists in advance, I testified on my differentiation among crazy, criminal, and crusading terrorists.

After suggesting simultaneous research and remedial social action, I argued that although the manifestations of modern terrorism are multifaceted and changing, they follow essentially few patterns; therefore, general principles and guidelines for appropriate counterstrategies can be developed. Based on my theoretical insights and practical experiences, I offered three general policy suggestions.

1. Action teams or task forces consisting of highly trained professionals from various fields, including but not confined to law enforcement officers, should be organized and permitted to start work immediately. These teams could operate under federal control or on a local level under the umbrella of a federal institution. Their function should be advisory, but it should be mandatory for the decision makers to consult them and inform them of all details of relevant events. In special cases, these task forces could be used for actual participation in negotiations, bargaining, and so forth.

2. The organization of action teams or task forces should have computerized data banks and similar resources at their disposal to keep track of the outcome of previous events and the countermeasures taken. The data-collecting center or centers could be empowered to conduct ongoing research into several areas: personality profiles and personality development of various types of terrorists; victimology; that is, the reasons why particular victims are chosen and their subsequent behavior (e.g., indignation, endurance, hysteria, sympathy for captors, erotic ties, identification with aggressors, poor-devil syndrome, effects of brainwashing and other forms of coercion creating conversion or increased resistance); behavior of terror objects (families, communities, nations, and so forth), including studies in group and mass psychology of behavior under stress combined with studies of deterrent effects

of higher penalties, particularly the death penalty, and special attention to the psychology of law enforcement officers and their sensitivity to loss of face and ridicule as well as their habitual use of quick confrontation rather than negotiations to resolve conflicts.

3. Various negotiation techniques and strategies should be evaluated in terms of effectiveness and morality. Such evaluations would consider, for example, which means are best suited to bring about the desired ends, who should negotiate, when and how, up to what limits. They would also provide empirical research data to assist in the decision about what is ultimately most important: the preservation of individual life, international prestige, or other considerations.

The authority, position, and function of such teams were discussed in the committee proceedings.[1]

CHAIRMAN ICHORD: Doctor, how do you envisage this team to work? Will it be a law enforcement team?

DR. HACKER: As a matter of principle in a democratic society, ultimate decisions have to be made by the duly elected or appointed officials. I do not believe one should delegate that authority to experts.

CHAIRMAN ICHORD: There must be legislative authorization and as far as that is concerned, I would say under the LEAA (Law Enforcement Assistance Administration) Act, which was passed by Congress, there is a very good grant of authority for the establishment of such a team.

In fact, I think the statute almost envisages the establishment of such a team. The executive branch does have the authority. I do not think there is any doubt about that. Now if the executive branch does not act, the Congress could specifically pass legislation establishing such teams. Specifically, how do you envisage this team operating? Will it be a law enforcement team, acting in an advisory capacity?

DR. HACKER: My preference would be that it be an advisory team whose advice must be sought, but not necessarily followed. But it ought to be compulsory and obligatory to consult with that team to get its counsel and advice. In case the advice is ignored or counteracted, there should be public explanations of why that has been done and for what reasons. By using that method, we can establish ongoing research. But certainly, I am against the present policy of treating a case as though it were the first and only case and treating it in a local jurisdiction that by necessity, in terms of information and skill and knowledge, is very, very limited.

COMMITTEE COUNSEL CRANDALL: Do you feel there are other areas that have significant relationship to this problem which would warrant this committee's consideration?

DR. HACKER: Yes, I do. The composition of and the responsibility for on-the-job training by that team is also of crucial importance. I think it should minimally contain a law enforcement person, psychologist, sociologist or criminologist, and it probably also should contain a nongovernmental lawyer, possibly a linguist, a media specialist, a cultural anthropologist and people of that sort.

There should be a central place where the administration of these teams is conducted. There should be a permanent staff to contact the various people and to coordinate them and have in the beginning regular monthly conferences of the prospective team members.

Also, this team or teams should certainly be in the position of having access to material, to research data that have been collected either nationally or internationally. I would very much favor a coordinated effort between service and research activity. In other words, what I think has hampered social research a great deal is the separation of research from action. I believe, in general, one of the bad things of modern research has been the isolation of the doers who do not think very much and the thinkers who do not do very much, and the twain never meet. We do not want to have one group of people who have all the information but cannot do anything about it and the other group who have all the power to act, yet don't know anything.

The chairman was apparently intrigued with some of these ideas. During the testimony of Ambassador Hoffacker, assistant to the secretary of state and head of the fight against terrorism, Ichord gave his approval to the proposed study-action teams: "I think it has a great deal of merit, that is, study and action teams could be stationed at several points around the nation and, when acts of terrorism such as kidnapping or some other acts occur, this expert team could immediately move in upon the scene and participate to whatever degree would be desirable." He also added, "I think there would be an even more important function and that would be as a teaching team for local law enforcement officials throughout the United States."

Answering specific questions about action teams from the chairman and other committee members, Assistant Attorney General of Legislative Affairs W. Vincent Rakestraw testified:

> Regarding the concept of regional study-action teams with special expertise that could be sent to the site of terrorist crimes to take charge of the investigation, we do not believe it is acceptable to dilute the authority of the operational agency having jurisdictional responsibility at the scene of such a crime.
>
> We would state that as a general proposition, domestic terrorist activities, including kidnapping, are not at this time of such a magnitude as to require or justify the creation of such study-action teams.

Later on, he added:

> Since terrorist acts necessarily involve state as well as federal crimes, study-action teams, if created, would necessarily raise important jurisdictional problems between federal, state and local law enforcement bodies. Such study-action teams would, in most all cases, have to coordinate their activities with competing federal, state and local law enforcement agencies and officials,

which would inevitably raise serious practical
problems, as well as jurisdictional problems.

Certainly, such study-action teams would raise
practical and jurisdictional problems concerning coordination. Rakestraw feels that it is better not to raise
these questions, to leave the situation as is, with its
present lack of coordination, which was so evident in
the Hearst case and in many similar instances. Yet,
there cannot be any disagreement that well-coordinated
command and decision structures are essential not only
for conducting negotiations but for ordering effective
confrontation.

Another witness, Dr. David M. Rosenbaum,
strongly emphasized the need for "unity of command."
But for opposite reasons, he arrived at the same conclusion as Rakestraw.

CHAIRMAN ICHORD: One of the expert witnesses appearing before the committee has advocated the establishment of so-called study teams,
which would be particularly applicable to, generally, kidnapping cases. They would be study-
action teams stationed at perhaps various points
around the country, consisting of criminologists,
psychiatrists, psychologists, news media analysts,
people of various disciplines that would be called
in to act in an advisory capacity, to participate
in negotiations with the kidnappers or to participate to whatever degree necessary. I have taken
this matter up with the Department of Justice
and the FBI and generally met solid opposition,
primarily because of the concern of the Department of Justice and the FBI of having outsiders
come in and perhaps work outside of the normal
discipline of the police officials who have primary
responsibility. Would you have any comments
upon such a proposal?

DR. ROSENBAUM: As well as I understand
the idea, I think it would be a bad idea also. I
think it is best to leave those sorts of climactic
situations to the police authorities, who are by far
best equipped to handle them. It is also necessary
to have a unit of command in such situations. I

think, however, that teams which would do studies after events to try to learn lessons from them after they are over would be very valuable, but I don't think it would be useful to have them in any way interfere in those few crucial hours when the police have to make a decision how to handle the situation.

Dr. Rosenbaum believes in maintaining the separation between thinkers and doers, between research and action. This was the pattern followed at Munich. The police psychologist was sent away from the scene of the Olympic tragedy because when the situation got really serious, fast shooters were preferred to fast talkers.

Inspector Thomas J. Smith from the FBI has conducted his own research into the motivation and behavioral patterns of terrorists. "In terrorist activity," he observed, "an attempt is made to determine two broad areas of affecting their action, namely, determining the emotional stability of the terrorists, and second, establishing their dedication to whatever cause they proclaim." The inspector also reported results: "Research on past terrorist actions indicates a high degree of paranoid and/or paranoic types of behavior existing within groups and individual terrorists actions." Absolutely correct. If the FBI can conduct psychological research and come up with findings confirming psychological insight, why, conversely, can't psychiatrists and psychologists advise and assist in law enforcement matters?

Advocating an in-depth study of skyjackers, Dr. F. Gentry Harris testified:

We would like to be able to take a look at him at any time from the moment of his apprehension until his disposition—imprisonment, hospitalization, freedom, whatever. We would like to have access to these people while in prison. As it is now with skyjackers, we have gotten together with their defense counsels before trial. The Justice Department has agreed to let us see these people only after their conviction, because it does not want any interference with the prosecution.

Dr. Harris had expressed what everybody knew. The government wants convictions and no nonsense regarding insanity, even if the state and federal prisons become swamped with mentally disturbed convicts. Psychiatric testimony that might induce the fact finders to declare the defendant legally insane or of diminished capacity is considered interference with law enforcement, although such testimony is a legally defined, legally enacted, and legally guaranteed procedure. Interference with what? Obviously, with sending people to prison. But what happens to them in prison and after they get out? People hate to think about that, but the public will have to start doing just that if it wants effective measures against crime and terrorism.

Inspector Smith conceded that modern terrorism is not just ordinary criminality, that it has novel features. Still, he came to the conclusion that "the proposal of an action team made up of non-law enforcement personnel responding to the scene of terrorist action would directly affect the operational function of any law enforcement agency. It would tend to confuse determining objectives and goals, as well as deter successful negotiations." On what evidence are such statements made? In the Patty Hearst case and in a host of similar kidnapping incidents, it was the confusion about the determining authority and the goals and objectives of law enforcement that deterred successful negotiations. Had the inspector never heard of Scheveningen (see page 284) and Stockholm, of The Hague and Vienna?

With regard to study-action teams, Ambassador Hoffacker stated:

> I know that the committee is considering the possible utility of other experts who might serve as advisers or managers of negotiations in this country or abroad for the release of victims of terrorists.
>
> I would recommend that the committee consult agencies in addition to my department which are directly responsible for such negotiations—the FBI and the Department of Transportation in particular—to ascertain the need for such addi-

tional expertise. My preliminary judgment, based on such information as is available to me, is that those agencies, as well as my department, are well supplied with psychiatric and other professional personnel who are automatically brought into kidnapping situations and who are valuable and active advisers and consultants as these situations evolve.

In an old story, a fellow is blamed for having broken a pot that he borrowed from a friend. Trying to absolve himself from blame, he explains "I haven't borrowed the pot"; "It already was broken when I got it"; "Somebody else broke it"; "I returned it unbroken." Following the same pattern, study-action teams, although suggested in an advisory function only, are considered by bureaucratic officialdom as: not necessary because "domestic terrorist activities, including kidnapping, are not at this time of such a magnitude as to require or justify the creation of such study-action teams" (Rakestraw); more or less impotent (having no decision power, they would just be in the way and could not assist effectively); confusing the issues and deterring negotiations by raising practical and jurisdictional problems; already functioning very well anyway within the existing bureaucratic and police structure.

Before the Internal Security Committee, Dr. David Hubbard testified: "The government knows no more now about terrorism, skyjacking, kidnapping and assassination, etc., than it knew 50 years ago. That same statement may still be valid 50 years from now. Bureaucratic ignorance and fear have fought these studies every inch of the way. Existing research institutions and their personnel are inadequate to the task."

Lip service is readily given to the novelty of the phenomenon of modern terrorism, but nobody dares touch the traditional law enforcement routines, heavily dependent on computerizable charts and figures, handbooks and profiles, managerial solutions, masses of paper work, and guns. Suggestions have been made about raising penalties, introducing the death penalty and forbidding the payment of ransom, increasing security measures, more surveillance of potential criminals, computer sharing of criminal record information by state and federal agencies (which has its own political and constitutional overtones). That is the scope of the problem as perceived by most law enforcement and bureaucratic officials. These days everybody is willing officially to acknowledge the necessity for novel measures in meeting moral challenges; but when it comes to brass tacks, the brass wants to depend on the old methods that have failed, on technologically embellished weaponry, and on violence.

Media Responsibility　Virtually all experts who testified before the committee pointed to the important role of mass media in increasing the contagious effect of violence by spreading the terrorist's message, thus providing him with important motivations. Some witnesses blamed the media for their greed and sensationalism; others insisted that the media fulfill their vital function in a democratic society by presenting what happens in violent reality.

　　Dr. David Hubbard (who also testified) uses rather strong language in *The Skyjacker*. After quoting a rather articulate skyjacker as saying, "The news is a whore. It will lie down and give itself completely to any man who skyjacks an airplane," Hubbard writes: "The others [skyjackers] have all shared his feelings. All have counted on the automatic media response. Guaranteed notoriety has been the most consistent gain sought by hijackers."[2]

　　Questioned by Representative J. Herbert Burke: "With regard to any adverse happenings that come about, do you think overt exposure by the news media generates further crimes by individuals?" Dr. Harris responded: "Yes, I think the news media people ought to get together with our group, and various other people, agencies, and so forth, and develop a mutual understanding about what should be done and should not be done under the circumstances."

　　In written statements submitted to the committee, the officials of "U.S. industry with large foreign operations" expressed the view that the news media are "the contributing factor in the popularization of terrorist groups—the publicity afforded the terrorist group contributes significantly to its appeal to those radical elements in any society who are attracted to violent groups."

Some officials claimed that they have refused to give the media any information about their negotiations with terrorists in kidnapping cases because such information mainly serves the terrorists. The officials noted that a frequent demand by terrorist groups is for press conferences, along with radio and television time to propagate the group's aims and objectives.

I had testified:

> Due to the undeniable fact that the mass media perform willingly or unwillingly the propaganda job for terrorism by providing national or international audiences with sensational mass entertainment, the possibilities for reasonable mass media presentation and appropriate controls must be studied and experimented with under strict observation of First Amendment protection and other guarantees for free speech and free expression. Various voluntary and compulsory control schemes, avoiding crude censorship, can be suggested to reduce or eliminate spectacular advertisement effects, and to minimize the multiplying contagion effect which leads to imitation and escalation of terroristic violence. All scapegoating of the media, who, after all, only do their job as presently defined and seemingly demanded by the public, should be avoided. Media experts (and investigations of media effects) could be used by the action teams and particular emphasis placed on experimental attempts to employ the media positively and productively through genuine information and education that nevertheless can be exciting and entertaining.

Dr. Hubbard believes that the First Amendment does not intend to protect the right to publish and report error. But who is to decide what is truth or error? After Vietnam and Watergate, can we trust government bureaucracy to make these ethical and factual determinations?

Censorship in any form, even if it is not used as a method of terror from above, is repulsively infantilizing and sets dangerous precedents. But you do not permit television crews to block the ambulance trying to get a man to the hospital to save his life because the public has a right to pictures and news about the fate of a prominent individual. In emergency situations, where there is clear and present danger to the community or to individual human life, certain rights have to be curtailed temporarily in order to safeguard other, more important rights. Voluntary cooperation regarding, for instance, an agreed-upon delay of publication, omitting names and photographs, and a ban on ongoing reporting to prevent the contagious "showification" effect that transforms a tragic event into a dramatic performance, is certainly not beyond the scope of realization. The equal-time doctrine specifically applied to coverage of terrorism would do little more than compel broadcasters to caution viewers that acts of terrorism are against the law and hazardous to health. But agreed-upon or imposed time lags and temporary blackouts would impede the copycat effect, deny the terrorists their otherwise guaranteed exposure, and serve as a deterrent.

Terroristic influence on the terror objects (i.e., the audience, the spectators, the general public) is the crucial part of the terrorist's overall scenario. If there is really nothing that can be done about this, for whatever reasons, so much the worse for our security, but at least we should not complain too loudly that we do not know what to do. We do know, but we do not want to make the sacrifices demanded by acting according to this knowledge. Thrills and kicks are highly valued consumer goods. Governments and revolutionaries, terrorists and antiterrorists vie for public attention and public sympathies. Terrorism could never have become the major contemporary menace that it is without its mass media-sponsored influence on public opinion everywhere.

In my testimony before the committee, I stated: "As a nation we pay dearly for our insatiable need for sensational entertainment. We don't have to capitulate in this country before this largely artificial and manipulated need which can be kept within certain bounds."

> COMMITTEE COUNSEL SHAW: Most of the television producers will tell you they have to have some kind of violence to hold public attention. Even your children's cartoons contain acts of violence. It is pretty hard to cope with.
> DR. HACKER: Let me be very hard-nosed about that. If this way of satisfying our desire to be tickled and entertained by violence is ineradicable within our society, then you have to write off the costs in excessive, surplus violence as a societal expense—as what you pay for entertaining kids of all ages.

Politization of Criminality

Correctional administrators look back with nostalgia to the days when con bosses kept things under control through racial segregation. Nowadays, criminals all over the United States represent themselves as political prisoners, as victims of racism, social injustice, and political persecution. The politization of criminality and the simultaneous criminalization of politics have been discernible modern American trends.

Chairman Ichord of the Internal Security Committee stated:

> This committee conducted a very sensitive investigation into subversive activities directed toward the nation's prison system. I say it is very sensitive because I think most people recognize there is a need for considerable prison reform. But I am particularly addressing myself to the problem that has arisen in the last two or three years, after certain court decisions making it extremely difficult to censor materials coming into our nation's prisons. We observed within the

last two years that our prisons, which are a sore spot that can be exploited, are being avalanched with propaganda materials along the line that you are not a real criminal, you are a victim of society.

The scandal of the prisons inflicting what Karl Menninger calls the debasing "crime of punishment" on its inmates has long been a topic of public debate, but not of public action. The prison population may or may not be politically polarized, but the communities outside the prisons certainly are. Hard-liners blaming outside agitators for all the trouble claim that contemporary violence is the harvest of permissiveness. They cite erroneous or faked atrocity reports (such as the officially supported but disproved story that at Attica hostage prison guards were slain by throat cutting) to justify massive retaliation. They frown upon negotiations as weak and immoral and proclaim that unrestricted violence, regardless of losses, is the sole means of effectively meeting illegitimate demands. In contrast, progressive softies point to the social and psychological motivations of the rebels and demand exploration of all other alternatives before violence is used. They favor honest negotiations for conflict resolution and therefore, in the case of Attica, blame the governor and the authorities for not having exhausted all nonviolent opportunities.

Raymond Procunier, chief of California's prison system, summed up the problem succinctly by stating that whatever is done at least one-half of the people will be disappointed and unhappy because those on the right want everybody to get the death penalty, while those on the left want the prisons blown up altogether.

There are fewer people in U.S. penitentiaries now than in 1960, in spite of the growing number of crimes committed. Statistics indicate that only 21 percent of all serious crimes result in arrests, and only 5 percent are resolved by conviction. It has been determined that the odds are about 200 to 1 that the offender who commits a serious felony will escape imprisonment, and the "success" rate for organized crime is even higher. In other words, crime pays; it pays well and is relatively safe. Most serious crimes are not reported. Most perpetrators of reported crimes are not caught. Most of those caught are not convicted (at least not sent to prison). Not the most dangerously criminal, but only the most inept, resourceless, poor, and unlucky go to prison, where the inmate population represents nowhere near an adequate sample of the offenders who actually commit serious crimes. The preprison selection process from arrest to sentencing is admittedly biased, immoral, and unjust, punishing predominantly disadvantaged and resourceless prisoners, most of whom come from the bottom of the social heap.

GOVERNMENT STRATEGY Recognizing that effective law enforcement is a matter of local control, Congress began allocating federal funds through block grants in 1967. Five years later, James Vorenberg, executive director of the President's Crime Commission, said that crime is an increasingly serious problem and that the criminal justice system, police, courts, and correctional systems seem to be increasingly less capable of doing anything about it.

Contrary to expectations, reported crime rates tend to go up in proportion to additional personnel and increased efficiency. But in an effort to maintain their image as successful crime fighters and in order to qualify for continued federal funds, the police manipulate their statistics to show a reduction in the crime rate.

Data in a 1972 survey show a substantial discrepancy between the planned and actual use of funds controlled by state governments under block grants. Money intended for training and for the prevention of crime and juvenile delinquency has been used to provide additional equipment that will reinforce traditional methods of law enforcement. Comprehensive criminal justice systems and crime prevention programs have received little attention. The police jealously guard the prerogative to fight crime all by themselves in their own way. They resist interference from federal and state governments and do not consider social service's crime prevention efforts and citizen participation as serious crime-fighting techniques. They measure success only by the rate of arrests but even by their standards, the war against crime has resulted in society's catastrophic defeat.

ROOT CAUSES   Violent crime is growing sixteen times as fast as the population. Patrick Murphy, former police officer in Washington and New York and current president of the Washington-based Police Foundation, has explained that until the instability of the cities, unemployment, underemployment, broken homes, alcoholism, drugs, and mental health problems are dealt with effectively, crime will continue unabated. As the McKay commission stated: "We have examined state rules and procedures, prison politics, the changing nature of the inmate population, and festering racism— a dangerously volatile mix. That the explosion occurred first at Attica was probably chance. But the elements for replication are all around us. Attica is every prison; and every prison is Attica."[3] One fact emerges undisputed: What has been tried has not worked, and new ways must be found if the crime problem, which costs uncounted billions of dollars and the incalculable suffering of millions of citizens, is to be solved.

Criminology is not an esoteric science. Almost everybody knows (or can know) what is required to battle crime effectively, yet the exact opposite course is usually the one chosen, with predictable results. It is as if the textbooks on criminology, psychology, penology, and psychiatry were used as instruction manuals in reverse. Punishment is effective, educational, and deterring only when administered quickly in direct connection with the prohibited deed. Yet we permit delays of months and years between crime and punishment and then, as a result of plea bargaining, punish the offender for a crime that is different from the one actually committed. The effectiveness of deterrence depends upon the certainty of apprehension and just punishment, not on long, debilitating, and brutalizing sentences. We permit the overwhelming majority of criminals to get away with what they have done. We selectively punish the poor, the disadvantaged, and the mentally disturbed and mete out the longest prison sentences in the Western world to those offenders we happen to catch, convict, and lock up. Impoverished, mentally disturbed, mostly uneducated, impulsive, and embittered people do not offer good prospects for fundamental change to begin with. But crowd them together; subject them to arbitrary rules, extreme brutality, and foul language; corrupt them with rampant homosexuality, the lucrative in-prison drug trade, and the generally prevailing adherence to criminal values, and rehabilitation has no chance at all.

The public and its representatives insist on concealing retaliatory urges behind the illusion of safety and the pretense of rehabilitative efforts. The President's Crime Commission opened its summary of recommendations by saying: "First, society must seek to prevent crime before it happens—war on poverty, inadequate housing and unemployment is war on crime."

President Nixon, in whose 1968 election the campaign promise to fight crime on the streets more effectively played a major role, stated: "I say that doubling the convictions rate in this country would do far more to cure crime in America than quadrupling the funds for the war on poverty." Vice-President Spiro Agnew, speaking for the administration as a whole, ironically denounced research efforts to investigate the root causes of crime and, to the thunderous applause of law enforcement officers, promised unqualified support for strong police measures. Governor George Wallace promised to rid the country of crime if, for only one year, constitutional safeguards could be suspended and the police could be given the opportunity to deal with actual and potential offenders "the way they deserve." Other, more liberal Democratic and Republican office seekers also expressed their unqualified support of stepped-up law-and-order efforts, such as stricter law enforcement, longer sentences, and more funds for crime detection and less for crime prevention. We build more and larger jails and penitentiaries with the money saved by nonsupport of community centers, health-care facilities, and state hospitals. Neither lenient judges who were sold a bill of goods nor bleeding-heart psychiatrists and social workers who never had any real influence are responsible; rather, the responsibility rests with that vast majority of the American people who desire or condone the tragic and scandalous conditions of our prisons that have now also become training grounds for terrorists.

Just as crusading idealists increasingly use criminal strategies to accomplish their goals, ordinary criminals have become politicized and, rather than admit any personal guilt, they blame the unjust, racist, capitalist, oppressive system for their plight. Criminals have elevated themselves to political victims or prisoners of war. By styling themselves casualties of an unjust social order, they acquire at least a semblance of dignity, which they have been deprived of by the prison regime. The selective inefficiency of the judicial process, the brutality and corruption of prison bureacracy, the hypocrisy of rehabilitation, and the pervasive prison atmosphere of ruthlessness and dehumanization make it possible for them to forge for themselves a new role definition as anticulture heroes.

Representatives of decent society have preached emphatically that finding and pursuing a meaningful occupation and a meaningful purpose in life are most important for rehabilitation, both inside and after prison. But these admonishments have remained oratorical, and the depressing dreariness of prison life, the anonymity of isolated individuals, and the pervasive sense of meaninglessness have worsened because of lack of interest, lack of funds, and the fear of appearing to mollycoddle offenders.

Recently, many convicts have made an effort of their own that seems to satisfy most of the criteria for successful rehabilitation. They have found a meaningful occupation: that of the revolutionary organizers and followers. And they believe they have a meaningful purpose in life: that of mercilessly fighting society by terroristic force.

Bloodshed at Attica

Like My Lai and Kent State, Attica, a maximum security prison in New York State, was to become a symbol and part of everyday language. Critics held the authorities responsible for a senseless bloodbath caused by the furious violence of unleashed guards and the inhuman indifference and ineptness of the authorities. Forty-two lives were lost at Attica.

Presumably hopeful negotiations between the authorities and the prisoners' spokesmen were terminated by the attack order (September 13, 1971) that resulted in wild shooting, causing the death of nine hostages by the guards' gunfire. Governor Rockefeller, the ultimate decision maker, felt that there was more at stake even than saving lives, that there was the whole rule of law to consider, the whole fabric of our society: "We have to look at these things not only in terms of the immediate but in terms of the larger implication of what we are doing in our society."[4] The governor based his views largely on Commissioner Oswald's opinion that at Attica the establishment could be made to buckle down. According to Oswald, the prison take-over was the swiftest and most skillful diversionary offensive since the 1968 attack on South Vietnam. If the defense of American national honor and the whole fabric of Western society were at stake, then indeed nothing else was indicated but a Vietnam-type attack, even though the warlike operation would destroy what it attempted to protect.

Saving face means sacrificing lives. The governor did not come to the scene, despite urgent requests, presumably in order not to encourage the terrorists by dignifying their uprising with the prestige of his presence. ("I do not feel that my physical presence on the site can contribute to a peaceful settlement.")[5] He also refused to contact the negotiation committee indirectly or to support the negotiating prison officials by adding the wise counsel of a rested, experienced man to the opinions of exhausted, deeply involved security officers. The rebels did not have a well-organized command structure, but neither did the state troopers, who were never given any clear instructions about when to fire and when to stop firing. They went on their "happy coon hunt," as one of them said later, with self-righteous courage, expecting to liberate the white hostages. "All the state officials, all the observers had believed explicitly that the inmates would kill the hostages if D-yard was attacked. But the inmates had not done it."[6] Commission findings and filmed evidence clearly showed that "There was clearly indiscriminate firing into congested areas by men who did not value the inmates' lives. Indeed, several witnesses told the Commission they heard troopers bragging later in the day about their exploits on the morning of the assault. . . . Their accounts would justify firing, but were, in many cases, unsupportable in light of other evidence. . . . When those statements are compared with all of the other available evidence, the conclusion is inescapable that many of them were exaggerated, if not fabricated. Indeed, one trooper testified that he and others in his troop were encouraged by their fellow officers to embellish their accounts of inmate activity."[7]

The New York *Daily News* reported an eye-witness story by a trooper who said he saw seven throats cut and quoted the man, "We were hit by gasoline bombs, makeshift spears, rocks, iron bars, sticks, and other missiles." In the words of McKay "officials did not wait to verify the reports and Commissioner Dunbar told legislators touring the prison that the 'castration' had been filmed from a helicopter. . . ." Governor Rockefeller's postassault statement referred to "militants who . . . forced a confrontation and carried out cold-blooded killings . . ." Senator James Buckley of New York commented: "The wanton murder of the hostages was an act of barbarism pure and simple . . . punishment of those responsible must be swift and authoritative."[8]

The sharp division of viewpoints along political

lines restricts on-the-spot decision making, which should be determined exclusively by the logic of the situation alone. An independent expert task force can indeed make the difference between life and death, even if such a group is only advising the decision makers. For obvious reasons, experienced task forces can make informed recommendations for action regardless of whether they are pleasing to the Left or the Right; whereas politicians, by necessity, have to consider their own political futures and the reactions of the electorate. Because polarization, escalation, symbolization, and dramatization are part of the terrorist strategy, the antiterrorist strategy must be to delay, to deglamorize, to de-emphasize, and to defuse. At Attica, exactly the opposite happened. The forces of law and order escalated and promoted the symbolic significance of the event.

Just as the main decision maker did not want to get too close to the scene in Attica in order not to bloody his own hands, the public continues to maintain an emotional distance from the bloody mess of brutalizing prisons unsafely removed from sight, stuck far out in the country, filled with racial strife, sexual perversion, and unmitigated power struggles.

A year later, the official commission appointed by Governor Rockefeller concluded that there was no excuse for the conduct of the peace officers, who, like those involved in the SLA shootout, celebrated their victory as a triumph of "white power." The question was raised whether the uprising of 1,200 rebels was the result of a radical conspiracy or a prisoner protest against inhuman treatment.

The commission's report indicates "that the Attica uprising was not planned in advance by a group of militant inmates. To continue to blame the uprising solely on a group of political 'radicals' and 'revolutionaries' merely perpetuates the dubious policy of isolating and transferring a few suspected 'trouble-makers' in response to mounting tensions, which prevailed prior to the uprising. . . . If these failures are not corrected, every flare-up of tensions—and under present prison

conditions there will continue to be such incidents—
has the potential to become another Attica."[9]

The McKay Commission's report on Attica and
prisons in general states the problem: "The question
we ask ourselves is whether what we say will be taken
seriously or simply regarded as a problem that others
should solve. The difficulty with that comfortable view
is that there are no others, we are they."

Lives Saved at Scheveningen

A potentially Attica-like emergency arose in Scheveningen prison in the Netherlands in 1974. Four convicts,
led by the imprisoned Palestinian Adnan Ahmed
Nuri, who together with the Algerian M. Koudache
formed a temporary alliance with two Dutch criminals
known for their violence and instability, had seized control of the Scheveningen prison gym, which also
served as a chapel. During mass, the convicts drew
their guns, taking twenty-five hostages, including visiting women and children.

Nuri insistently demanded that Sami Houssin Tamimah, his friend and mentor in a joint hijacking at
Amsterdam airport who was imprisoned in a different
jail, be permitted to join him. Using "precommission
bargaining" tactics (see Chapter 11), the authorities
had promised Tamimah a reduced sentence if he would
decline to cooperate with the prison bandits. Tamimah
refused to be taken from his cell and then played a major role in the negotiations. Four times he talked with
his friend Nuri, who would not believe in the sincerity
of his refusal and threatened to kill the hostages one by
one, pointing out to each hostage the part of the body
in which he would be shot. The threat was not carried
out. Instead, several hostages, who were subsequently
able to give valuable information about the terrorists
and their state of mind, were released at various times
in order to prove the terrorists' good faith.

The terrorist team, composed of two crusading terrorists and two criminals (one extremely violent, the
other mentally defective), made vague and contra-

dictory demands. Negotiations, conducted by a team in which psychologists and psychiatrists played a decisive part, depended on traditional time-winning tactics and granting requests for getaway vehicles, even though the authorities knew that they would eventually have to use force. The psychiatrists advised on the best timing, and in the early morning hours prior to another promised visit by Tamimah, it was assumed that the convicts would be confident, off guard, and fatigued. The meticulously planned assault from three sides was accompanied by wild howling, the whining of a huge siren, and swirling searchlights, thus prolonging the crucial shock seconds. The attacking officers cut through the metal lock of the closed chapel door and entered the room in full force, shooting wildly at the ceiling. The specially trained police squad immediately seized three prisoners, discovered the fourth in the midst of the hostages, and within minutes successfully terminated the action. A barrage of shots had been fired, not at people, but at inanimate objects. The hostages were liberated, and the convicts were taken back to their cells. Nobody was wounded; nobody died.

After Attica, many critics expressed the belief that there must be a better way. Scheveningen proved that there is.

11

Let's Make a Deal

Under the rule of law, everyone accused of an offense is presumed to be innocent until he is proved guilty and convicted. He is constitutionally entitled to a speedy and public trial before his peers or, if that right is waived, before an impartial judge. But actual public trials, in which prosecution and defense attempt to persuade a judge or jury by arguments and the weight of evidence, are in fact a comparatively rare method of judicial disposition. "In the interest of justice," trials are avoided in over 90 percent of all criminal cases in the United States through plea bargaining, a process in which the prosecution and the defense strike a compromise somewhere between total guilt and total innocence.

Most frequently the defendant, with the agreement of the prosecuting attorney, waives his right to a trial by pleading guilty to a reduced charge or charges. In consideration of the plea, the prosecutor confers some benefit on the defendant, such as a promise to charge him with a lesser offense, to drop charges, to recommend leniency, probation, or nonrevocation of parole. Obviously, the benefit ranging from a lesser sentence to full immunity is something that the defendant finds important enough to exchange for some of his rights.

When the plea to a lesser charge is accepted by the prosecution and the judge, only a hearing to fix sentence is necessary, and a time- and money-consuming and possibly publicity-attracting trial is avoided.

History of Bargains

Most contemporary observers justify the practice of plea bargaining as facilitating the complex modern judicial administrative process. Negotiated agreements have played an important role throughout the course of Anglo-American legal history. Bargains have been around as long as legal institutions, resulting from the inherent tension between rigid statutory mandates and the need for flexible responses determined by individual situations.

In the traditional tribal sanctioning process, the widely recognized right to a personal retributive feud was rarely claimed until an attempt had been made to reach a satisfactory money agreement or its equivalent. Detailed tables of compromises were provided for such bargains. As official legal institutions became more predominant, the personal relief processes were withdrawn, bargains diminished, and institutional punishments became frozen by law. Still, the bargains continued in an attempt to sort out equitable compensations for particular injuries. Rigidity increased, however, as the state began to define itself as an interested third party in criminal acts. This is the origin of the King's Peace, which assumes an injury to the state's authority in all antisocial acts.

The king could be satisfied and vindicated only by administering the predetermined statutory punishment, by which the offender "paid for" disturbing the universal harmony of things. The recipients (although not necessarily the beneficiaries) of this payment were those who had been "upset" and "offended" by the crime, namely, the king, God, the state, or justice and the equilibrium of peace in general. In principle, opportunism, convenience, or compassion could not be substituted for "justice," but the reality always was and is different. De facto bargaining continued and is now all the more prevalent where the prescribed punishments are severe.

Most U.S. citizens are shocked to learn that in some civilized democratic countries as well as under certain totalitarian regimes it is quite customary to buy one's way out of most crimes, on the spot or later. Americans would be even more shocked if they had to acknowledge that in most instances the same is true in America, although the consideration offered is not always money. The public might have to recognize that the law compromises some of its ideals to cope with practical problems. Plea bargaining and similar deals approximate the reality of law enforcement; they are manifestations of on-the-spot justice, of law in action.

Plea bargaining also helps speed up the judicial process. In view of the contemporary trend to solve more social and political problems by invoking criminal sanctions, legalized bargaining is likely to become even more widespread.

Philosophically, it could be argued on a different level of abstraction that social measures based on an absolute separation of good and evil do not take into account the actual human condition and are therefore impractical. Plea bargaining recognizes the ineradicable presence of evil in this world and makes necessary concessions to crime without actually approving it. Bargaining negotiations and compromises may therefore be held to be an improvement over the rigid either/or choice between complete guilt and total innocence, and negotiated bargains may be appropriate options for social conflict resolution.

Plea bargaining is the preferred method whenever the prosecution is not absolutely sure that it can conclusively prove the guilt of the accused for the crime charged or when the defendant is not certain that he can convince the jury of his innocence or does not have the financial or emotional means to engage in the risk of a full-fledged trial.

For centuries, litigation was found to be the most adequate means of assuring justice. A speedy and public trial is thus the community's duty and the defendant's right; it is also a bargaining chip for the accused, to be exchanged for various benefits from the state. The state profits from the deal by obtaining a higher rate of convictions (although not necessarily for the offenses committed) without delay, additional expense, and trouble. With various qualifications, the American Bar Association, the President's Commission on Law Enforcement and the Administration of Justice, and the U.S. Supreme Court have all approved the practice of plea bargaining.

If no agreement can be reached, the defendant is simply tried in open court without allowing the state to use the previous, unsuccessful negotiations as evidence or admission of guilt. But if the deal is concluded effectively, all parties are obligated to perform accordingly. Bargains must be kept according to the fundamental concept that voluntary contracts must be upheld and obeyed.

In the landmark case of *Santo Bello* v. *New York,* the court ordered the honoring of a plea bargain that had been breached by the government's attorneys. It was held that broken promises violated the defendant's due process rights and that the prosecution must not be permitted to take advantage of such a breach of faith. The court decreed that after the defendant has fulfilled his part of the bargain by testifying, the people must fulfill theirs. Double-crossing cannot be allowed.

The court said: "The disposition of criminal charges by agreement between the prosecutor and the accused, sometimes loosely called plea bargaining, is an essential component of the administration of justice. Properly administered, it is to be encouraged. If it further appears that the defendant performed his part of the agreement while the government did not, the indictment may be dismissed. For the judiciary not to act would create a void, leaving the defendant hopeless and the court responsible."

Postcommission Plea Bargaining

Bargaining after the commission of an offense but before or in lieu of a trial has evolved progressively in the last forty to fifty years because of its efficiency, economy, and practicality. If plea bargaining were to be abandoned, ten times as many cases would have to be tried in open court, and no speedy trial would be possible under the present system. Plea bargaining has become an administrative necessity.

Yet the obvious consequence of plea bargaining is that a large majority of offenders do not suffer the legal consequences for the offense they have committed. They are either guilty or innocent of the crime with which they have been charged, but the lesser offense for which they are punished was either not committed at all or was not all for which they should have been punished. Because the punishment meted out has no direct relationship to the offense committed, it is not likely to have any deterring effect.

No genuine remorse or even regret can develop under these circumstances, only cynicism and bitterness. The defendant does not experience deprivation of money or freedom as a consequence of his deed. Instead, either he feels that he has gotten away with something, or more often he regards his punishment as the aribitrary outcome of a gamble in which he was the loser. Criminal justice reduced to commercial bargaining or to a game of chance has little educational value. Divorced from the crucial issues of justice, the legal game, which indeed offers significant advantages to the well-represented wealthy party and to the professional criminal, is experienced by the losers as cruel and arbitrary, lending credence to the view that every sentenced criminal is the political victim of a biased system.

Some social scientists and penologists believe that this method of criminal disposition may be at least partially responsible for the rising crime rate, for the notoriously high recidivism of convicted criminals, for prison restlessness and revolts, and particularly for the curiously high tolerance of the American public for all types of crime. Nevertheless, plea bargaining appears to be here to stay.

Precommission Bargaining

In view of the fact that we are willing to accept the bargaining procedure, with all its moral flaws, there is no sound reason why it should not begin to operate earlier, to avoid crime rather than to dispose of the criminal and to serve as crisis prevention rather than as crisis intervention.

If plea bargaining is realistic, why is it not equally realistic to suggest that the same principle be extended to produce socially beneficial results? Customary plea bargaining is postcommission (after the criminal deed and in order to negotiate the consequences of the deed for the defendant) and pretrial (or in lieu of trial). Why should not legal arrangements be proposed, not to avoid the trial, but to avoid the commission of a criminal act? In short, why should we not legally authorize precommission bargaining?

Instead of the state offering reduced punishment or no punishment at all in exchange for a guilty plea to a reduced charge or for testimony against another culprit, the state would grant similar concessions in exchange for the offender not committing any, or any further and more serious, criminal acts. Instead of the defendant cooperating with the authorities to save the expense and trouble of a cumbersome trial, the offender would cooperate in saving lives and other social valuables.

In instances of blackmail, extortion, and threats to hostages, bargaining procedures are customarily initiated even now, although usually ineptly and too late. We ask: What do we have to pay or do or guarantee so that you don't throw the bomb, blow up the plane, kill the hostages? Even now, precommission bargaining, prior to or more hopefully in lieu of violent confrontation, is practically the preferred coping device for meeting the terroristic challenge when security precautions have proved insufficient and highly valued objects or persons are in danger.

Precommission bargaining requires that offenders be accorded the status of comparative equality as negotiation partners for a limited time and for the purpose of protecting the threatened persons or objects. The terror objects have no choice but to trust the terrorists as long as they have control over the victims. The terrorists know that nothing but the possession of the hostages guarantees that the negotiated agreements will be kept, and so they hold on to the victims until the last moment. Fatal accidents, misunderstandings, or impulsive reactions most frequently occur in these final phases of an episode that has been prolonged by the terrorists' not-unfounded suspicions. As long as actual hostage control is the only way to prevent a double-cross, innocent hostages will be endangered unnecessarily. In the interest of these victims, the terrorists should be able to have confidence that the authorities will not renege on the deals that presently are not considered morally or legally binding because they are negotiated under duress and coercion. Legalizing the guarantee of promises by a kind of escrow arrangement vouched for by judicial authority would unquestionably increase the chances of successful negotiation and would preserve human lives.

I propose the official introduction and legalization of precommission bargaining through which the performance of negotiated agreements would be guaranteed and enforced by a properly authorized agency. I consider my proposal neither radical nor even particularly original; it simply carries widely used, effective, and realistic procedures to their logical conclusion. The reasoning behind these suggestions is obvious: Because precommission bargains are frequently negotiated anyway, let's make them better and safer for the victims and the community.

At first glance, the suggestion of legalizing precommission bargaining may appear morally reprehensible and thus unacceptable. It seems to put a premium on coercion and violence, to grant terrorists the prestige of coequal negotiators, to guarantee them legally enforceable agreements made under pressure, to reward present and encourage future violence, and to promote the spread of moral indifference. If that is true, we are guilty of such terroristic encouragement right now because almost without exception, we do engage in precommission bargaining with blackmailers, but we do so in a haphazard and disorganized manner and accompany our actions with moralistic self-reassurances.

That some machinery, some legalized, binding negotiation guarantee is necessary for the most dangerous national and international emergencies is generally, if often belatedly, acknowledged. The Geneva convention is not regarded as condoning or encouraging war just because it spells out rules and regulations for conducting warfare; it merely acknowledges that wars do occur and that in case they do the interests of humanity are better served by some kind of agreed-upon legalized procedure, even between implacable enemies.

Recently, the PLO organizers and perpetrators of the Munich, Lod, Ma'alot, and countless other massacres succeeded in bombing their way into the United Nations, which invited them and gave them a standing ovation. Leaving aside all moral considerations, would it not have been more sensible to have them admitted prior to, and in order to prevent, their committing all these atrocities, if they are worthy of being admitted at all? Certainly, innumerable innocents could have been saved.

But possibly moral considerations should not be left aside, even in the harshest of realities. Then what about conventional plea bargaining, immunity grants, and pardons?

After the Watergate episode, in which the staunchest defenders of fundamental law-and-order concepts were the most adept at obtaining all the advantages of plea bargaining, the myth that justice can be accomplished through the undiluted functioning of adversary litigation only will be increasingly hard to maintain. The American public tolerates, apparently without great difficulty, a morally outrageous, probably criminogenic (crime generating) practice as the practical price of justice. If postcrime immunity is accepted, why should precrime immunity not be accepted on a case-by-case basis? Why should the extension of exactly the same principle not be tolerated as the price for saving human life?

All over the world, police departments engage in precommission bargaining. They grant immunity, penalty reduction, or other privileges to informers or accessories not just to apprehend culprits but to prevent crimes. Usually this is done informally and without public knowledge in order to avoid offending a morality that cannot be maintained without its unofficial violation. But the success of these practices depends on a previous relationship of mutual trust, no matter how limited and qualified, between offenders and police. Such trust simply does not exist in just those cases where it is needed most: headline-making terrorist crimes.

The Manson murders were "solved" because of participant Susan Atkins's confession compulsion. She subsequently withdrew her confession, and another active participant in the murders, Linda Kasabian, served as state's witness, helped to convict her accomplices, and went scot-free. The court honored, as a matter of course, the prosecution's agreement to grant full immunity to the cooperating witness. Yet nobody effectively protested against letting the coldblooded killer go free.

But what would have happened if Atkins or Kasabian or any other member of the Manson gang had notified the authorities of the homicidal plans prior to the murders or even in the midst of them? Under present circumstances, nobody could have concluded and kept an immunity deal with a guilty participant to save innocent human lives. What would have been the chances for maintaining the bargain after everybody was safe, in the midst of an inevitable public outcry against rewarding a conspirator? Yet, it is not unreasonable to conjecture that the possibility of such an arrangement might have saved one or more of the victims.

On August 17, 1974, after the disastrous Los Angeles airport explosion, Alan Cranston, senior senator from California, attempted to make contact with the Alphabet Bomber (see pages 22–26) through a publicly broadcast radio message: "Call me right now before you do anything else." Cranston agreed that many of the immigration and naturalization laws to which the bomber objected were unfair and should be changed. He added: "Violence is not the way to improve things. Hurting or killing innocent people will only make things worse, not better. Violence will harden the opposition and make it far more difficult to achieve justice." Cranston pleaded with the bomber to contact him at any time. The terrorist never responded, and two days later he was arrested.

Senator Cranston had made a spontaneous attempt at precommission bargaining. Although by that time it was known that the bomber was responsible for several deaths, the senator wanted to prevent him from committing any more crimes. For that reason and in order to start negotiations, Cranston publicly announced that he and the bomber shared certain views about the unfairness of naturalization laws. It is doubtful whether the offender ever heard the message. If he did, he might have asked himself what the senator conceivably would have been able to offer that was of sufficient benefit to him to prevent him from committing further offenses.

The answer would have been: nothing. Neither Senator Cranston nor anybody else could have guaranteed the bomber any leniency, diminution of punishment, or protection of privacy during ongoing negotiations. Such promises would not have been legally binding.

After a crime has been committed, no matter how monstrous the offense, it is not only perfectly permissible legally but desirable in the interest of justice for the defendant to make his arrangements with the authorities in plea bargaining and immunity trades for testimony. But to make similar arrangements before the commission of the deed, in order to prevent maiming and killing, is considered illegal, immoral, and corrupting.

Does the United States prevent foreign governments or private companies from making monetary and other arrangements for the release of hostages? Of course not. Was the Hearst family not permitted and encouraged to negotiate indirectly with the captors of their daughter and to make ransom payments through the food giveaway program in spite of the constantly reiterated no-ransom policy of the government and law enforcement officials?

The decision about whether to negotiate and/or yield obviously depends, not on abstract morality, but on what is actually at stake, on what value the good guys place on whatever the bad guys have effectively jeopardized.

Troubleshooters as well as national and international peacemakers shuttling back and forth between the various sides in Ireland, in Cyprus, in the Middle East, and elsewhere are in fact precommission bargainers. They attempt to negotiate the noncommission or nonresumption of overt hostilities for a price; a definite, bargained-for, and agreed-upon premium is put on a party's renunciation of destructive conduct. The negotiators then serve as escrow officers, guaranteeing against double cross, enjoying the trust of parties who do not trust each other.

Nobody expects to buy the parties' peacefulness without paying heavily in concessions, compromises, and sacrifices. Yet this type of activity is not considered immoral or contemptible. On the contrary, the successful practitioners of international precommission bargaining are highly praised and awarded Nobel Peace Prizes.

Similar, if less widely advertised, methods are used for problem solving between fiercely competitive power groups within a national society. Not so long ago, U.S. labor unions were regarded as gangs of blackmailing thugs whose rebellious violence was to be met by counterviolence. Today, negotiations between employer and employee groups enjoy overwhelming public approval and government sponsorship. Arbitration and bargaining are official, well regulated, legalized activities that have by and large eliminated violence from labor relations and are generally seen as indispensable, stablizing social endeavors. There is no good reason why similar practices should not be used in dealing with the new social problem of modern terrorism.

Authority for Bargaining

A great deal of thought would have to be given to who should be authorized, and under what circumstances, to negotiate such precommission bargaining. What should the roles of the police, the district attorney, or the representatives of the study-action teams be? Should immediate judicial approval be sought in spite of time pressure? Or should the reasoning of the *Santo Bello* decision, preventing the state from profiting from a broken promise, be relied upon? How can the necessary wholehearted cooperation of law enforcement agencies, conditioned to independent and face-saving tactics, be enlisted for procedures that are contrary to all their traditional customs?

Establishing the proper perspective will be crucial. Well-regulated precommission bargaining will have to be understood as just another discretionary tool on the shelf of available remedies, to be resorted to whenever deemed necessary by the authorities. There will undoubtedly be tremendous, possibly insurmountable, resistance to the idea. Still, an open public debate should explore whether law enforcement and the public will tolerate legalizing procedures that are universally practiced anyway.

The art of effective government involves spotting potentially dangerous problems and disruptive conflict areas before they become dangerous and disruptive

and bringing appropriate resources to bear. The most
important advances in labor, race, and minority relations and in relief measures for the poor, the old, and
the sick were achieved either after actual outbreaks of
violence or in order to prevent violent protest.

In a sense, all peaceful social advancement is
based on some kind of precommission bargaining. For
the prevention of terrorism, certain explosive situations
and endangered areas could be pinpointed and studied
well in advance of any violent demonstration. Social
scientists (possibly the suggested study-action team)
could help by acting as radar for social problems, as
troubleshooters and ombudsmen. Because terrorism
is spawned by the terrorists' belief that they suffer
injustice that cannot be corrected by any means other
than violence, public awareness of existing trouble spots
and a willingness to seek nonviolent remedies are
sound and indispensable bases for social policy decisions.

Can we imagine that any sane person or government would refuse to negotiate if heads of state, presidents, cabinet members, or their relatives were taken
hostage or if fissionable material by which whole cities
could be eradicated fell into the hands of threatening
terrorists? (Furthermore, should the lives of anonymous citizens be considered any less important than
the lives of the prominent and the powerful?) Let's
face it: What is intended as toughness against the terrorists actually turns out to be toughness against the
victims. Such a response requires nothing but rhetorical courage. Rigid sanctions that have not been very
successful in curbing ordinary crime will not work at
all against crusading terrorism; they just create a false
sense of security.

Why, then, persist in the obviously hypocritical
deception that denies the value of negotiations while
at the same time engaging in them or permitting interested parties to do so? If negotiations become inevitable, why not make them more effective by the precommission bargain option and by guarantees against
double cross?

Why not admit that certain situations, which cannot be avoided in the absence of wartime or totalitarian controls, constitute emergencies that call for unusual emergency measures? Why not prepare for these emergencies in order to increase the chances for the survival of innocents by making adequate psychological and legal arrangements before an incident becomes a catastrophe?

PART IV

The
Overview

12

Terror and Terrorism Revisited

The distinction between terror (from above) and terrorism (from below) cannot be found in the literature, yet this differentiation appears convenient and plausible. In ordinary usage, "terror" and "terrorism" are terms of disapproval often applied interchangeably to any intimidation by means of violence. Terror or terrorism, like aggression, is what the other does; one's own violence is given different names through label swindle. Some apostles of violence extol terror or terrorism as aesthetically beautiful (see De Quincey, Shelley, Keats, and Sartre); others praise violent intimidation for utilitarian reasons as necessary means to achieve a desirable goal (see Marat, Trotsky, and Fanon). However, violence cannot always be equated with radicalism and revolution, nor nonviolence with gradualism and reform. Not only Mao and Lenin, Hitler and Franco, and practically all nationalistic politicians but also Saint Thomas Aquinas have declared that the fight against tyranny in the defense of one's homeland or in order to achieve a more equitable social order constitutes a "just war" (*bellum justum*)

303

justifying the lesser evil of violence to ward off a larger political evil.

Responding to an initiative of the secretary-general, the U.N. Plenary Session of September 1972 decided, after the Munich Olympics tragedy, to refer the discussion to its Committee for Legal Questions. The Soviet Union and the Afro-Asian bloc protested against the mere condemnation of terrorism without examining its root causes. The majority of the nations represented in the United Nations wanted to make sure that any measures adopted could not be used against national liberation movements similar to those to which they owed their existence. They rejected any resolution categorically condemning terrorism as favoring strong, established states over the weak and helpless, whose only means of redress is spectacular violence. They insisted that the organization examine "the underlying causes of those forms of terrorism and acts of violence which lie in misery, frustration, grievance and despair and which cause some people to sacrifice human lives, including their own, in an attempt to effect radical change."[1]

The subsequent committee discussions reflect the irreconcilable conflict among the varying viewpoints. Some representatives felt "that an inalienable right of all people should not be affected; people who struggle to liberate themselves from foreign oppression and exploitation have the right to use all methods at their disposal, including force."[2] In contrast, the report of the secretary-general argued that "even when the use of force is legally and morally justified, there are some means, as in every form of human conflict, which must not be used; the legitimacy of a cause does not in itself legitimize the use of certain forms of violence, especially against the innocent." One committee member stated explicitly: "International terrorism originates in the pursuit by certain countries of policies of colonialism, occupation of foreign territory, racism, apartheid, domination and exploitation." National terror from above was seen as an integral part of the overall problem of terrorism, but national sovereignty is an international sacred cow. The committee excluded from the issue "all those activities that are the inner affairs of individual states." But terror and terrorism cannot be treated separately. They perpetuate each other as components of the same complex problem.

The same word, "terror," designates both a state of mind and the means by which this state of mind is brought about. Both the intimidation by the mighty to perpetuate their rule and the intimidation of the powerful by the so-far powerless implants terror in the hearts and minds of men by the brutal introduction of fear into the most intimate and private spheres of the individual's life. Both terror and terrorism attempt to commit rape of the mind.

Terroristic actions are purposeful and goal-directed, yet unrestrained and indiscriminate; rank, status, noninvolvement, and innocence are no protection. Threats are not directed against any single target group; the jeopardy is universal, admitting no exceptions. This is the message of terror and terrorism: Anyone can be struck anywhere at any time. The arbitrary selection of the victims is calculated. The unpredictability of terroristic action is predictable. Apparent aimlessness is the terroristic aim. Seeming senselessness is the true sense of terroristic activities that are calculated to establish and perpetuate permanent, pervasive insecurity as the normal condition of life.

Terror and terrorism aim to frighten and to dominate by frightening others. They want to impress. They play to and for an audience; they desire nothing more than audience participation. They stage and choreograph their attention-getting appearances and disappearances. Grievance claims, self-display, theater, and propaganda are all wrapped up in the spectacular performance. The creation of general insecurity and the stimulation of universal fright by intimidation are the intended primary effects of the terrorist performance; the aim is to elicit audience reactions of pity and sympathy, of indignation and hatred.

Terror from Above

Terror from above creates the one-dimensional universe of naked power in which it thrives best. All personal relationships are forcibly reduced to the master-slave, lord-servant, hammer-anvil formula; whoever does not want to be terrorized must terrorize.

TERROR IS BOTH THE FORERUNNER AND THE HEIR OF TERRORISM Terror from above is the intentional choice of a policy, strategy, or technique of domination that is deliberately represented as inescapable and inevitable. Terror from above claims to be imposed for the benefit of those who have to be shaken up in order to be shaped up. The nature of the terror objects, their ignorance or helplessness, their evilness or weakness, presumably compels the terrorist from above to protect, educate, unite, and lead his wards through terror, advertised as the sole remedy against terroristic disturbances of law and order.

As a matter of principle, terror from above is totalitarian and total. It respects neither privacy nor any sphere of intimacy. The inner circle discloses nothing, but it has the right and the duty to disclose everything about everybody at its discretion. The ruling clique is not accountable to anybody except the leader, who is responsible only to his conscience, to history or to the will of the people, which he represents; but everybody else is held strictly accountable for every thought or action. There is no such thing as illegal search or seizure or any other constitutional guarantee; everything that the masters deem necessary is by definition legal, legitimate, and in the interest of the sacred cause. Everybody is exposed; only the chief and his clique must be fully protected by silence and stonewalling. It is as if he and his clique, having absorbed and preempted all available rights and, for that matter, most committable crimes, leave only a few for anybody outside the inner circle.

TERROR SCENARIO   Under a totalitarian regime, everybody has been sentenced in advanced and lives on probation under unknown conditions. Deliberately vague threats create the terror atmosphere of constant and pervasive dangerous uncertainty. "The threat of death is the coin of power"; absolute power over life and death constitutes the order of terror. The potential death sentence can be carried out whenever necessary or desired.

The convicts on death row in France were not told, for "humanitarian" reasons, when they were going to be guillotined. In the early morning hours, the execution platoons went through the prison corridors on felt slippers to pick up those who were to die that day. Every night, all the condemned convicts listened with concentrated attention for even the slightest sound. Their fear often made them "unrealistic"; they imagined they heard the muffled noise of the felt shoes. This paranoia amused the guards; they laughed heartily at the "crazy behavior" of the fear-stricken prisoners. The convicts were relieved when the platoon did not appear or when it passed by their cells; but the next night, their fear was even more intense. This is a typical example of terror from above in its "ideal" state.

TERROR PROVIDES ITS OWN JUSTIFICATIONS   Terror regimes are often launched and maintained on the promise of protection that they alone can effectively provide against terrorism from below. The Russian Bolsheviks explained that draconian terror measures were necessary to combat imperialist-inspired terrorists. The Greek colonels presented themselves as the only remedy against impending Communist terrorism; yet, in subsequent free elections, the Communists received less than 20 percent of the vote, and no Greek terrorist activity has been reported since the new democratic regime took control. The German Nazis mercilessly smashed all terrorism that they themselves had organized and led during their rise to power; they also invented terrorist upheavals in order to justify their occupation of Austria, which they claimed was necessary to restore law and order in that country.

Supreme rights and highest principles, national survival, the will of God, or general welfare are forever invoked to justify shabby, brutal, or outright criminal acts. The sacred cause sanctifies everyone and everything in its service. Terror is the temptation of power to transcend its legitimate limits by having illegitimate, easily justified practices accepted as regular administrative routines. The introduction of terror from above constitutes a declaration that civilized politics are bankrupt. Yet violence is not necessarily a sign of institutional breakdown; rather it often cements and maintains the institutions that are legitimized by the will of the ruler.

In the Watergate affair, criminal activities for the sake of reelecting a president were carried out under the sheltering umbrella of the highest authorities. National security was supposedly being protected against vaguely defined threats by obscure insurgents, who conceivably might be aligned with the opposite political party. The perpetrators of these illegal acts merely followed orders, perhaps believing that they were just doing their patriotic duty. Sincere conviction, not corruption, often sanctions lies against liars, deception to fight deception, and crimes in the war against crime. Many who consider themselves to be decent, moral people see nothing wrong in forgeries, robberies, and assassinations for the good of the country or the cause; incorruptible police chiefs have gone on record* stating that they could not enforce the law if members of their departments, in order to protect the community more effectively, were not occasionally permitted to violate the laws they are sworn to uphold.

TERROR COPIES DIVINE ATTRIBUTES   The terrorist ruler becomes either the representative of or the substitute

---

*Like, for instance, Los Angeles Police Chief Parker in a television speech.

for divine power; total authority must come from God or from some other godlike, nonhuman source of indisputable legitimacy.

Hierarchically organized according to the power-pyramid model, with the leader at the top, terror from above copies and arrogates the features of the divine triad: omnipotence, omnipresence, and omniscience. The leader and everyone acting in his name may do anything to anybody with impunity because he is all-powerful. Through fear and the workings of secret police, he and his clique are everywhere, even in the thoughts of people, which they aim to control. The leader is the great destroyer and the great benefactor, the most dangerous threat and the best protector; he is all-knowing and never wrong, the only true prophet. He will see to it that the history of his people, which he will dictate, will ascribe to him all conceivable desirable qualities and describe his reign as the culmination of all previous historical developments.

The leader, in his role of superhuman authority, is inaccessible and inscrutable. Yet, he is the sole arbiter of the fate of the people at his mercy; he combines within himself the supreme legislative, judicial, and executive authority. Decisions that are never publicly debated or announced in advance hit the community like lightning; every ordinance has the force of eternal natural law, to be obeyed without hesitation or question.

Ordinary written law is superseded by a higher unwritten law that is embodied in the natural, "healthy" feelings of the people as interpreted and represented by the leader. Every life situation is predetermined by the interconnection of carefully balanced rights and duties that are defined and imposed by the highest authority. Such arrangements exert a magnetic attraction on unformed, dependent, confused, or alienated persons, who long for the mythical solidarity of community.

The vice of uncontrolled arbitrariness is transformed into a virtue. Because terroristic decisions are often irrational and incomprehensible, they are inter-

preted as expressing a justice and wisdom beyond the
limited scope of the human mind; their obscurity serves
as further proof of higher inspiration. In total terror,
the ruler becomes totally infallible.

TERROR METHODS THAT APPEAR CAPRICIOUS TO THE
VICTIMS ARE RATIONAL FROM THE RULER'S POINT OF
VIEW   In the heyday of the movie industry, which
used to be dominated by authoritarian bosses regarded
as veritable giants by all those subjected to their tyrannical rule, the jocular question was asked quite seriously: "Is everybody crazy in Hollywood?" The answer
was: "No, but it helps."

The belief in the leader's infallible intuition is reinforced by his bizarre idiosyncrasies and fits of rage.
Whether real or playacted, violent outbursts of temper
are vastly exaggerated in the imagination of the terrorized and can become rituals that confirm the unusual
character and extraordinary charismatic qualities of the
chief. Accounts of the peculiar behavior of dictators,
Mafia bosses, and Hollywood tycoons fill whole li-
braries. In a terroristic atmosphere, the oppressed are
always preoccupied with the presumably unique
thought processes and behavioral peculiarities of the
ruling clique, who are feared, envied, joked about, and
imitated. The institutionalized psychoses of the powerful also help to excuse the powerless, who are incapable of resisting the "craziness" of their rulers. Distinctions between reality and fiction become blurred when
fictitious, paranoid, and delusional notions of the
ruler (Stalin, Hitler, Idi Amin, some Zulu rulers) become the social reality of the oppressed, who willingly
participate in the fictionalizing of reality and the realization of fiction.

TERROR CREATES THE NEED FOR OMNIPOTENCE THAT
LEGITIMIZES THE TERRORISTIC CLAIM OF OMNIPO-
TENCE   The terrorized want their ruler to be omnipotent and omniscient so that they can participate in his
power through total surrender and submissive identification. The notions of reconciled unity and magical

wholeness unconsciously attract the impatient, alienated, community-hungry members of a deeply split,
antagonistic society dominated by hostile competi-
tiveness. People intimidated and indoctrinated by fear
will not tolerate the tarnishing of the image of the omnipotent ruler; they will force him to continue and
even to reinforce the terror from above that they have
internalized so that they can console themselves about
their own "inevitable" fate.

At times, the ruler is so sure of his subjects' internalized need for his omnipotence that he can effectively threaten them with the end of his rule. Zulu
despots sometimes organize ritualistic games of rebellion against themselves. The general indignation provoked by the thought of revolution strengthens the regime, which then proceeds to suppress with increased
vigor all thoughts and actions even remotely reminis-
cent of rebellion. Occasionally, the Zulu ruler, pretending to be hurt by the ingratitude of his people, retires
into solitude and threatens to abandon his subjects, who
insistently implore him to return, promising even more
complete obedience and submission.

In the absence of a feasible alternative, victims
who have accepted the terror regime as inevitable will
soon regard it as desirable. Modern dictators are in a
much better position than Zulu chiefs to organize all
aspects of life under their control, including opposition
to the system, which in turn necessitates the leader's
continuing protection. The ruler may be dangerous, but
he is also indispensable.

TERROR ARRANGES FOR SUBMISSION RITUALS Time
and again, the indissoluble unity between leader and
led must be demonstrated by pompous ceremonies and
choreographed rituals that celebrate the leader's indomitable will to power and his people's readiness for
total submission. The helplessness, dependency, and
personality impoverishment of the terrorized are af-
firmed and at the same time denied in the ceremonial
surrender to the all-powerful father or Big Brother figure, who is simultaneously the source of all fear and

the incorporation of all wisdom and justice. Social forms depending on terror from above to provide unity and cohesiveness were vastly underrated in their appeal and effectiveness by rationalistic observers, who classified them as obsolete developmental stages in the progress of Western civilization. It is precisely this simplistic primitiveness of terror from above that causes many of civilization's malcontents joyously to extol slavery as the wave of the future.

TERROR LIBERATES AND LEGITIMIZES VIOLENCE   The complexities of modern society impose burdensome duties and instinctual sacrifices on the individual, and those demands of civilization are represented and administered by an anonymous, depersonalized, and depersonalizing bureaucracy. In contrast, the charismatic leader who sees, hears, and knows everything need not depend on bureaucrats and computers; he needs no intermediaries because he is in direct intuitive contact with the highest superhuman authority and with the people, whom he promises to liberate from the dehumanization and depersonalization of modern society.

In the interest of the whole, all possibilities for individual freedom, expression, and self-realization are blocked; but at the same time, terror from above is extremely permissive and encourages instinctual gratification in the service of the regime. In carrying out their duty, the practitioners of terror need not postpone, control, or renounce their gratification; aggression in any form can be employed with impunity against arbitrarily selected scapegoats and victims. Permission to engage in unlimited aggression in the service of terror from above is the reward for total submission. Because the ruler and the ruling clique are deliberately and ostentatiously violent, all their followers are encouraged to violence, which invites new imitation and identification. As the king's representatives and executioners, innumerable people become little kings in their own right. Contagious violence, widely copied, gives innumerable people the opportunity to act as sovereign mini-tyrants within their private sphere. The climate of business and everyday life changes, giving bosses and domestic despots permission to act in conformity with the prevailing style. Terror made respectable becomes invisible and pervasive because it is immanent to the system and personality syntonic for victimizers and victim.

TERROR IS REPRESENTED AS AN ACT OF GOD Natural disasters are often conceived of as divine punishment for wickedness. Because there is no insurance or protection against such acts of God, as disasters strangely enough are called, the population is expected to remain passive, happy, and tranquil, no matter what sacrifices are demanded. Similarly, the terror regime is represented as a cataclysmic event of world-shaking importance. It is to be regarded with awe and accepted as inevitable.

Terror from above deliberately uses the model of natural catastrophes to spread the same kind of indiscriminate fear, to inspire awe, and to convey the impression that no resistance is possible or reasonable. The suspense of not knowing what comes next but fully expecting that something drastic will occur keeps everybody confused, anxious, and disoriented. This pervasive insecurity erodes all security structures, family bonds, and ties of friendship.

This state of affairs leads to the defensive attitudes of withdrawal, isolation, and alienation and to the development of utter distrust and paranoid suspiciousness, which further reinforce the individual's atomization and helplessness. The potential victims lose trust, particularly trust in themselves. After a time, pervasive insecurity produces low-key hopelessness and despair; nothing seems to matter anymore. Original resistance becomes passivity; fear-dictated noninvolvement changes to genuine indifference.

The aim of terror from above is the total subjugation of its objects, not through crude force, but through seemingly voluntary submission. Cleverly manipulated terror, being the extreme abuse of the universal human need for belonging, can depend on the spontaneous hunger for community of individuals who have been deliberately isolated and made to doubt the loyalty of their environment and the reliability of their former social bonds.

If the terror is complete and there is realistically no escape and no possibility of overthrowing the regime, accommodation to its demands becomes quite realistic and is accepted and internalized not only by cowards and opportunists but also by upstanding citizens, who in their despair see no other feasible option.

TERROR PROMISES UNITY AND WHOLENESS Terror from above is obsessed with Platonic notions of unity, wholeness, cohesion, and unanimity. The pure idea of the one and only good and eternally unchangeable truth inspires the terror regime to battle against the rest of the world, which is seen as dangerous, changing, polluted, tainted, and corrupt. Iron discipline is the way to restore lost purity and wholeness. The unity of the reborn people is sealed with the spilled blood of nonbelievers and half believers. The climate of terror is moralistic, ritualistic, and magical. The French Revolution's Reign of Terror enthroned the goddess of reason to justify the blood myth of violent purification in the name of virtue. The Nazis chanted: "One empire. One people. One leader," celebrating wholeness and unity as the highest values while burning churches and books and smashing heads. Bizarre dreams of a rebirth of the Russian people through the Christian-inspired ferociousness of the Cossacks were later realized by mass starvations, deportations, and killings carried out by the Bolsheviks in the holy spirit of dialectic materialism.

In planning and executing its monstrous enterprises, terror from above ruthlessly exploits the passions, illusions, and infantile expectations that it has created. Many terror systems are characterized by the juxtaposition of sober Machiavellianism and magical intoxication, by a combination of technological operationalism and sectarian crankiness, and by a mixture of administrative matter-of-factness and romantic spiritualism.

TERROR NEEDS ORGANIZED PROPAGANDA AS AN INDISPENSABLE TOOL Propaganda and organization, including the organization of propaganda, are indispensable to bring about the terror effect. Terror that cannot stand up under reflection and criticism needs a propaganda campaign replete with justifications. Hence terror often conceals its anti-intellectual, antirationalistic, antihumanistic bias behind pseudoscientific praise of life and celebration of nature. All philosophies that stress the importance of power and vitality over that of intellect and rationality lend themselves to the popular doctrine of Social Darwinism, which asserts the right of the stronger over the weaker as natural law. Existence in and of itself is declared absolute and absolutely creative, also absolutely barbaric and nonrational.

TERROR ATOMIZES AND ISOLATES All independent organizations that could form rallying centers for resistance are immediately eliminated because they are incompatible with the terroristic need for total power. The very first terroristic measures are directed against freedom of assembly; thus, after a while, the highly organized terror regime confronts only a mass of disorganized, isolated, mistrustful, and powerless individuals.

In order to escape their demoralizing isolation, the alienated masses soon ask for guidance from the masters of terror. The victims who have succumbed to the contagion of psychoterror come to depend on the image of omnipotence that has victimized them. The oppressed masses then demand that everybody be subjugated as they themselves have been. In order to confirm their own experience, they expect resistance to be nipped in the bud by brutal precautions. The terror techniques of domination produce and reproduce in the manipulated terrorized subject those needs that are essential for creating and maintaining the terrorist's claim of omnipotence, omniscience, and omnipresence.

Through propaganda, bribery, compulsion, threats, and brute force, terror reduces people to helpless, anonymous, atomized, and dehumanized masses that indeed require control by terror.

ONE PEOPLE, ONE ENEMY   In order to justify the merciless use of violence, the terror regime must find or invent an equally ruthless enemy. According to the simplifying and polarizing regime, everything evil is concentrated in that one enemy. The crafty opponent may take on many different appearances, but he always represents the same persistent danger.

Nobody can really hate a vague abstraction, so the enemy must have a recognizable, clearly defined personality profile. Surface appearances are deceptive, as is innocence, which may be only a clever cover for guilt. Everybody may be a potential agent or informer or assassin, and everything is suspected of being different from what it appears to be. The cunning and wicked enemy appears in all kinds of disguises. The dangerous enemy, capable of everything, particularly of terrorism from below, is the constant companion of terror from above, indispensable to the justification of its methods.

The existential basis of terror is the death fear of the powerful, which becomes the state's reason to exist. The ruler persecutes because he feels himself persecuted. Because he is gripped by paranoid fears for his life, he instills paranoid fears in his subjects. Paranoia has become the law of the land and determines the reality of everyday life, so that reasonable caution is replaced by paranoid suspiciousness.

TERROR CLAIMS INTIMIDATION TO BE NATURAL AND FEAR TO BE THE LIFE-PRESERVING, NORMAL HUMAN CONDITION   Terror interprets the sacred principle of the preservation of life (its own) as permission to threaten and destroy the lives of all those who are arbitrarily declared threatening and destructive. The state of continuous intimidation artificially and artfully produced and maintained by terror from above is pronounced as universal and normal, the essence of the human condition.

Hence terrorists from above have no difficulty convincing themselves and their captive audiences that the most drastic forms of intimidation are the best, most natural, and most humane because they produce the desired effect in the quickest and most direct way. If no system can survive without compulsion, then the employment of the most extreme compulsion is the most desirable. Executions demonstrate the danger of resistance more dramatically than imprisonment or fines, shooting suspects is more impressive than locking them up. In the production of terror the collective goal is represented as taking precedence over any individual interest; notions of national inferiority, master race, and world salvation justify any and all violence to individuals in the service of the sacred cause.

TERROR MAKES TRUTH INOPERATIVE For terror from above, the difference between truth and falsehood is as irrelevant as that between guilt and innocence. Whatever seems to help the terrorists is a fact; true is what is promoted and accepted as true. Plausibility is more important than accuracy. The various propaganda claims need not be correct; they need only be credible and easily understood. Incessant repetition provides the emotional impact that actual proof cannot and need not provide.

The captive audience of the terrorized public, lacking any independent source of information, needs only to be distracted and entertained. Therefore, the propaganda of the terror regime works with sensational effects, spectacular performances, and big lies.

In the deliberately created climate of universal uncertainty, doubts about the accuracy of official statements cannot reduce their effectiveness. Under no circumstances are the audience permitted to ask "silly" questions or to interfere with what goes on. They have to be satisfied with being amused by "harmless," ideologically tinged entertainment; by morality plays in which the villain always loses and preferably is executed at the end; and by the comic relief of "funny" humiliations of victims.

Behind all effective propaganda, there must always be the threat of a sharp sword (Goebbels), and that threat is even more important than the use of force itself. Ostentatious strutting, bragging, and demonstrative macho behavior are integral parts of terroristic propaganda.

TERROR CREATES ITS OWN LANGUAGE   The establishment of a consensus or its semblance is vitally important to the terror regime because it enables the regime to represent itself as the expression of the will of the people. Any ideology simplifies and stereotypes; terroristic ideologies use particularly tedious, crude, and repetitious arguments in order to glorify the simplicity of justified violence. Mass propaganda is pitched to the lowest possible common denominator; the same few polarized descriptions appear over and over again in easily remembered, impressive slogans. Terrorist propaganda explains everything and clarifies nothing. Every concrete event is tied to universal abstract schemes that are empty of verifiable content. Novel and original ideas are banned, but the familiar stereotypes continually emerge in new examples that illustrate the unvarying guides to the regime's idea of proper conduct.

The monotonously ritualized terror system provides a never-ending topic of conversation and a focal point for everybody's interests. The widely imitated terroristic jargon, suggesting affiliation with the inner clique, consists of clichés repeated over and over again that do not communicate or inform but rather demonstrate loyalty and unanimity. Adapted to the purposes of indoctrination and command, terror language is language in uniform. The easily recognizable, familiar slogans only reiterate what everybody knows anyway. The repetitiousness and monotony of these slogans accurately reflects, expresses, and contributes to the monotony and dreariness of a frightened existence under the rule of terror.

TERROR CORRUPTS Through terror systems, order is not abolished but perverted; morals are not eliminated but corrupted, even in the victim. Witch-hunts and show trials not only prove the system's ability to detect and punish its enemies as it has predicted but also serve as warning examples. The grotesque enormity of the alleged crimes justifies the extreme measures taken against the perpetrator while at the same time confirming the propaganda that only a strict and vigilant regime can protect the community from a breakdown of law and order.

Many potential victims believe that they can escape their fate by not attracting any attention and by not seeing or hearing anything evil. They soon find out that at best their inconspicuousness only postpones the inevitable. In the meantime, terror from above greatly profits from the citizens' ultimately futile attempts to protect themselves through mimicry, camouflage, and noninvolvement. Indifference extorted by fear meets with the desire of average people for peace and quiet. This favors terror by exploiting the unwillingness of potential victims to accept any responsibility voluntarily. Forced to make a choice, the individual selects the lesser evil of submission or even of alliance, with or without the sacrifice of previous beliefs. But in the long run, nothing can save a number of potential victims from becoming actual victims—neither their lack of involvement, their lack of interest or information, nor their innocence.

The thought of self-preservation, inertia expressing the need for continuity and the desire to be included in the unity of the whole at first provide excuses for serving the regime. Eventually, participation in the terror enterprise, which offers protection and security at least for awhile, becomes less a matter of a definite decision than of gradually not resisting the routine requirements of daily life any longer. The payoff for cooperation is the permission to participate in terror. Submitting to terror from above entitles one to the practice of terror from above.

TERROR DRAMATIZES EXISTING OR IMAGINARY DANGERS Witch-hunts and show trials, the most extreme forms of terror, are reserved for special occasions. Nevertheless, they dominate all modes of life in totalitarian countries. Witch-hunts are moral exercises, and the witches (enemies of the people or of God) serve as concrete examples of the threatening evil that has to be put to death so that the community may live.

Coerced, widely publicized confessions confirm the most bizarre propaganda claims of the regime, which are ordinarily made in smear campaigns and public denunciations. The accused will most likely be abandoned by his friends and associates, who fear that their interest or sympathy might make them suspect, too. The degree of terror—the terror quotient, so to speak—can be gauged by the extent and speed with which the innocent victims of terror are abandoned by the community.

All the participants in the witch-hunts or show trials fervently desire that the accused be guilty; otherwise, they would be guilty of injustice. In show trials the accused always confess, the confessions being coerced by torture, drugs, sensory deprivation, and most often, the promise of salvation. Those who can no longer save their lives make the last supreme sacrifice for the regime in the hope of purifying their souls. Physically and mentally broken or not, they confess because they have been coerced into believing that it is necessary and heroic to confess.

Terror from above is based on the irrefutable presumption of everybody's guilt, and it both demands and assumes total involvement. Everybody is a potential criminal, not because he has done or thought anything specific, but simply because the regime can mark him a criminal at any time and treat him accordingly.

TERROR ATTRACTS THE TERRORIZED AND THE CRIM-
INALS Cruelty is fascinating and impressive. Those
who have been brutalized are the first to seek admission
to the group that can brutalize others with impunity.
The terror regime anticipates its attractiveness to psy-
chopaths and criminals, whose enthusiastic participation can be counted on in seizing and maintaining power. The corrupted corrupters—spies, sycophants, and
yes-men—who participate in terror from above for their
personal profit usually report only what their superiors expect them to report. Successes are greatly exaggerated, and failures or delays are denied or minimized.
The ruling clique, which has erected between itself and
the masses a high barrier that is lowered on special
occasions at the discretion of the authorities, is intent
on confirming its self-fulfilling prophecies. Often the
members of the inner circle acquire a distorted picture
of reality because they listen only to those whom they
themselves have indoctrinated. The experts in the manufacture of surprising effects are then often stunned by
developments they have not foreseen; the masters of
deception are deceived by the threats and lies they
have invented.

TERROR REDUCES ACTIVE INDIVIDUALS TO REACTING
PUPPETS Terror from above treats the individual as a
passive, merely reacting infantile creature. The infantile
needs of the masses, requiring satisfaction and control through terror, are the results of infantilization,
carefully arranged and accomplished by the terror regime. Terror from above uses its human subjects not
only as objects and means but also as raw material
to be shaped and manipulated. Human nature is transformed by terror in order to justify the continuation
and perpetuation of the regime. Terror cripples and
mutilates its victims, who then require, as a result of
their injuries and deformities, the continued services of
their torturers and masters. Terror strikes the wounds
that presumably only terror can heal; the damage is
inflicted for the purpose of being cured by the terror

perpetrators, who indeed then act as teachers imparting the proper knowledge, as pharmacists doling out the prescribed medicine, and as doctors administering the right treatment.

The normal, healthy human being permitted to live in reasonable freedom is potentially active and spontaneous, with nearly inexhaustible possibilities for developing a creative and unique personality in interaction with an environment that neither completely controls him nor is totally controlled by him. But terror from above can restrict the interchange between outer world and inner personality to a simple reflex pattern, by which the terroristic programmers reduce the people under their control to passively submitting or automatically reacting marionettes.

No terror regime is ever fully effective or permanent, because the totality of control required is difficult to establish and maintain in an interdependent world. But this observation is no more consoling than the fact that there are always some individuals and groups able to retain their integrity and dignity even under the most vigorous terror regimes. The danger of terror from above lies in its capacity to create and exploit pervasive fear and to bring about obedient passivity, collective irresponsibility, and coerced cooperation in many, if not in most, people who are subjected to its ministrations. Terror from above must be combated with as much effort and imagination as is channeled into the fight against terrorism from below.

TERROR REPRESENTS A CLEAR AND IMMINENT DANGER
Terror from above is a social invention, a deliberate strategy of domination that is chosen whenever other alternatives have failed or are claimed not to exist any longer. This is the strongest argument for making these other alternatives work. Terror from above is not restricted to any barbaric national character or to any particular region or stage of social development. It can happen anyplace; it can happen here; it can happen now or tomorrow. The universal historical process, contrary to Platonic or some Marxist notions, is not

restricted to any preordained development with a fixed outcome. Terror from above, including an international coalition of terrorists from above, is not inevitable, but it is certainly possible. Because even the most cruel, irrational, and inhuman terror from above succeeds in self-justification and coercing the voluntary loyalty of the terrorized at least for a while, the clear and immediate danger of terror needs to be recognized and denounced in all its ramifications and effectively exposed before all of us become its victims.

Terrorism from Below

VIOLENCE AND THE EXPERIENCE OF INJUSTICE Remediable injustice is the basic motivation for terrorism from below, which has multiplied in modern times because both the awareness (if not the incidence) of injustice and a belief in the availability of remedies have increased enormously. The successive waves of terror and terrorism, advertised and imitated like fashions, are neither isolated events nor part of a deliberate, conspirational master plan; rather, they are the symptomatic, logical, and psychological expressions of a novel situation prevailing all over the world. Not deprivation or oppression as such, but the perception and experience of injustice and the belief that such injustice is, not natural or inevitable, but arbitrary, unnecessary, and remediable, are the root causes of terrorism. In an inflation of rising expectations, the unfulfilled promises of abundance, equality, independence, and sovereignty provoke bitter frustration and a spreading feeling of needlessly suffered injustice that can and should be terminated by violence. Highly advertised and eagerly copied, spectacular violence has had its most impressive success after violence had been officially declared futile, unrealistic, and an obsolete coping device.

Modern terrorism, which combines utter ruthlessness and self-sacrificial dedication with a fanatic belief in the justification of any, even the most excessive, destructive acts, has raised the ultramodern question of whether anything but violence and counterviolence is appropriate, effective, and realistic in the contemporary world. The terrorist's motto is "Destroy in order to save." Should it be countered with the equally simplistic and equally terroristic response "In order to save, destroy the destroyers"?

MASS MEDIA IMPACT   Terrorism is part of a chain reaction; terroristic deeds are episodes of a series of follow-up, copycat, or imitation crimes. Some forms of terrorism (such as skyjacking and kidnapping) occur in waves and follow definite patterns, influenced and even produced by spectacular, dramatic mass media coverage.

Realistically and instantaneously, the mass media show examples of widespread hunger, torture, and oppression all over the world; they also show occasional instances of successful uprisings and revolutionary changes employing violence. Even though these reports may be purely factual, they are inflammatory. When the mass media tantalizingly dangle the availability of goods and services before everybody's eyes, those who cannot afford to buy the products of abundance experience their limitations not just as scarcity but as deprivation and injustice. Poverty, oppression, and the domination of man by man are no longer accepted as part of the world's design or as natural catastrophes: they are attributed to inadequate and exploitative arrangements that can be altered by appropriate measures.

Discrimination and domination appear grossly unjust today; the individual's right to freedom and equality is recognized nearly everywhere. With racial and ethnic distinctions celebrated as unique, beautiful, and worthwhile, the denial of identity claims seems intolerably unjust. The failure or unwillingness of obsolete and inadequate institutions to react is regarded as rank injustice by those whose expectations have been stimulated by countless promises of imminent change. The evidence of false promises and the discrepancy between reality and its official representation have led to a vast credibility gap and a general suspiciousness that all the ills of the world are caused by the greed, power lust, and evil intentions of the powerful, who can be made to respond only by the most ruthless violence. The simultaneous experience of actual progress and continued frustration makes for the modern combination of frustrating progress and progressive frustration. The sense of injustice combined with the belief in available remedies, is the dangerous mixture that explodes in terroristic action.

Theatrical, mass media-oriented terrorism and terrorism-oriented mass media thrive on the sensational, surprising, and exceptional event that occupies total audience attention for a period of time. Terrorists intentionally manufacture, direct, and perfect the sensations they need to captivate their fascinated audiences, who temporarily forget their private concerns and worries.

JUSTIFIED VIOLENCE Modern expressions of violence are indissolubly tied to justification. There is hardly any violence that someone, somewhere will not attempt to justify as defensive, educational, or serving a higher cause. By the same token, there is hardly any justification scheme that will not condone violence. We teach our children to eschew violence except in certain circumstances, and these exceptions become the conditions for the use of violence in adult life. Because the child has learned that it is not only permissible but desirable to be aggressive in self-defense and in the service of an honorable cause, the adult uses the same rationale to justify every aggressive act.

Not all aggression is manifest and visible; most of it is concealed by false labels or otherwise hidden away. At the individual level, the conscience permits only the repression of "legitimate" aggression, legitimized by some cause or social group. Social institutions and organizations, reflecting the conditions of their origins in force, authorize violence for the maintenance of their power. Permission for individual violence is granted in the service of the institution, which is held together by its structural aggression.

Terrorists from below believe that the violence of

these social institutions, which is concentrated in the hands of a few who perpetuate the unequal distribution of power, is the true, original violence and that their terrorism is merely reactive, defensive, and hence fully justified. The system's structural violence is considered the original violence that cannot be removed by political action, only by military action. Resistance against this polluted and polluting system is perceived as self-defense and as devoted service to the sacred cause of a more equitable and just society.

TERRORISM ALARMS AND SIGNALS   Terroristic acts are often intentionally provocative in an effort to make the system's latent structural violence overt and manifest. The successful proof of the system's violence is used to gain sympathizers and allies and to justify attempts to change or overthrow the system.

Terrorism never takes place in a vacuum; it occurs against a background of social conditions and of emotional reactions to these conditions. Terrorist acts are often parts of a master plan, but equally often the act itself is the whole plan. Previous injustice suffered supplies the terrorists with their imperative to do something violent in retaliation. Costs and sacrifices do not matter, and the immediate usefulness or advisability of the action is of minor interest. Terrorism is a sign, a signal, a symptom, and a symbol; it alarms, awakens, advertises, and accuses; it is a spectacle, a game, a ritual, and a performance. Spectacular violence is designed to attract attention and to give notice to the world that the terrorists will not be ignored or neglected any longer. The terroristic action points to the actual or alleged injustice, which has to be terminated at all costs. Terrorism from below wants to stimulate and galvanize resistance by awakening the population from its indifference; it seeks to arouse the oppressed brothers and sisters to join the common cause. The terroristic act is both a severe reproach directed against an indifferent world and an appeal to that world for sympathy and help.

TERRORISM IS USUALLY A DELIBERATE POLICY CHOICE
Terrorism, at least the crusading variety, is neither senseless, mindless, nor irrational. It is the purposeful use of strategic aggression to achieve its objectives. Terrorists deliberately create extreme fear and, in its wake, indignation, helplessness, or even paralysis in order to command attention to themselves and the causes they presumably represent and in whose name violence is perpetrated. Terrorism mainly serves to alarm, to prove the powerlessness of power, to advertise, and to propagandize. Victims chosen at random or for their publicity value are used or abused ruthlessly to intimidate the objects of terrorism (who are not to be confused with the victims) through extortion, blackmail, and spectacular cruelty. The objects may be a small (family) or a large (nation) community or even the whole world.

TERRORISM, REFLECTION, AND INTIMACY There is an inverse proportion between terrorism and reflection (and humor). Deadly earnest modern terrorists are outraged by compromise and appalled by hypocrisy. They tolerate no subtlety, no laughter, no qualified approach. They consider their bluntly militant deeds more eloquent than any words and more forthright than any deliberation or discussion. In comparison, the scruples of yesterday's terrorists, insisting on a separation between combatants and the uninvolved, appear old-fashioned, almost quaint.

Conservative aristocrat Helmuth von Moltke, a member of the resistance movement that staged the July 20, 1944, attempt on Hitler's life, refused to participate in the assassination. He wanted Hitler forcibly removed, but he could not condone murder: He believed that murder would undermine the resistance's right to condemn the slaughter in the concentration camps.

The Russian revolutionary Kulyayev, a member of a terrorist organization of Social Revolutionaries, considered terrorist violence not just a practical means of carrying out the demands of the party program but also an absolute act of liberation in which the perpetrator must be ready to die along with his victim. On February 2, 1905, after months of preparation, Kalyayev stood in the shadow of a doorway in Moscow's bitter cold waiting to carry out his assignment to assassinate Grand Duke Sergius. The grand duke's car appeared according to plan, but as Kalyayev raised his hand to throw the bomb, he noticed the grand duke's wife and two small children. He lowered his arm, put the bomb away, and reported to his organization that he could not bring himself to kill two innocent children.

At first, Kalyayev's comrades accused him of prolonging the suffering of thousands of innocent Russian children who would starve to death because of his squeamishness. But after considerable debate, they approved Kalyayev's decision.

For most terrorists the agonizing choice between giving up worthy ends and resorting to unworthy means either does not emerge or is immediately pushed back into the depths of the unconscious; thoughtlessness and humorlessness are preconditions as well as results of terroristic devotion. Often the terrorists are actually the terrorized, who escape into the extreme deed in order to liberate themselves from their own anxiety. In the exclusive emphasis on action, the deed is experienced as self-liberation, although it is performed in the interest of a collective cause.

Most terroristic activity is carried out in the name of goals, no matter how remote; but action for its own sake can acquire "functional autonomy" and become "purified" into a nonutilitarian, transcendental, and spontaneous performance. Action, presumably a means to an end, can become the end itself as apocalyptic destruction and self-sacrifice.

In the magical moment vibrant with life that is close to death, terrorists seek the intimacy denied to them in their ordinary existence through the extraordinary group experience in whose service they test the limits of the possible and experiment with extreme danger and with their own lives. Terrorists no longer passively accept their fate; they activistically arrange their frequent rendezvous with destiny.

TERRORISM IS MEMORABLE The group protects the individual, giving him aggressive license and freeing him from doubt or guilt. Crusading terrorists confirm their group loyalty through terrorist acts, which serve notice on friends, foes, and the world that they are determined to risk everything, including their own lives, to end the existing oppression. The terroristic act is experienced as an unforgettable occasion. Overrating their importance and the significance of their inner change, the terrorists interpret their actions as unique events that mark the beginning of a new era. For the terrorists history is not a narrative sequence of interrelated developments but a series of dramatic kairos (opportune and decisive moments). To have participated in or to have brought about such historic events is to gain historic stature.

Because the crusader feels in his gut, not just in his brains, that he has become different, he is convinced that the world must have changed too. Passive suffering of injustice and humiliation may have prevented him in the past from becoming a full human being, but now the new person, violently self-made, fearless and feared, will prove the durability and extent of his own change by his unlimited readiness to act aggressively.

The terroristic act is a cry for help, signifying an underlying sick condition in the society; but at the same time, it is also a demonstration of self-help, announcing that violence is the only remedy left. The extreme situation of human desperation and human hope transcending the narrow limits of individuality is symbolized by the terrorist's willingness to sacrifice his life for a high purpose.

TERRORISM IS MYSTICAL AND RITUALISTIC Ancient religious tradition combines with new social revolutionary fanaticism to produce the mystical act of the

terroristic ritual. The willingness of the terrorist to give
his life confirms and seals the convenant with spiritual
entities, divine forces, the holy mother soil, and the
immortal sacred community. Beyond the pursuit of
political goals, terrorism testifies to the importance of
values higher than self-protection and self-preservation.

The terroristic performance is directed toward the
audience of terror objects, but it is also calculated to
influence the terrorists themselves. The ritual of communal action is the best way to fortify the bonds of
the terrorist group and create identity feelings. Through
blood sacrifice the insignificant mortal transforms himself into the immortal hero.

Barbarization performed and condoned in the
name of a higher purpose constitutes regression to infantile states of automatic obedience and ecstatic emo-
tionalism. Brutalized children of all ages invest their
"direct actions" with historic significance. (Ralph
Waldo Emerson: "Terrorism feels and never reasons,
and therefore is always right.") The groups of humor-
less infants who justify their impulsive game playing
with the ponderous self-importance of sovereign states
have become civilization's mortal danger; their feelings
lead heroes to extremes, or rather, they seek extremes
in order to become heroes.

TERRORISM IS A THEATRICAL PERFORMANCE DE-
SIGNED FOR AUDIENCE PARTICIPATION   In 1893, the
French intellectual Laurent Tailhade, anticipating the
development of terrorism from private deed to public
event, exclaimed: "What do the victims matter if the
gesture is beautiful?"

Intent on setting an example for imitation, terrorism always plays to and for an audience. Audience
participation is invited and, whenever possible, coerced.
Publicity seekers do not particularly care whether the
comments they provoke are favorable or critical, as
long as their names and the name of the cause they
represent are spelled correctly and become generally
known. By the same token, terrorists prefer to be un-

derstood and praised, but they do not mind being denounced and feared so long as they are recognized and taken seriously.

Terroristic acts interrupt the dreary repetitiveness of everyday routines and offer occasional dramatic situations that momentarily reveal the essential conflict, as in a play. Pity and horror are the miniature terror effects that, according to Aristotle, make dramatic catharsis pleasurable and educational. In a play, the true nature of man is dramatically revealed through cruelty, suffering, despair, and sacrifice; the extraordinary case becomes the model for deterrence, encouragement, or identification. Sensational actions are also invigorating for the actors, who thrive on image and illusion. The danger inherent in their risky endeavors is likely to make the terrorists counterculture heroes in their own eyes and in the eyes of the community. Many terrorist acts are demonstratively theatrical, carefully staged and choreographed for maximal dramatic impact. The emphasis on intimidation and publicity blurs the distinction between falsehood and truth, guilt and innocence, show and reality; the terroristic show is the reality and the provocative scandal.

In 1894, the French intellectual Emile Henry, after randomly exploding a bomb that killed several bystanders at a Paris coffeehouse, proclaimed that there were no longer any innocents. He justified his deed by stating that anarchists could not have any pity on the wives and children of the bourgeoisie because the bourgeoisie did not have any pity on the wives and children who starve in miserable quarters.

TERRORISM PROMISES INSTANT SALVATION The terroristic deed is intended to alarm **and** to illuminate; in the glaring searchlight of explosive action, presently imperfect society is shown to be totally evil, perverted, and hopeless. The unembellished face of oppression is revealed by terrorism's shortcut to truth which tears off every hypocritical disguise.

The kingdom of heaven on earth is to be accomplished either totally and immediately or never; the

big jump into salvation is to be made now. Terrorism does not propose piecemeal societal changes. It
promises, by propaganda and deed, the advent of a
totally perfect society instantly. Having become the focus and projection screen for smoldering community
dissatisfaction, the terrorists become infatuated with
their own image and begin to believe that they can indeed redress the grievances they have dramatized and
thus implicitly promised to remove. As catalysts of discontent, they represent the injustice and at the same
time the remedy for the injustice. The terroristic demand creates its own supply of solidarity feelings with
the masses, who do not dare give vent to their anger
and frustration by violence but who envy and admire
those who do.

TERRORISTS FIGHT FOR RULES   Terrorists are not recognized as a force capable of engaging in "legitimate"
warfare; they, in turn, refuse to accord any recognition to the authorities against whom they fight. Terrorists equate the observation of society's rules with
their own former image as losers, which they want to
change. They are convinced that the established rules,
devised for the oppressor's advantage, need to be sabo-
taged and discarded. Yet they have a deep yearning
for those rules; they also fight to be admitted to the
club of rule-devising and rule-enforcing sovereign nations, in which they hope to be given the same privileges. The terrorists know that aside from economic,
political, and military power, it is the power of authority to define reality that counts. The uncontested capacity to determine what is right and what is wrong
confers the very real power to distinguish between attack and defense, between justifiable homicide and
wanton murder. The terrorists attack violently in order
to avail themselves of the opportunity to judge their
own violence as defensible and legitimate.

DAVID AND GOLIATH   The enormous discrepancy between the numbers and military power of the establishment Goliath and the terroristic David can be

turned to more than just a psychological advantage for the weak and outnumbered who like to cast themselves in the role of the small, courageously fighting the big against all odds. The total amount of terrorist violence "comes to something less than the annual homicide rate of any major American city and is trivial compared to the casualties of any war" (Brian Jenkins); it is not easily comprehensible why terrorism should be more reprehensible than war itself (Walter Laqueur).

Although terrorism, guerrilla warfare tactics, and war strategies may merge, there are differences between them. Terrorism is an "irregular" and smaller-scale activity, although often well organized; guerrilla activity is more like ordinary warfare, aimed primarily at the destruction of definite objects of economic or military importance. Guerrilla tactics depend on a degree of participation or at least sympathetic toleration by the local population. Terrorism is usually indiscriminate in the choice of means and publicity-conscious in the choice of targets. Destruction that is not necessarily aimed at definite persons or objects is sought mainly for its spectacular effect.

Guerrilla warfare often uses terroristic attacks as part of its available action repertory. Starting from a position of comparative weakness, guerrilla activities conduct the war of the flea. Terrorism, in turn, wages the war of the microbe; terroristic activity is aimed at "infecting" and affecting the people. It is often performed by various individuals or small groups intent on "invading," awakening, and alarming a hostile or indifferent population in order to destroy the image of the system's efficiency and to create a violence prone "climate of collapse."[4]

Modern terrorism, in spite of its international ramifications and implications, always originates in protest against the "internal affairs" of certain countries. Many modern states have become sovereign through liberation struggles that were terroristic or at least had a terroristic phase; many sovereign states give open or clandestine support, aid, comfort, and sanctuary to the terrorism of other sovereign countries, whose national or social structure is actually or allegedly the cause of terroristic activities.

TERRORISM USES SOPHISTICATION IN THE SERVICES OF BARBARISM   The progress of technology and gadgetry tends to equalize the power differences between the big and the small. Faithful mercenaries and experts will sell their skills to promote, not the person or the cause that convinces them, but the one that pays most in affluence, comfort, or prestige. Not the takeover of power by the experts, but the exploitation of their skills for any given task beyond their control and responsibility presents an acute, growing danger.

In former times, those who had reached a higher degree of civilized development shaped and directed the human raw material of the less advanced. Colonial powers trained, educated, and exploited native labor and native armies. Today, the opposite is also happening. The technological skill and the trained manpower of advanced civilization can still manipulate primitive strivings for its purposes, but conversely, archaic primitivism can employ the sophistication of technology and justification for its crude, simplistic ends.

GOING NUCLEAR   Socially aware and responsible scientists tend to join the conspiracy of silence regarding the use of fissionable material for terroristic purposes. The concern about giving new ideas to actual or potential terrorists is quite legitimate; mass media presentations of scenarios for terrorism invite imitation and emulation, regardless of whether these presentations are science fiction, drama, news, or scientific reports. Cautionary tales, in trying to arouse fear of (rather than through) the terroristic deed, may have an opposite, counterproductive effect. Detailed descriptions and warnings against terroristic attack have often been used as blueprints and instructions. Terrorists are more avid consumers of information about terror and counterterror than most law enforcement officers and peaceful citizens. Scientists and security officials have, probably quite correctly, hesitated to go public so that the terrorists might not be helped to go nuclear. Nobody responsible wants to take the chance of aiding and provoking what he wants to warn against and prevent: atomic blackmail. But it may be too late for such delicate discretion and fastidiousness; the horse is out of the stable, and there is no use closing the stable doors now.

At the same U.N. meeting in 1972 during which the major powers used reciprocal vetoes to prevent any effective resolution against terrorism or any investigation of its causes, the Soviet delegate suggested that a future Robin Hood armed with biological weapons or perhaps even stolen atomic devices would be in a position to blackmail any government. What used to be a nightmare or a lunatic's fantasy has become a frightful possibility today. Because everything that can possibly happen often does happen by design or by random selection, there is a strong probability that atomic terrorism could indeed be a reality tomorrow.

In 1971, the city of Orlando, Florida, was subject to nuclear blackmail when the mayor received a single threatening note containing a crude drawing of an atomic device. After studying the sketch, armament officials at McCoy Air Force Base reported that they believed it would most likely work. When a fourteen-year-old high school student was arrested and confessed to making the drawing and sending the note, alarm turned into relief and somewhat uneasy laughter. Nevertheless, an adolescent who had purchased a small uranium souvenir at Oak Ridge was able to terrorize a whole city for several days by a threat the credibility of which was authenticated by competent scientists.

In a test run by the Atomic Energy Commission, two young physicists with no more experience than their Ph.D. degrees were given the task of designing a nuclear weapon. In six months, they made a bomb and fairly accurately predicted its yield. Another AEC study group investigated the problem and concluded that the information needed to make nuclear weapons is widely available and that major changes in security measures are therefore essential. According to nuclear consultant Theodore Taylor, basement nuclear bombs are a real potential danger; with fifteen pounds of plutonium obtained by hijacking a nuclear transport truck or by "bit by bit diversion," a knowledgeable individual could construct a crude atomic weapon in a matter of weeks. Edward Gills, AEC assistant general manager for military application, disagrees; he claims that it is not quite that easy but that a crude atomic device presenting a viable threat could indeed be manufactured by private physicists or educated laymen.

A pound of plutonium is more expensive than a comparable quantity of gold or even heroin; yet some loss of nuclear materials is inevitable in the nuclear fission cycle. At every nuclear facility there are sometimes as many as several hundred pounds of uranium unaccounted for in a period of several years. The possibilities of obtaining fissionable material illegally would be multiplied if Project Independence, designed to minimize the threat of oil blackmail, succeeds in constructing several hundred nuclear plants around the country.

In 1974, the public became alarmed when passengers on a commercial airline were inadvertently exposed to dangerous radiation as a result of the faulty packaging of nuclear material that was being carried in the cargo area of a plane. Given the necessity to manufacture bombs to maintain the balance of terror that guarantees peace in the world, such incidents are as deplorable as they are inevitable. The spectacular development of technology has created a new type of terrorist: the unconscious, inadvertent, statistical terrorist who may unintentionally and unwittingly terrorize and victimize innumerable people by engaging in high-risk activities such as nuclear production.

Assuming the continuation of nuclear production, there is no absolutely or even reasonably safe protection against the danger of illicit use of atomic materials. Security precautions could be stepped up; the various materials necessary for putting an atomic device together could be "spiked," although the production of a "hot" atom that would kill any potential thief is costly and complicated. But the very purposes for which atomic bombs of any size are manufactured (defense, buildup of threat potential, experimentation, research, and so forth) preclude the effectiveness of stringent safety precautions. Even if a "garrison society" with strict police measures were instituted, it could not prevent smuggling or the import of the big bang in a small package.

David Hall, a pioneer A-bomb scientist at the Los Alamos Scientific Laboratory in New Mexico, distinguishes five classes of potential atomic thieves: one or a few individuals acting on their own in an irrational manner (crazy terrorists); organized activity for money (criminal terrorists); an organization dedicated to the destruction of a country and its leaders (crusading terrorists); a minor, undefined nation engaged in a border dispute or internal rebellion; and a major nation desiring to join the atomic club.

Dr. Hall omits the most likely possibility: terrorism by proxy or by delegation, a nation offering training, sanctuary, safe research space, and experimentation possibilities for hire or to dedicated terrorists acting on behalf of that country. These individuals or groups could, by credible or actual atomic threats, hold whole cities or nations hostage and easily enforce their blackmailing demands on their own or their patron's behalf.

DIFFERENT MEASUREMENTS Transnational or international terrorism would indeed be totally eliminated or confined to the occasional acts of "crazies" if a type of international agreement were possible that in present reality is precluded by the guarding of exclusive, absolute sovereignty rights of the existing states and through the insistent demands for such sovereignty rights by the would-be states. Ambassador Abdulrahim Abby Farah of Somalia remarked at the United Nations: "It must be realized that this phenomenon [terror and terrorism] is not new; it has only been brought closer home because the world which has accepted violence and terror as the natural lot of the poor, the weak and the oppressed is shocked to see these evils applied to the rich and successful."[5] The United States and other powerful nations outlaw terrorism without at the same time dealing with the grievances that motivate it; this approach appears to weigh violence by government with measurements different from those used for violence against government. It is this very application of a double standard that appears inflexible, inequitable, and unjust to all those who feel that tolerance of terror from above is one of the causes of terrorism from below.

The modern possibilities for transnational terrorism by export and internationalization have made terrorism immensely more attractive to the audiences and to the terrorists themselves, who can now deliberately choose their target according to where and when they are likely to command the most attention. This new terrorist potential has not gone unnoticed by numerous established sovereign states that support, finance, and organize terroristic activities in other sovereign countries, thus demonstrating the perfect compatibility of terror from above with terrorism from below. Terroristic brutality pays; it pays handsomely, at least in the short run, particularly in its unholy alliance with a high-sounding universal doctrine that demands and commands the total destruction of the enemy. The terrorists see themselves as soldiers on duty; sometimes they are precisely that, commandos on a paramilitary mission for the command structure of a country other than their own. The deniability of terrorist acts is an immense advantage to their use in surrogate warfare against another nation. The organizing country can avoid all responsibility and sacrifice the expendable terrorists without loss of prestige.

Large parts of the world do not search for cures or remedies to terrorism if terroristic violence serves their ends. Many young nations, comprising a solid majority in the United Nations, owe their existence, their sovereignty, and their new respectability to revolutionary strategies that included terrorism. For them, violence is the favorite and sometimes the only means for the liberation of the weak. They want to eliminate only terror from above, which to them is the sole cause and perfect justification for terrorism from below.

Another larger part of the world either refuses to acknowledge the interrelatedness of terror and terrorism or considers it irrelevant; terrorism is regarded as a crime to be fought, like any other crime, with traditional or reinvigorated methods of law and law enforcement. The dependence on ordinary local police or national military measures betrays a parochial shortsightedness that chooses to ignore the worldwide implications and ramifications of terrorism, which is a symptom and an expression of worldwide disturbance and change. But the overt or passive support and toleration of terrorism, out of sympathy or out of feelings of helplessness, is just as shortsighted because universal terrorism, respecting no rules of human cooperation, must quickly lead to universal chaos and the perpetuation of pervasive fear, or more likely to oppression on the largest scale imaginable.

HUMAN NATURE? The infliction of crude inhumanity is part of the aggressive repertory of human capabilities. Undeniably, terror and terrorism are viable possibilities for overthrowing, changing, organizing, and perpetuating power relationships. Intimidation is an effective mode of influencing human behavior. Intimidation, once internalized, produces and reinforces the terroristic temptations. Those who have been beaten are inclined to beat; those most frightened are often most to be feared; having been subject to intimidation increases the likelihood of trying to control by intimidation. If the tendencies to employ terror and to yield to terror and terrorism were not part of human nature, or rather, part of what human nature crippled by fear is capable of, terror and terrorism could never have become the widespread, contagious disease and life-threatening danger they are today.

Terrorists are evil because they believe that their opponents are totally evil and need to be not just

fought and defeated but completely smashed and eliminated. Terror and terrorism are in the same rut. Counterterrorism is not the opposite of or the remedy for
terrorism, but its counterpart and mirror image. The
cure is worse than the disease; in fact, the cure may
be precisely the disease that it pretends to cure. Yet
sweeping, spectacular actions holding out the promise
of promptly relieving helplessness and distress have an
irresistible appeal to the desperate. The immature, the
impatient, and the primitive, hankering for clear-cut,
simple answers, are sorely tempted. There are terrorizing terrorists all around us; there is some part of
the terrorized terrorist even within us. The democratic
forms of government all over the world are put to the
crucial test in deciding whether and how they can meet
the challenge of eliminating or reducing terrorism without engaging in warfare or lapsing into the slavery of
a totalitarian state.

FIGHT AGAINST TERRORISM   Terrorism can be eliminated or reduced to insignificance in any of three different ways: by war, by terror from above, and by
appropriate social action to remove the political, social,
and psychological causes of the experience of remediable injustice.

In war against an external enemy, terrorists disappear, although their violent activities do not. Their
exploits may even be stepped up, but they are called
commandos "carrying the fight behind enemy lines" in
"total warfare." Their formerly irregular activities are
given different labels, suggesting "regular," ordinary
actions, even if they continue to do exactly what they
did before. The sovereign nation committing and even
commanding destructive violence against an external
enemy provides all the necessary justification that in
peacetime had to be imagined, manufactured, or copied
by the terrorists. What used to be terrorism from below acquires new impact and new dignity in war as
part of a destructive and terrorizing effort that is supported and sanctioned from above.

The most popular way to eliminate terrorism

from below is by terror from above. There is no terrorism from below in totalitarian regimes; the government has preempted and monopolized all terroristic activities, which are organized, governed, and justified from above. The ruling circles practice what they prohibit: gaining and maintaining influence and power through universal intimidation and indiscriminate arousal of fear. Oppressive police state measures in small dosages tend to stimulate and increase terrorism from below, but under ideal conditions of totalitarian control, terrorism, blanketed in silence and anonymity by nonreporting media, can be crushed by draconian measures, including population transfers, torture, and deprivation of civil rights. This method, widely advertised by strategists of terror from above, is the most likely to succeed. Assisted by the widespread belief that an end with terror is a lesser evil than terrorism without end, justifications for intimidation and terroristic brutality are always found most easily in exalted nationalism, in radical socialism, or in fundamental religious goals.

Nonviolent social action is the most reasonable and also the most unpopular approach to the problem of terrorism. But social justice does not come cheap. Necessary remedies call not only for intensive and extensive alterations of existing structures but also for fundamental changes in patterns of thinking and feeling. As long as national consent requires the paranoid distortion of an enemy image and the self-righteous insistence on absolute sovereignty that no longer exists, no meaningful international cooperation, which is required for effective antiterrorism, is possible.

THE FUTURE OF TERRORISM   Terrorism is a growth industry that demands little investment. It is comparatively cheap and has a miraculous political effect; the modern mixture of identity, territoriality, and sovereignty has proved its explosive power over and over again. What makes the future of terrorism even brighter is the present state of international disunity and the lack of imagination on the part of conventional law enforcement. The terrorists of tomorrow can go atomic, setting up the blackmail potential to the point of irresistibility, they can go even more fully transnational and international in a permanent "simultaneous revolution of terrorists," or they can perfect terrorism by proxy and by any or all of these devices plunge a more and more fragmented world into constant miniwars between smaller and smaller fanatical groups. The prospects of this development, most likely to happen if nothing decisive occurs to counteract it, are neither pleasant nor hopeful. It is precisely the hope for and reliance on financially expensive but morally and emotionally cheap patent medicines that constitute the problem. The easy solution of violence has been preempted by the terrorists from above and below; to use the same methods and the same justifications means to imitate, not to combat, them. The time to act nonterroristically is now.

Epilogue

In the mid-1970s, terrorism strikes everywhere and is mushrooming at an alarming rate. On its own terms, terrorism has literally been a smash hit. Thought and behavior control by intimidation used to be the prerogative of the powerful few. Today, with homemade Molotov cocktails, guaranteed media coverage, and ideological justifications, the means of intimidation are available to practically everybody. The little guys and the little groups make the big difference. As in the stock market of old, which thrived on the increasing participation of the formerly excluded public, it is the small investors in terrorism who are getting more experience and independence and who, added together, have a significant impact on world opinion and world politics. The prestige of terrorism has risen like the price of gold which may go down temporarily but is expected to rise to new heights eventually. Terrorism is in, and it is the golden opportunity for the disinherited and disenchanted who formerly were unable to acquire the growth and glamour stock of spectacular action.

Terrorism has come a long way from the horse-and-buggy days of dagger and poison. Weirdly disguised kidnappers and gunmen appear on the television screen, impressing everybody with their self-assurance and self-sacrificial single-mindedness; they have had more effect on the world's imagination and on powerful governments (both those that possess the atomic bomb and those that do not) than all the political pundits and economic wizards put together. Yet, in all probability, we have seen only the ominous beginning; the growth potential of terrorism is still largely unexplored. The forming of worldwide terrorist alliances, coalitions, and organizations, so far erroneously assumed by simplistic conspiracy theories, seems very likely within or outside of the United Nations or other agencies instituted for very different, peaceful purposes. National governments will get into the terroristic act more systematically by employing terrorist groups and tactics in substitute, surrogate, or supplementary warfare, declared or undeclared, against other nations. The use of fissionable material or nerve gas for blackmailing purposes obviously opens up brand-new vistas for more effective terrorism in the future.

Even the most dastardly acts, involving large numbers of totally innocent people, including children, do not always provoke worldwide condemnation; indignation often seems restricted to those who oppose the politics of the perpetrators. There is no global outcry against terrorism; instead various interest groups, often enough decent people and sovereign states, silently or openly support terrorists or terroristic anti-terrorists no matter how gruesome their deeds.

Lulled into complacency by their own rhetoric, many individuals and states persist in their righteous belief that the outrage they feel about a certain atrocity committed by the opponent will and must be shared by everybody. They deceive themselves with the futile hope that someday the pervasive feeling of general insecurity and disgust will produce a world climate in which terrorism will be universally outlawed. Their opponents feel exactly the same way, and outrage is answered by counteroutrage, and so on ad infinitum, just as violence is answered by counterviolence and terrorism by counterterrorism. The injustice of the excessive punitiveness of violent counterterrorism, provides terrorism with new converts and new justifications. The escalation of mutual outrage, accompanied and followed by "just" retaliation, is regarded by the majority of the world's population first with horror and then, as habituation occurs, with boredom, impatience, and resignation. The feeling that there is no escape and that nothing can be done about the problem spreads, which is exactly what the terrorists want.

The mood of resigned acceptance also favors terrorism and may eventually turn into sullen outrage, thus beginning the cycle of violence all over again. There is no sense in hoping that something as simple as world unity against terrorism can be achieved in the foreseeable future. In many places, the demands for social improvement and equality cannot be accommodated within the existing structures, and certain national aspirations can apparently be satisfied only by new territorial sovereignties. Large parts of the world have a vested interest in retaining their sovereignty while promoting fundamental change in other places.

Simplistic ideologies stipulate the existence of only one enemy; conspiracy theories maintain that one monstrous foe, such as the Wall Street capitalists or the Leninist-Marxist conspiracy, is pulling the strings of terrorism everywhere. This assumption contains a clearcut direction for remedial action: Destroy the enemy, and everything will be fine. Yet, it is precisely this trust in instant salvation through total eradication of the opponent that has inspired terror and produced terrorism.

We will not be so helpless as the terrorists want us to be if we can succeed in freeing our hearts and minds from the contagious effects of terroristic feeling and thinking. Patent medicines are phony; the promise of instant salvation is fraudulent; perfect justice cannot be achieved by a leap of faith or by intimidation, bombs, and guns. But that is no reason not to research for and experiment with measures to relieve social ills, or not to work toward possible and necessary improvement of the human condition by correcting those injustices that are remediable.

Terror and terrorism always coexist; they condition each other and need each other to justify their existence. We should be consciously and deliberately involved in a simultaneous two-front struggle against both of them. I believe that a firm stance against terrorism can be morally justified and credibly maintained only if there is equal firmness in rejecting totalitarian terror methods. There are alternatives to the dreary choice between tyranny and anarchy, but only if we do not impatiently succumb to the temptations of terrorism's direct action or of terror's police state.

Although I have described the meaning and effect of totalitarian methods of domination in great detail, I have not offered many examples of terrorism in countries under "successful" police state regimes simply because there aren't any. The total institution of the tightly organized police state is indeed capable of curbing terrorism, together with "educating" people through tough control and enforcing the social tranquillity of the graveyard. Terrorism can be subdued by terror from above or absorbed by war. The choice of eliminating terrorism from below by imposing terror from above is a definite option. Do we want to take that option or, by not finding alternatives, have it imposed on us?

We already know a great deal about what to do and particularly what not to do. Unhappily, most of what we are currently doing or failing to do falls into the category of the don'ts, usually involving an escalated imitation of terroristic methods and an obstinate reliance on fail-safe "monitor and shoot" postures.

Peacetime thinking, to which the United States and other civilized nations are presumably officially committed, permits change through the nonviolent means of persuasion, negotiation, and compromise. But we have turned to the methods of full-fledged warfare brought home from our overseas encounters. Weapons and styles of attack used in Vietnam are used against domestic dissidents. By allowing the practically unrestricted sale of automatic weapons and bomb cookbooks, we permit ourselves to be a nation armed against itself. The inhabitants of a major American city, for instance, possess more handguns than the entire U.S. army. We not only allow terrorists unhindered access to our mass media but permit and encourage the "showification" of ongoing violent events, thus adding the thrill of authenticity.

More violent crimes are committed in the United States than in any other place in the Western world, but our rate of apprehension of culprits and the proportion of offenders punished for their crimes are the lowest. It takes us the longest time to impose and execute the stiffest sentences. And there is considerable support for the reintroduction of the death penalty. We continue to allow our jails and prisons to be run as schools for crime and terrorism, complete with instruction courses and identity-inspired insurgencies. We permit law enforcement, known to be corrupt in some places and not always alert to the newest developments in others, to function without any "interference" from or accountability to outsiders. And we continue to suspect that even the most legitimate demands for necessary social changes are enemy-inspired.

What has all this to do with terrorism? A great deal. It is plain to see that the interdependence of the modern world makes it mandatory to export the methods of internal social control to the international arena, rather than to import the methods of external warfare for use against an internal "enemy." No international covenant banning terrorism is possible overnight; this is mostly because no similar agreement banning terror is possible, as terror is considered an internal affair of sovereign states. But limited agreements between international opponents are feasible; the mere existence of the punish-or-extradite treaty between the United States and Cuba has done more to stop skyjacking than all other measures combined.

Free people everywhere retain their freedom even when they are not permitted to purchase guns and explosives. Some free nations have found ways to prevent the reporting of ongoing violent events and the full identification and heroizing of the participants, without oppressive censorship. Many free countries can do without the death penalty and can maintain law and order without having to resort to excessive penalties. Practically all free countries have better, less brutal, brutalizing, and rebellion-breeding prison systems than we have in America. It can be done; it is even well known how it can be done.

Because of the international nature of modern terror and terrorism, every country, civilized or not, is at times forced to negotiate with and occasionally even yield to blackmailing terrorists. Most countries manage to do so without sacrificing credibility by negotiating while simultaneously claiming that they will never negotiate and never yield. The United States proudly proclaims that it will not be blackmailed when human lives are at stake, and thus it permits innocent people to be killed (as it did in Khartoum). Without gaining either respect or deterrent clout, the United States in 1975 refused to provide food but permitted the government of Lebanon to distribute it in exchange for a kidnapped American officer in Beirut. A U.S. government spokesman and prominent expert on counterterrorism commented that all governments should pay back terrorists in their own violent coin and urged that promises to terrorists should not be honored. But we are not tough at all when it comes to oil, although sometimes the same parties alternately use oil and human beings as commodities for barter and blackmail.

Governments and police departments all over the world have found it perfectly compatible with their honor and their professional dignity to seek the advice of experts in various fields. In several countries, independent psychiatrists and psychologists have been members of teams responsible for advising officials and devising the strategy and the timing of negotiations or for actually conducting those negotiations. What American police department would grant that much authority to behavioral scientists outside their department discipline? What American police department would publicly acknowledge that something more than routine measures might be required to handle an incident within their jurisdiction, and that, in the case of the terrorist situation, special expert intervention might be needed? Qualified specialists with legitimate research interests were denied access to data after the SLA shoot-out in Los Angeles. The idea that such expert advice may have been helpful not only after but during the event or that it might have helped to prevent the shoot-out undoubtedly appears absurd to authorities who are more interested in justifications for, rather than alternatives to, their own violence.

Tremendous risks had to be taken at Vienna, at Scheveningen, and in many other similar situations. All kinds of things might have gone wrong and spoiled the favorable outcomes, which depended partly on luck and partly on the decisions of clearly defined command structures with specially trained forces and advisers exploring all the possible alternatives to violence based on the logic of the situations and previous experiences. Mixed strategies (delay, negotiation, promises, firmness, consistency, force) used flexibly in different, changing situations and not chained to any preconceived political or other biases produce the best results. I do not advocate softness; to yield under any circumstance is just as unprofitable and futile as to decide in advance never to yield. Rigid commitments either to surrender or to face-saving, life-wasting, massive Munich- and Attica-type approaches predictably cost the lives of the guilty and the innocent alike.

Playing it by ear is the best tactic most of the time because it is appropriate to the changing nature of modern terrorism. But it makes a great difference whose ears are listening to what signals and what signals, information, and advice are available to those who call the shots—preferably without calling for shoot-outs. Winning does not mean scoring higher than the opponent; it means saving irreplaceable human lives. If the employment of force becomes truly inevitable as a very last resort and ultima ratio, it must be used sparingly and must be limited to the necessary minimum of "violence without pleasure."

Corruption, double-crossing, high-handed hypocrisy, emphasis on image making (rather than on real change), violence, and the perpetuation of remediable injustice all promote terrorism. Everything that increases the belief in the credibility, fairness, and non-violence of the authorities is antiterroristic. All measures that redress remediable injustices are directly, if not immediately, antiterroristic. The reason crusading terrorism (despite Black Panthers, Weathermen, and SLA) has been relatively rare in the United States is the existence of accessible agencies and institutions for the peaceful resolution of conflict and, even more important, the belief that such machinery for cooperation exists.

The commitment to real peace and security calls for the extension of those international and particularly national agencies that aim at disclosure, avoidance, and nonviolent resolution of conflict to deal with the causes of potential trouble before the trouble occurs.

Violent resolution of conflict is all the more likely the more the participants on either side become fanatically indoctrinated with feelings of righteousness and convinced of the sacredness of their cause. The evident connection between violence and its justification (in the minds of the perpetrators) deserves particularly careful attention. Rational terrorists who rely more on strategy than on symptomatic violence may be sincere, unselfishly motivated, incorruptible, well trained, and well organized, but that only makes them more dangerous.

Negotiations with terrorists are often negotiations in name only. They are conceived by the authorities as a cover for more or less sophisticated strategies of deceit. Delay is sought, and every imaginable trick is pulled, not to gain concessions, but to stall the opponent until he can be subdued by force, without any concessions whatever. Highly immoral means, such as lying, false promises, treachery, and dirty tricks, are condoned by the authorities in their uncompromisingly self-righteous stance. However, reckless, dedicated fanatics are usually neither idiots nor raving lunatics, and they cannot be tricked out of their demands by delay and guile. They are not deterred by the threat of severe penalties; in fact, they are attracted by dangerous risks and the expectation of a heroic death.

But modern terrorism is a novel challenge that must be met with new ideas and new approaches. Law enforcement officials have a hard time accepting this fact of modern life. Accustomed to dealing quickly and decisively with lawbreakers, they are inclined to meet force or threats of force with superior counterforce and to make use of delay only in order to muster sufficient strength to overwhelm the offenders. It is not just adherence to professional routines that makes law enforcement officers employ force as the primary means of handling lawbreakers. Acting for the sovereign state as its sole legitimate practitioners of violence, the army and the police easily slip into the habits of sovereign independence. Prestige and a strong sense of righteousness, legitimacy, and power are important compensations for the danger and constant criticism inherent in the security officer's immensely difficult job. They do not fear the criminals, but they fear the appearance of impotence or inefficiency in dealing with criminals. Like all those whose main business is violence they are afraid not of danger, but of mockery and ridicule. What scares them is not loss of limb or life, but loss of face. They regard alternatives to violence or hesitation in the use of force as despicable weakness. Because they have been trained to act tough, they are inclined to regard toughness as a virtue in and of itself.

Modern terrorism is an international problem, an import-export growth industry that is exchanging trade secrets and personnel. This fact needs emphasis over and over again in order to make the necessary "diplomatization" and legalization of strategies of negotiation and compromise more palatable. Modern-day terrorists move around quickly, using psychological and technological weapons of considerable sophistication and dangerousness to support their extortion and blackmail demands by threats to highly valued property or lives. Terrorists cannot be prevented from attacking almost anyplace in the world, but measures should be taken to minimize the damage that cannot be avoided.

The terroristic enterprise consists of conflict

polarization and the escalation of dramatized and glamorized violence; therefore, antiterroristic tactics have to depolarize, de-escalate, deglamorize, and defuse. The moralistic luxury of name-calling and blame-calling will have to be sacrificed to the more imperative need to save human lives, which is not only a humanitarian consideration but also the best chance to prevent copycat and follow-up terrorism.

The alternative to and the remedy for violent direct action is innovative social action. All progress would stop if there were no new inventions and practical improvements. But no industrial firm would put a product on the market without having first conducted extensive experiments to find out whether it works. Why not engage in systematic and intuitive social experimentation?

The mass media serve as outlets for propaganda and instruments of blackmail for modern terrorism because the desire for widespread spectacular publicity is one of the main motivations of crusading terrorism. The terrorists clearly create and exploit the public's needs to be tickled and enthralled by the adventure of thrilling, violent spectacles. Although the right of the public to unhampered information and entertainment has to be respected in a democratic society, it should not be impossible to devise effective means to prevent "showification" and reporting of ongoing terroristic attacks. With the cooperation of media representatives, constitutional lawyers and other experts could devise ground rules to reconcile the legitimate needs for information, entertainment, and a chance for expressing divergent views with the equally legitimate need for public safety.

Dramatic, spectacular violence is imitated or avenged by more spectacular violence. Nonviolent solutions to conflict have an educational impact that reaches far beyond the specific occasions of their successful employment.

On the international level, every conceivable effort should be made to strengthen existing impartial supranational institutions such as the Red Cross, the

International Commission of Jurists, Amnesty International, and agencies of the United Nations, even if such support means that nations must yield some aspects of their sovereignty. Agreements between opposing nations could be worked out along the lines of the U.S.-Cuban treaty to curb skyjacking: that is, by accepting the opponent as he is, carefully evaluating his strengths and weaknesses, and basing the negotiations on such evaluations.

For the most part, international law regulates relationships between sovereign states only; it does not recognize or accommodate those groups that aspire to national sovereignty. By the standards of established states, they are irregulars operating outside of any law. Theirs is all the exposure, but also all the freedom of movement, of the outlaw; they strike whenever and wherever they choose. They are socially irresponsible because their only responsibility is to their cause and their organization, which in turn is not responsive to or responsible for anything other than its own code of conduct, unrestricted by any customary limitations. Attempts could be made to grant some of these groups some kind of internationally recognized status. That might give them added prestige, but it would also compel them to accept certain restrictions of rule-regulated behavior.

Our officials and statesmen conclude agreements with foreign powers whose politics and morals we may not like but accept because they control something we want. Why not try the same type of approach with terrorists and other blackmailers? Any community that abandons the unjustly persecuted shows a degree of disintegration which invites (rather than curbs) further terroristic activities. Obviously prison reform and improvements in the efficiency and fairness of criminal proceedings are needed, as well as regulations regarding the manufacture, sale, and availability of guns and explosives. Precommission bargaining should be seriously discussed and considered, and the protection of the human mind's integrity (criminalization or rape of the mind) should become part of a multinational bill of rights. The forcefully emerging modern needs for justice and belonging must be recognized and accommodated by novel measures.

Aleksandr Herzen, whose gradualistic proposals did not prevail against the violent teachings of his pupil Mikhail Bakunin, wrote prophetically a hundred years ago:

> Reasonable people will forgive the Huns, the terror reign of the French revolution and even Peter the Great, but they will not forgive us. Let's not appeal to the hatchet, the ultima ratio of the oppressed, if there is the smallest hope of change without hatchets. Russia needs brooms, not hatchets.[1]

What does this country, what does the world need? Will we act in time so that reasonable people can forgive us?

Postscript

Modern terrorism, a continuing spectacular with many more episodes to come, is a thriving growth industry yielding enormous profits in notoriety and political influence for a relatively minor investment. It is not likely to wither away in response to sanctimonious admonitions or tough talk, nor will it surrender to the unimaginative matching of terrorist violence with reciprocal violence under the label of antiterrorism. Books about terrorism cannot hope to keep up with the accelerated pace of crusading violence; something new and perhaps bigger is bound to occur on the terroristic scene between writing and publishing.

Like everyone else, I knew that whatever deadline was set, my book would be dated by the time it reached the public. But the surprise strike by Israeli commandos and the ensuing liberation of over a hundred hostages at Entebbe, Uganda, on July 4, 1976, the two hundredth anniversary of American independence, was too significant to leave out even though it occurred after my book was in proof. This event, unique in some respects and very typical in many others, aroused strong emotions all over the world; there was jubilation in Israel, and the whole Western world rejoiced in the spectacular success of a daring venture, extolled as an example to be followed from then on. The message was clear: teach the terrorists once and for all that there are no more safe havens in the world and, for the sake of national self-esteem, retain the option to use "surgical strikes" any time, any place in order to eradicate the spreading evil of terrorism. The Entebbe episode, a morality tale with a happy ending, was more than an exciting adventure story; it was an instruction in how to deal with international terrorists.

No doubt lessons are to be learned from Entebbe, but what are they? Has Entebbe really illustrated that bold decisiveness, taking or ignoring the risks of daring action, is the method of choice for combating terrorism? I don't believe so.

The Entebbe story was instantly recognized as great material for mass entertainment to be told, retold, and reproduced with all the familiar ingredients of a heroic tale: the brave and determined good guys stealthily invade the seemingly impenetrable fortress of the vile criminals and, at the last moment, spirit away their captive comrades from among the midst of their bloodthirsty foes. The high drama of this impressive story crowned by the happy ending of improbable success is almost too clearcut and simple to be real; but happen it did, demonstrating to our complicated, contemporary world that now, as ever, dedicated virtue will triumph over the dark powers of evil.

As congratulatory messages arrived in Israel from practically all of the Western nations (with the notable exception of France), jubilation, dancing, and flag-waving broke out and continued in the streets of Israeli cities and towns. Anger flared up briefly over the U.N. Secretary General's statement that the commando raid was a "serious violation of the sovereignty" of Uganda (Kurt Waldheim later denied that he had used the words "flagrant aggression"). The father of nineteen-year-old Maimoni, one of the accidentally killed hostages, was respectfully heeded when, in the midst of the ecstatic joy, he demanded silence to commemorate his dead son and the others who had perished. But the pause for mourning and reflection lasted only a short time, then back-slapping celebration resumed as U.S. President Ford in an "unprecedented message" thanked the Israelis for a great Fourth of July present and the president of B'nai B'rith declared that Israel's gift to the world on the occasion of America's 200th birthday was "the eleventh commandment—thou shalt not bow down to terrorism."

Clearly, the daring rescue mission, planned with ingenuity, coordinated with impeccable precision, and carried out with brilliant flexibility (and a great deal of luck), was a master stroke. Hardly anybody, not even Idi Amin and many of his fellow African leaders, could hide their admiration for the military and technical achievement of this surprise attack, staged in hostile territory over 2,600 miles away from the starting point to which all of the over 100 hostages, except three, were returned with the loss of only one of the attackers. Of course, Israel was able to use all of the vast resources of a well-prepared, excellently equipped, powerful nation on constant war alert. Intelligence reports could be obtained and updated through Washington, Kenya, and various other African nations, all of whom were kept in the dark as to the intended use of this intelligence. During a period of friendship between Uganda and Israel, Israeli soldiers had trained Ugandans in the use of weapons, many of them purchased by Idi Amin on a veritable buying spree in Israel. Hence, the Israeli secret service possessed a great deal of information about the Entebbe Airport, about Idi Amin and Ugandan military routines at Entebbe. Israeli "tourists," flown to Uganda's next-door neighbor Kenya during the postponement of the terrorists' deadline, provided additional intelligence and probably made the necessary arrangements for the waiting hospital airliner and the refueling of the cargo planes in Nairobi. Although many hundreds of people must have known or guessed what was intended, no slip of the tongue betrayed the secret. Everything went according to intricately coordinated plan. The attackers could take full advantage of the anticipated surprise effect on which the success of the venture depended. Even the slow, inefficient response of the Ugandan soldiers, untrained in flexible techniques and intimidated away from the habit of independent decision making by their tyrannical boss, was not so much a stroke of luck as a credit to Israeli imagination and ingenuity. Nevertheless, the rescued hostages were quite right when they exclaimed, "It was a miracle."

Though the lives of the prisoners of Entebbe were in constant jeopardy, the aim of the hijackers certainly was not to murder their victims, a majority of whom had been voluntarily released on previous occasions; in true terrorist fashion, the hostages were intended to be used instrumentally to blackmail the terror objects (Israel and other nations) into releasing the terrorists' jailed comrades. The decision makers actually had to weigh the raid's risks against the feasibility of releasing several dozen political prisoners, most of them terrorists. Only the refusal to grant such a release made the danger to the lives of the hostages imminent and left military rescue as the "only remaining option." The Israeli government, which could hardly have survived the failure of this operation, estimated that between twenty and fifty lives would have to be sacrificed. Compared to those figures, the actual loss of "only" four lives represented a major success (in the gruesomely fashionable practice of "body counts" the number of killed opponents is either multiplied many times by the "prestige factor," as in Vietnam, or else not mentioned at all and pushed out of consciousness: the twenty dead Ugandan soldiers did not count, and, of course, the dead terrorists did not count at all). The twenty Ugandan soldiers and the seven terrorists killed in the raid were buried in Uganda with military honors; the Israeli commander was given a hero's funeral in Israel, the mourners expressing their proud belief that he had died for a worthy purpose and had helped Jews all over the world to hold their heads high again.

Nobody denied that the daring rescue mission was a gigantic gamble, which could have had disastrous consequences for all the participants. But the gamblers' (and their sympathetic kibitzers') joy and relief over a successful outcome is greatest when devastating defeat has been narrowly avoided; those who have taken the biggest chances feel most exalted, graced, and loved when benevolent fate smiles on them and grants success against all probability. High stakes and near prohibitive odds enhance the thrill of victory.

Threats and thrills reinforce each other from earliest childhood on. Danger is also alluring and exciting. Aggressive satisfaction combines with sexual (pregenital) pleasure, when rigid impersonal rules (experienced as inhuman) can be circumvented or broken by playing tricks on authorities, outsmarting them, or snatching something away from them. Pranksters who expose corrupt and brutal authorities as dupes and dopes become almost heroes; the rule-breakers may be rascals, but they are wonderful, lovable rascals who are pardoned for their transgressions and admired for having the courage to do what others secretly wish, but do not dare to do. Pranksters and rascals thus personalize and dramatize the protest against restrictions that call for instinctual renunciation. Counting on the general discontent with rules and regulations, and representing the underdog, they invite identification and permit others to enjoy vicariously otherwise prohibited, aggressive satisfaction.

The precedent-setting Entebbe raid may have been unprecedented in some respects—in the magnitude of the enterprise carried out from afar and in the total surprise of a magnificently executed venture—but in other respects it was a repeat of an old, familiar performance. No two events are ever exactly alike, but there have been several similar exploits with striking analogies that come to mind.

The liberation of compatriots from deep within enemy territory was attempted by the U.S. in 1970. Parachutists from the Army Special Forces and the Air Force went on a mission to rescue fifty-five American prisoners of war believed to be held at San Tai prison near Hanoi in North Vietnam. Due to the bungling of intelligence, it was not learned until later that the prisoners had been moved from the compound. Although all the raiders returned safely home, the mission was considered a dismal failure because the would-be rescuers found all the prison cells empty. But at that time, the U.S. was at war with North Vietnam, or at least officially involved in a "police action" lasting for many years.

Then there was the *Mayaguez* incident. Affirmative action demonstrating a government's strength is at first always applauded by the people who, together with their government, bask in uniting national glory. In May 1975, Cambodia seized an American ship in Cambodian territorial waters. As neogitations dragged on for several days, the American government ordered a rescue action that was again plagued by serious flaws of intelligence. The U.S. Marines invaded Tang Island, twenty-five miles away from the island where the ship's crew was actually being held. Although Cambodia had offered to release the American crew before the assault was made, the offer was ignored because it was "too late" to halt the action. A second strike, presumably to protect the Marines, had definite overtones of a punitive expedition rather than a rescue.

Fifteen Americans were reported dead, three missing, and fifty wounded in this incident. Counting Cambodians, an estimated forty to fifty lives were sacrificed in order to save thirty-nine that were never in serious jeopardy to begin with. Nevertheless, the tough action was greeted with intense popular enthusiasm. "When Ford entered the Cabinet Room to inform the assembled congressional leaders of his decision to use force to free the *Mayaguez,* the legislators—all veterans of similar sessions held by Presidents Johnson and Nixon during the Vietnam years—rose to their feet and applauded," according to the New York *Daily News.* President Ford and Secretary of State Kissinger were filmed laughing and patting each other on the back; the jubilant response of the public was explained as an understandable reaction to national frustration over Vietnam. Senator Goldwater gave voice to the popular sentiment that we had had enough of "little half-assed nations" attempting to push us around.

In the *Mayaguez* episode, one of the mightiest superpowers reacted (or, as some critics would have it, overreacted) against what it felt was an unwarranted provocation from a small, hostile nation. The act was labeled piracy, although the American ship was reportedly seized in Cambodian territorial waters. Hence, the choice of a limited option by a nonbelligerent, large nation for a rescue operation against another nonbelligerent tiny sovereign country did not have the same moral impact as the rescue of innocent civilians at Entebbe, where the terrorists appeared to be the primary offenders and the host country only an accomplice. But despite the differences, the psychological effect on the countries adopting the hard-line warlike approach was very similar: back-slapping jubilation, self-congratulation, and applause from all those upright people who, because of their deep-rooted differences, can produce a semblance of national unity only in short-lived coalitions against an external enemy, against pirates, terrorists, and criminals. *Mayaguez* proved that even a bungled incident can be cosmetically treated by public relations methods to give the appearance of success. The Israelis had no need for such manipulation after their brilliant venture. Critics of *Mayaguez* warned the administration that the jingoistic mood created by their machismo diplomacy would incite further follies or provoke counterfollies and that military force should never be a substitute for realistic nonviolent methods.

The U.S., incidentally, has not always been as tough (at least not against the same parties) as the present stance of "no concessions to terrorists" would suggest. Using the International Law Doctrine of reprisal in an effort to justify the Israeli raid, Professor Adrian Fisher, authority on international law and Dean of Georgetown University Law Center in Washington, D.C., recalled an incident in 1904 when the Sultan of Morocco, disdaining to negotiate with criminals, refused to pay ransom for the release of an American kidnapped by a Moroccan rebel. President Theodore Roosevelt ordered the American fleet to stage a naval demonstration off the Moroccan coast and to show the flag. The Sultan responded to this show of force by paying the demanded sum, and the American was released. At that time, U.S. might was thus employed not to punish the offender at all costs but to make certain that the innocent victim's interests were protected to the fullest.

Daring rescue missions leading to surprise liberation of hostages or prisoners are no prerogative of any particular nation or creed. In July 1943 Italian dictator Mussolini, whose wartime alliance with Hitler's Germany had brought Italy to the brink of defeat, was, after a stormy session of the Fascist Grand Council, deposed by the Italian king, taken into custody by a new Italian government, and held prisoner on a seemingly inaccessible mountaintop in Ponza in the Abruzzi. Several weeks later, German paratroopers led by dashing S.S. Colonel Otto Skorzeny staged a surprise rescue mission. Landing with gliders on the mountaintop, they overwhelmed the startled guards, and, without any casualties, whisked Il Duce away to a meeting with Hitler in Munich. The liberation of Mussolini by a brilliant, imaginatively planned, and perfectly executed stunt was jubilantly celebrated by the Axis powers; nearly all Germans, even opponents of the Hitler regime, found themselves caught in the tidal wave of enthusiasm. ("We did it; nobody but us could have brought off a mission impossible like this one.") Sagging German morale received a powerful boost as friend and foe, including British wartime leader Winston Churchill, could not withhold admiration for the ingeniousness and courage of this highly successful operation.

May sovereign rights and basic legal principles, such as that the accused and/or victim should not serve as judge, be suspended in extraordinary circumstances? In 1960, Israeli intelligence located Nazi mass murderer Adolph Eichmann living under an assumed name in Argentina. A carefully selected team of Israeli experts managed to smuggle the drugged Eichmann out of the country, transporting him to Israel after he had been held captive in Argentina for several weeks. Eichmann was tried in Israel and eventually executed. The magnitude of his crimes seemed to reduce the impact of the admitted kidnapping and of the infringement of Argentina's sovereign rights; no decent person wanted to be suspected of sympathy for the monster who had arranged to kill hundreds of thousands of innocents or for the tyrannical Hitler regime in whose service the massacres were performed. For the Israelis, the moral issue appeared clearcut and indisputable: a law higher than any ordinary written law demanded that one of the worst mass murderers in history be brought to justice even if he was to be judged by a court of his victims and their descendants.

The same imperative directs some of the Israelis' more recent activities and legitimizes otherwise criminal deeds—and occasional mistakes. Incensed by the alleged spinelessness and ineffectuality of several European police departments in dealing with Arab terrorists, Israeli counterterrorists, intelligence, and execution teams were organized to deal more decisively with Arab terrorists wherever they might be. Mortal strikes occasionally also killing bystanders in Rome, Paris, Cyprus, Beirut, and other places testified to the deadly accuracy of the professional experts, who left no doubt about their identity and yet were never caught. Once, however, the seemingly infallible Israeli intelligence made a mistake, and a tragic mishap occurred in the small Norwegian town of Lillehammer. Intending to eliminate a top organizer of Arab terrorism, the highly trained Israeli team instead mistakenly executed an innocent Arab totally unconnected with any terrorism, mowing him down in front of his pregnant wife as he left a movie theater. All four executioners were caught, tried, and given relatively short prison sentences in Norway.

Let there be no misunderstanding: many hundreds, if not thousands, of acts of ruthless and indiscriminate terrorism or antiterrorism could be enumerated that were performed by South Americans, Germans, Irish, and particularly by Arabs. This book, not at all pretending to be comprehensive, gives many significant examples of such atrocities (regularly experienced by the perpetrators as responses to atrocities) in an attempt not just to deplore terrorism in a futile fashion, but to understand in order to help eliminate this virulent modern plague. I see my task as more than to condemn blindly or to assume the stance of nonjudgmental intellectual detachment. I also take sides and, after examining all the evidence to the best of my knowledge and conscience, I judge certain attitudes and acts right and others wrong, or more often some better than others that I consider worse. I admit, reluctantly and without pleasure, that in some very rare instances, resorting to force and violence offers the only morally and pragmatically acceptable solution to a desperate situation. But my passionate commitment to the protection of individual human life compels me to approve of violence (the military option) only after all other nonviolent alternatives have been carefully explored and honestly tried.

Whether or not I approve is of little importance; what does matter, however, is the exposure of clearly emerging repetitive patterns of justification by label-swindle, of self-righteousness by omission of evidence, and of disregard for law and order (often in the name of law and order). I have tried to show how these mechanisms of deception and self-deception originate, operate, and succeed in legitimizing any kind of terror, terrorism, antiterrorism, and counterterrorism, from above or below, by states or individuals. I believe that only decisive action based on insight into similarities and connections between terrorism and antiterrorism can liberate us from the dominance of fear and violence, which is the gravest threat to our security and happiness.

This is more than an expression of intellectual convictions; I confess to experiencing strong emotions whenever an action infringing on the rights of others is to be justified by a "higher law" based on some group's identity needs and whenever the discussion about legality or morality ends with the declaration that only a member sharing a certain identity is competent to judge. No matter how honestly felt and sincerely made, statements such as "You have to be an Israeli" (or an

Irish Catholic or an Irish Protestant or a Turkish
Cypriot or a Greek Cypriot or an Arab or an Aryan
or whatever) to really understand and to know what
is required in this or that situation provokes in me an
association with the Nazi regime, which proudly proclaimed, "Whatever benefits the German people is
good and right and just." *Das gesunde Volksempfin-
den* (healthy popular consensus and common sense)
of German Aryans as interpreted by the Fuehrer and
his clique was not so long ago considered the sole
basis for determining what was in the interest of
the holy German nation's survival and welfare. All
morality and all rules of law were suspended by the
Nazi leaders, who seemed invincible for a while because of their courage and decisiveness, in the name of
a higher law (survival of the master race) that plunged
the world into a devastating war and legitimized the
brutal slaughter of millions in the holocaust. Claims
made by no matter whom that a unique emergency
calls for the disregard of conventional morality and
law should, in memory of the disastrous Nazi experiment of just over thirty years ago, be viewed with utmost suspicion. Action based on such claims must not
be authorized only by those who stand to benefit and
who forever assert that there is no other or better
way than violence.

At a meeting of the U.N. Security Council after
the Entebbe incident, called at the urgent request of
the African nations, Israel's representative, Ambassador Herzog, refused to accept the role of the accused party, stating instead, "I stand here as an accuser
of all those evil forces which in their inherent cowardice
and abject craven attitude see blameless wayfarers and
innocent women and children—yes, even babes in
arms—as legitimate targets for their evil intentions. I
stand here as an accuser of the countries that, because
of evil design or lack of moral backbone, have collaborated with those bloodthirsty terrorists." He spoke
of the worldwide wave of approval that Israel's action
had given rise to, offered "overwhelming evidence" of
Uganda's prior knowledge of and complicity in the

terrorists' actions, found that "the weight of international law and precedent lie fully in Israel's favor," but added that "the law we find in statute books is not the only law of mankind. There is also a moral law, and by all that is moral on this earth, Israel had the right to do what it did. Indeed it also had the duty to do so." He concluded, "There is a time in the affairs of man when even governments must make difficult decisions guided not by considerations of expediency but by considerations of morality. Israel was guided by these considerations in risking much to save its citizens. May we hope that others will be guided by these principles too?"

The representatives of Uganda, Somalia, and Tanzania, among others, indignantly called the Israeli raid a dastardly, unprovoked, and unlawful act of aggression which was "an unprecedented and direct attack on the Republic of Uganda and its government. It also constitutes an arrogant insult to the dignity of Africa and mankind as a whole and contravenes all norms of international behavior and conduct." Deploring the "wanton killing of many innocent people by the Zionist agents," they vowed that "the legitimate struggle of the Arab Nation to liberate the Zionist occupied territories shall not be stopped by these acts of [Israeli] terrorism and shall continue until final and complete victory is achieved." President Amin was given credit for his success in having more than half the hostages released, for having brought about the continuation of negotiations through which the lives of the remaining hostages were saved, and for humanitarian efforts on behalf of the prisoners. In the further course of the debate, the Israeli spokesman rejected the Africans' allegations "of Israel's habitual transgression and its unbelievable barefaced inclination to indulge in an unrestrained attitude." He expressed his surprise that the government of Mexico could be led "to attack a small state defending itself against a common enemy of Mexico and Israel, namely international terror," and could not hide his amazement that Yugoslavia again saw fit "to intervene in a debate on the side of those condemning Israel in order to demonstrate [its] loyal alignment with the remarks of the so-called nonaligned countries."

In repudiation of the foreign minister of Mauritius' statement acquitting President Idi Amin of complicity, Israel's ambassador had commented that the eloquence of the foreign minister's speech was equaled only by his eloquent silence. Indeed, the African accusers at the U.N. and their allies carefully omitted mention of how Uganda had warmly welcomed the terrorists and permitted them to be joined by their waiting comrades, which could not have occurred without Ugandan cooperation. Idi Amin's public fraternization with the terrorists and his unqualified support of their demands was not mentioned, nor was there even the slightest condemnation of the brutal hijacking, the segregation of Jews from non-Jews, or any reference to the horrible fate of the helpless elderly woman left behind. But the Israeli representative was also eloquently silent on many points. It would have been hard to maintain his stance of absolute moral purity and at the same time admit that Israel had indicated its willingness to negotiate, had tried to cajole Idi Amin even after he had divulged his sympathies for the terrorists, and had used the extended deadline to prepare a military strike. The repeatedly made claim that the raid was the only possible way to save more than a hundred lives is incorrect on the record. There was another way, the one suggested by the terrorists: the release of the fifty-three political prisoners would have provided equal, if not more effective protection for the hostages. That, of course, would have meant what the Israelis considered "capitulation," but it cannot be argued that the raid was the only means of rescuing the hostages, nor is it likely that the release of a few dozen jailed terrorists, probably no more dangerous than thousands of their brethren in spirit and deed who are at large, would have significantly increased the terroristic danger in the world. Israel's authorities had used cunning and deceit in order to invade a sovereign country with which they were not at war, the commandos had destroyed a sizable part of the Ugandan Air Force, and, before they were able to defend themselves, killed twenty unaware soldiers guilty only (to the extent that it can be determined) of being Ugandans and subject to the tyrannical rule of a crazed fanatic. Of course, in any war innocents are killed, enemy soldiers intentionally and civilians, women, and children accidentally or carelessly. We may grant that even in peacetime, extraordinary circumstances like terroristic attacks or criminal assaults may justify the jeopardizing of human life, but should the death of innocents then be regarded with indifference or celebrated with jubilation?

Consider the following hypothetical situation: instead of exuberant rejoicing, the authorities responsible for an action like the Entebbe raid order a day of mourning, not just out of respect for the dead but to indicate that what they thought had to be done was done out of necessity and without joy. This scenario won't become reality in the near future; it is utopian and "unpsychological" to expect that the mourning for human lives (possibly needlessly) lost will be permitted to spoil the great fun of celebrating the opponent's humiliation. Just because, most of the time, this was and still is the way it is, the suspicion arises that the mood of self-congratulatory triumph and of grandiose self-aggrandizement confirming identity and community belonging (we are the greatest, we showed them, we won't be pushed around) is not a byproduct or fringe benefit of such a violent act, but its most important purpose, motive, and goal.

Commenting on the Entebbe raid, Harvard scholar, former U.S. ambassador and delegate to the U.N., and present Democratic senatorial candidate in New York Daniel Moynihan declared that it was "the judgment of mankind that what the Israelis did was honorable and brave—and done for all of us." Moynihan could not have meant that statement as a realistic appraisal; in fact, he predicted in the same sentence that the U.N. would seek to condemn Israel for the Entebbe affair. What Moynihan did imply was that those who did not agree with him were not part of mankind any longer, not quite human, and hence they could be ignored or treated accordingly. This pompous reasoning follows an old totalitarian tradition that has many contemporary imitators. Predictably, after an acrimonious debate, the U.N. split into two camps, each side proposing their own resolution. Both motions failed: Israel was not censured for its "aggression," terrorism and its accomplices were not censured for their actions that led to the Israelis' intervention.

According to a report in *Newsweek,* Israel's Defense Minister, Shimon Peres, in a cabinet meeting soon after the hijacking, called for military action "to counter the image of a weak and indecisive government." Allegedly Prime Minister Rabin "turned crimson with anger." " 'We are talking about military feasibility,' he snapped, 'and not about politics.' " The record indicates that Rabin and his cabinet explored other possibilities before adopting the military option, which seemed to them a last resort measure. Acts of violence performed with a clear conscience indeed appear irresistibly attractive even in peacetime; they strengthen the government, are glorified by the media, and at first are enthusiastically applauded by a public starved for adventure and eager to communicate the impression of indomitable strength.

There are also other deeper reasons for giving in to the yearning for heroic adventure than the wish to overcome enraging feelings of impotence and helplessness through a memorable deed. The public's (short-lived) euphoria signifies more than mere identification with the national heroes who, by their actual conduct and the "logic of the deed," seem to express generally shared emotions in a direct, spontaneous, genuine fashion. The general enthusiasm, often mounting to emotional highs of orgiastic ecstasy, indicates a kind of non-intellectual mystic participation with the heroes in which everybody becomes part of a unified whole and the separating ego boundaries of the individuals are temporarily dissolved. In the communal rejoicing, celebrating the moment of perfect control over one's fate, death is defied and conquered, when in transcending the narrow limits of individuality, the oceanic feeling of belonging to an eternal community conveys a sense of absolute security, immortality, and bliss.

The preference for the use of violence without regard for human lives will always find easy rationalizations disguised as necessities of self-defense and survival and as demands of a higher lawfulness. Provocations are often greatly exaggerated or even invented to explain and excuse self-serving violence, considered expedient for political purposes or desirable for the psychological impact of glamorized force. According to that very same pattern and for these very same reasons do terrorists perform their spectacular deeds to arouse public attention and to enhance their own importance and self-esteem.

Terrorists have been compared with the germs of an infectious disease; but the terrorists also consider the systems or nations they fight with bombs and "a swift knife" to be decayed, polluted, cancerous, and sick. If a "surgical strike" (as the Entebbe raid has been called) is at times necessary, when all "conservative" treatment possibilities are exhausted and there is no time to deal with the underlying cause of the illness, the surgeon should not be motivated by desires similar to if not indistinguishable from those of the disease carrier. Terror and terrorism are horrifying, malignant afflictions whose greatest danger is their contagious effect on the disease fighters, who become contaminated by the same malady and mistake the symptoms of the disease for the cure.

Since the time that the semiliterate ex-boxing champion Idi Amin (who insists on being addressed as "Excellency al-Hajji Field Marshall Dr. Idi Amin Dada, holder of the British Victoria Cross, DSO, MC") was described in this book as one of the rare examples of a "crazy" terrorist from above, considerable evidence has been added to his record confirming the suspicion of serious mental disturbance. "Craziness," however (due to syphilis, drug abuse, brain injury, or whatever), may not sufficiently explain his actions, which, although bizarre at all times, often also display cunning, cleverness, and a talent for bombastic self-display. There is some comic relief in the ironic detail that his first inkling of the Entebbe raid came from Tel Aviv, 2,600 miles away, because his terrorized underlings, fearing for their lives, dared not inform him of what had happened right there. His intemperate rage attacks (one of which resulted in the deaths of the four delinquent radar operators), allegedly costing the lives of as many as 400,000 Ugandans during his reign, could be interpreted as a cruel and primitive dictator's indulgence in unrestrained power use. But Idi Amin's self-serving conduct before, during, and after the negotiations at Entebbe was so grotesquely incongruous, his utterances so irrationally inconsistent, and his strutting yet vacillating conduct so inappropriate that only the assumption of serious mental derangement can account for his behavior. And who but a severely disturbed individual would believe that the Israeli commandos used nuclear grenades to put the Ugandan soldiers out of commission, would claim that "the most modern and sophisticated Soviet antitank weapons were operated by the president, his wives, and some of his children under the age of seven," would proclaim that his conflicts with Britain stemmed from his refusal to marry an English woman, and would order the shooting of a few hundred Ugandan children in the school in which his son presumably was ridiculed?

Uganda was certainly not the first or only nation to shelter and support terrorists (Libya, Algeria, Kuwait, South Yemen, and several other countries do more than that—they instigate and finance Palestinian terrorism). But Uganda's ruler is such a contemptible and bizarre figure that from sheer dislike of his person and his despotic rule, it became easy to minimize the violation of his country's sovereignty.

The guarantee of a national sovereignty is not a minor issue, although Uganda may be a minor country, cursed with a frenzied dictator who deserves neither sympathy nor protection. Sovereignty is a preconceived construct, a legal presumption granting the nationals of a certain territory the right to choose their government and to arrange their affairs in any way they see fit without outside interference in their "internal affairs." The presumption of sovereignty is admittedly often more fiction than fact. Numerous countries are not truly independent financially or politically, and many nations in our contemporary world were and are denied the right of free choice by a dictatorial regime imposed upon them. Idi Amin's Uganda may serve as a prime example of the extremes of merciless exploitation and inhuman cruelty tolerated nowadays under the protective umbrella of sovereignty. Yet whatever exists of a contemporary international order, guaranteeing at least some continuity and stability, is based on this presumption and protection of national sovereignty; in fact, no different organizing principle for the regulation of international relations is presently imaginable. Chaos would be inevitable if one country, large or small, were permitted to invade another one without notice or declaration of war, for whatever reason deemed vital or defensible by the attacking country. If any law and order is to prevail, no nation, disapproving of what a neighboring country's regime is, or does, must be allowed to intervene violently in another nation's territory to establish its own standards of law and order.

Of course, such interventions, often disguised as rescue operations, have occurred without the sanction of international law; Nazi Germany invaded Austria and Czechoslovakia in peacetime, Soviet Russia intervened "peacefully and with brotherly intentions" in Hungary and Czechoslovakia, and the Colonels' Greece invaded Cyprus, but all these actions are examples of the worst kind of totalitarian aggression. They endanger human survival if they are not stopped and contained by some force committed to the observation of international treaties.

Law by necessity restricts immediate reactions; hence it often seems counterintuitive. It goes "against the grain" to have to submit to frustrating legal restraints. It has taken civilization a long time to become habituated to the rule of law, which, in delaying judgment and delegating the punishment function to an impartial agency, calls for a renunciation of the "instincts" for lynch justice and immediate revenge. But it is just this imposed delay and restraint, accepted by all civilized mankind in one form or another, that protects the weak and otherwise helpless and, through justice, guarantees security. Clearly, the protective provisions of international law benefit small countries in particular; their very existence depends on the respect of more powerful nations for their sovereign rights. The higher law commanding and justifying the redress of injustice according to one's own intuition and power is the law of the jungle, the law of lynch justice, and the credo of the terrorist.

The provisions of international law, flexible and amenable to various interpretations as they are, will have to be stretched very far to accommodate the Israeli interpretation of the Uganda events. It could be argued that in the absence of any effective international police force carrying out the judgments of an international court, a country has the right and even the duty to protect its citizens victimized by criminal attacks wherever they might be. But this conception of a state's rights and duties clashes head on with the accepted doctrine of national sovereignty. The commandos were not in hot pursuit of the offenders, they were not acting out of "necessity of self-defense, instant, overwhelming, leaving no choice of means and no moment of deliberation" (the definition given by former U.S. Secretary of State Daniel Webster, as quoted by Daniel Moynihan). Other means were contemplated and there certainly were many days and nights of agonizing appraisal and deliberation. But the sad truth of the matter is that nobody on either side worried too much about any international or other law until after it was all over.

Most people in the Western world just plain liked the action and were quite satisfied, even relieved, not to have to give any explanation for their spontaneous pleasure. Without any intellectual effort, it just felt good to join in the celebration and to take delight in the success of brave people doing what comes naturally: the "right" thing. Spectacular actions invite the identification of spectators who, from a safe distance and free of guilt, can vicariously participate in seemingly permissible (socially syntonic) aggression; as in fairy tales, one side (ours, of course) is completely just and right, and the other completely wicked and totally wrong. In the prelogical fairyland of absolutes, there is no disturbing emotional ambivalence, no upsetting intellectual doubts, and no intriguing moral conflict. Everything is clear and simple; good is good and bad is bad, and the good wins over the bad. Who would not like that! The nostalgia for this primitive state which has never existed in reality is an understandable wishful fantasy compensating for confusion and frustration. But the attempt to bring about that paradise through justifiable violence is bound to create hell on earth.

Praising the Israeli action, James Burnham wrote in *International Review,* "The counterterrorist Israeli operation was itself a terrorist operation." Burnham poked fun at such "moral" notions as have led to outrage over "the doings of the CIA, FBI, the Pentagon and the Nixon White House." He was amused by such statements as "the end does not justify every means; the president and CIA director are not above the law; no nation has the right to intervene inside the borders of another nation." Do those who think as Burnham believe that the end *does* justify the means, that the president and the CIA *are* above the law, and that a nation (preferably ours or one of our allies) *does* have the right to intervene inside the borders of another nation? They do. And who determines which end justifies all means, which ruler or secret organization is to be considered above the law, and which nation may intervene? They do, or at least they would like to. Burnham further stated, "The Entebbe affair proves the inadequacy of an abstract moral attitude toward political terrorism. It is a simplistic fallacy to believe you can settle the moral problem of terrorism by declaring all terrorist action wrong." Of course, it does no good to disapprove of evil and declare it morally wrong. But the acknowledgment that it is futile to denounce evil verbally does not mean that every evil has to be accepted with resignation, condoned, or, worst of all, used for one's own benefit. While ethical absolutism is unrealistically abstract and can become tyrannical, complete ethical relativism is totalitarian and despotic from the start, because it leaves the ultimate determination of values to the whims of the most powerful and most ruthless.

It is a simplistic and cynical fallacy to believe that any significant conflict among human beings can be satisfactorily resolved without regard to the moral principles of truth and justice. To be sure, most complex human actions are the result of a variety of motives and represent an ethically mixed bag. That the good and the bad often intermingle with each other, that the truth does not emerge by observing surface appearance only, that justice is difficult to achieve and hardly ever perfect, does not mean that these values —morality, truth, justice—do not exist or should not be the guidelines of desirable behavior. In his categorical imperative, Immanuel Kant demanded that one should "Act only on that maxim whereby thou canst at the same time will that it should become a universal law." Only despicable nonchalance about the ethical aspect of human action can will or tolerate that terror and terrorism become universal laws. Violence, war, and particularly terror and terrorism are destructive and morally wrong. Nonviolent conflict resolution and the correction of injustices are morally good, or at least better than the unrestrained violence of everybody against everybody. There is nothing naive or ineffectual about this belief if it becomes the motivating impulse for remedial social and political action.

All the tough talk about the eleventh commandment, not to bow to terrorism, inspired by the Entebbe success, has not given a single new clue as to what actually should be done now in order to "stamp out terrorism." Everybody agrees that an Entebbe-like situation is highly unlikely to develop again; a similar strike would no longer have the advantage of surprise. Even the Israeli government and its most optimistic supporters, hoping that the Entebbe raid would prove an inspiration and example to other countries, did not expect that Entebbe would be the last act of terrorism. Unless an opponent can either be persuaded by political means or else totally exterminated, the escalating tragedy of terrorism versus counterterrorism remains a deadly zero sum game in which one side loses what the other side gains and therefore feels compelled to recapture his losses on a subsequent occasion. The more demonstrative triumph is displayed on the one side, the more humiliation is experienced by the other, which then compels retaliation to restore self-esteem. It is better to win than to lose; it is better to be disliked than pitied. But for reasons of self-preservation, as well as humanitarianism, it is better to respect the enemy even in defeat than to humiliate an opponent who cannot be eliminated.

No prophetic gift is required to predict that international terrorism will continue if not escalate; after Entebbe and because of it there will be retaliation raids, revenge operations, and demonstrations of "senseless" brutality. In August 1976, as a prelude to bigger things to come, two Arab terrorists prevented from boarding an El Al flight to Tel Aviv opened fire at Istanbul's airport lounge in revenge for the Entebbe action. Two Israelis, a Japanese, and an American were killed by the random shooting. The would-be hijackers, members of the Popular Front for the Liberation of Palestine, stated after their arrest: "Our aim was to kill as many Israelis as possible." In the same week, Rhodesian commandos, in retaliation for guerrilla attacks from Mozambique, crossed the border and killed over three hundred black guerrillas or, as Mozambique claims, six hundred civilians in a refugee camp, twenty-five miles within Mozambican territory. The raid was ecstatically celebrated with champagne as "Rhodesia's Entebbe" and "did wonders for the white Rhodesians' morale." (*Time,* August 23, 1976.)

According to popular opinion, compromises with terrorists, usually thought of as capitulation, set a bad precedent and only encourage terrorists to repeat their actions. Over and over again it is said that violence is the only language "they" (the terrorists? the criminals? the children and adolescents? or everybody?) understand. Of course, violence is no language at all, but a means of communication widely employed precisely because it requires no understanding whatever. Indeed violence makes any language or understanding superfluous.

Negotiations and compromises do not stop terrorism, but neither do deceitful tricks and shootouts. It is not quite as simple as that, not an either/or proposition. The question of what method works best, or at least better, in the long run has to be answered by factual research, not by passionate beliefs that remain impervious to experience. I have written, "Mixed strategies (delay, negotiation, promises, firmness, consistency, force) used flexibly in different, changing situations and not chained to any preconceived political or other biases produce the best results. I do not advocate softness; to yield under any circumstances is just as unprofitable and futile as to decide in advance never to yield."

Deterrence through the use of force and through humiliation has never worked. To the contrary, the intended deterrent punishment is, according to all experience, likely to act as a provocation and stimulation for future revenge, to even the score and prove equal or superior courage. If violent fanatics were in the habit of making rational profit-and-loss calculations, they would not be crusading terrorists. The announcement never again to engage in negotiations with terrorists will only make the terrorists step up the intensity and widen the scope of their enterprise. And who could refuse to bargain if, for instance, the lives of top officials, hundreds of children, or the fate of a whole city (atomic threat) were at stake? Next time, because of Entebbe, deadlines will not be quite so readily extended by terrorists, who will regard any request for delay as a crafty attempt to gain time for deception. Increasing the risks to the terrorists only increases the risks to the victims; it is the victims who will be further victimized.

I realize more than ever that in the short run sensible arguments, realistic experiences, and moral considerations are of little avail against the massive impact of dramatic violence, staged as a heroic deed and represented as "the only way" to deal with a difficult situation or as the final solution to a complicated problem. But I still believe that in the overwhelming majority of conflictual situations, violence, suggested or suggesting itself as the simplest, most courageous, most effective course of action, is self-defeating in the long run. Worse than primitive violence is glamorized violence, performed with a clean conscience, celebrated as a lesson, and proposed as an example for others to follow.

To justify violent deeds in the name of a higher than ordinary law, regardless of the risk to life, is terrorist ideology. To simultaneously arouse worldwide attention and scorn world opinion with a spectacular performance, regardless of consequences, is terrorist intention. To use such a deed to enhance communal pride and to raise one's own self-confidence is terrorist magic.

While terrorist "solutions" have a powerful attraction to those who consider themselves antiterrorists, the belief that all that needs to be done about terrorism is to get tough and shoot it out is also a dangerous simplification and a self-deception. As I said earlier in this book, "Genuine negotiations, not morality plays or exercises in doublecrossing, are always preferable to quick confrontations. Meeting complicated challenges with simplistic solutions that have proved ineffective in the past renders us even more hopeless and terror-prone. Only the ignorant and the fanatic are sure that simple remedies will solve everything in a hurry." The complex manifestations of terror and terrorism, interwoven as they are with governmental strategies, traditional beliefs, aspirations for liberation, and a variety of other motivations, present extremely complicated problems that should not be simplified just to make them appear solvable by violence. The infantile insistence that there must be a quick, decisive answer to every question (the answer being violence) should finally be recognized for what it is: childish, wishful thinking as well as a seductive temptation to dangerous terrorism.

World opinion is divided. International law, often ill-defined and weak, has no effective enforcement machinery at its disposal; also it certainly would be wiser to gradually reduce rather than to strengthen national sovereignty. Yet, if the Entebbe model were to become universal practice, small mobile forces of any state or would-be state, either official execution teams or vigilantes, would soon be busily roaming the earth engaged in police actions against other states or hostile groups within other states all over the globe.

Then the practice of on-the-spot executions would become widespread regardless of what legislatures, judges, and law books might have to say. Since by his very existence every jailed terrorist represents a liberation challenge to his comrades and increases the chances of dead innocents abroad, why keep him alive? To depend on highly trained, freewheeling, revenge-rescue-and-killer squads for security and the protection of national (or other identity group) rights, rather than on legal or moral provisions, is to advocate and instigate an insane war of all against all.

In a continuous, ongoing effort, human beings have devised laws and certain ritualized game rules, the sum total of which is called civilization, to regulate human interaction without regular recourse to violence and in order to prevent a permanent state of universal war. Terrorists routinely disregard the rules of civilized conduct. They are most dangerous not when they behave like children or lunatics, but when they act like sovereign states, recognizing no law but that of survival and self-assertion as they interpret it. Yet the truly lethal menace of terrorism lies not in what the crusading terrorists do, but in what they induce others to do—that is, to imitate the tactics that are certain to eliminate freedom and security for all and to plunge the world into a never ending violent struggle between competing tyrannies.

On rare occasions, it may be necessary to use violence without pleasure; but the terrorists' motto "destroy in order to save" should not regularly be countered with the equally simplistic and equally terroristic response: "In order to save, destroy the destroyers." There are different, better ways, more humane and more effective. Entebbe was a memorable episode in the escalating terroristic-antiterroristic enterprise, but it should not become a precedent or a model. The human needs for survival in dignity and freedom command that rather than indulge in the satisfaction of communal self-righteousness, we create and maintain a world in which there are no more Entebbe-like problems, no more Entebbe-like "solutions."

There will always be conflict within and between human beings and groups; and there will always be power-seeking sponsors of glamorized violence. But every age must develop its own definition of courage. Winston Churchill's prophecy of 1955, "We shall, by a process of sublime irony, have reached a stage in history where safety will be the sturdy child of terror and survival the twin brother of annihilation," need not come true. But to tenaciously explore the possibilities of nonviolent conflict solution will be the difficult but not impossible mission of modern heroism, neither intimidated nor tempted by terror and terrorism.

Source Notes

Chapter 1

1. General Assembly Official Record, 29th Session, Supplement 31 (8-9631). Resolutions adopted under report of the 6th Committee, Article 2, page 143.
2–4. Interview with Jonathan Broder, *Oui* magazine, May 1976.
5. *Der Spiegel*, July 29, 1974.
6. *Newsweek*, July 29, 1974.

Chapter 2

1. *Newsweek*, January 5, 1976.
2. *Terrorism, Part 2.* Hearings before the Committee on Internal Security, House of Representatives. Washington, D.C.: Government Printing Office, 1974.
3. *Newsweek*, September 30, 1974.
4. *Newsweek*, European Edition, May 24, 1976.
5. Frank B. Walters, *Seven Years of Terrorism: The FLO.*

Chapter 3

1. *Newsweek*, September 25, 1972.
2. Gerald Frank, *The Deed.* New York: Simon & Schuster, 1963.

Chapter 4

1–2. Simma Holt, *Terrorism in the Name of God.* New York: Crown Publishers, 1965.
3–4. Trial transcripts.
5. *Newsweek*, November 2, 1970.
6. Seymour Pollack, M.D. Report to Judge Manual Real. U.S. District Court, May 15, 1972.

7. Frederick Hacker, M.D. Report to Judge Charles H. Carr. U.S. District Court, July 13, 1972.

Chapter 5

1. *Newsweek*, September 10, 1973.
2. Official Police Report, Swedish Ministry of Justice.
3. *Chicago Tribune,* August 27, 1973.
4. *Newsweek,* September 10, 1973.
5. *Die Presse,* August 30, 1973.
6. *Chicago Tribune,* August 29, 1973.
7. *Newsweek,* September 10, 1973.
8. *Die Presse,* August 29, 1973.
9. *Newsweek,* September 10, 1973.
10. *Die Presse,* September 8, 1973.
11. *Chicago Tribune,* August 23, 1973.
12. *The New York Times,* August 30, 1973.
13. *Chicago Tribune,* August 23, 1973.
14. *Die Presse,* September 8, 1973.
15. Geoffrey Jackson, *Surviving the Long Night.* New York: Vanguard Press, 1974.

Chapter 6

1–2. *Time,* October 28, 1974.

Chapter 7

1–2. Steven Weed, *My Search for Patty Hearst.* New York: Crown Publishers, 1976.
3. Jerry Belcher and Don West, *Patty/Tania.* New York: Pyramid Books, 1975, pages 337, 343.
4–5. Probation Report of David B. Calhoun, Centinela Area Office, December 6, 1968.
6. Thomas T. Noguchi, M.D., Chief Medical Examiner and Coroner, County of Los Angeles, 1974.
7. Vincent Bugliosi, *Helter Skelter.* New York: W. W. Norton and Co., 1974, page 234; paperback edition: Bantam Books, 1975.
8. *Patty/Tania,* page 334.
9. M'Naughten's Case (1843) 8 Eng. Rep. R. 718.
10. *Federal Reporter,* 2d. Series, 426, Henry White Edgerton, Cite as 426 F. 2d 64 (1970), pages 64–86, Wade vs. U.S.
11. *Time,* March 29, 1976.
12–13. *Patty/Tania,* page 345.

Chapter 8

1. Richard Maxwell Brown, *The American Vigilante Tradition in the History of Violence in America.* A Report to the National Commission on the Causes and Prevention of Violence, June 1969, pages 1–3.
2. Golda Meir on Ma'alot, *Newsweek,* May 27, 1974.
3. *Time,* September 20, 1974.

Chapter 9

1. "The Events of September 28–29, 1973: A Documentary Report." Issued by the Federal Chancellery, Vienna, Austria, 1973.

Chapter 10

1. *Terrorism, Parts 1, 2, 3, and 4.* Hearings before the Committee on Internal Security, House of Representatives, Washington, D.C.: Government Printing Office, 1974.
2. David Hubbard, *The Skyjacker.* New York: Macmillan, 1973, pages 268–69.
3. "Attica: The Official Report of the New York State Special Commission on Attica," Chairman Robert B. McKay, 1972, page xii.
4. "Attica: The Official Report of the New York State Special Commission on Attica," pages 322–323.
5. Russell G. Oswald, *Attica: My Own Story.* New York: Doubleday.
6. Tom Wicker, *A Time to Die.* New York: Ballantine Books, 1975.
7–8. "Attica: The Official Report of the New York State Special Commission on Attica," pages 402, 403, 456, 457, and 458.
9. "Attica: The Official Report of the New York State Special Commission on Attica," page 112.

Chapter 12

1–2. U.N. General Assembly Report, November 9–29, 1972.
3. Canetti, *Masse und Macht II.* Reiche Hanser, 1960.

4. Walter Laqueur, *Can Terrorism Succeed.*
5. U.N. General Debate, Plenary Session 2063 VI 1363.

Epilogue

1. Hans Kohn, *Die Welt Slawen II: Russen, Weisrussen, Ukrainer.* Frankfurt am Main: Herausgeber, 1962.

Index

ABOUT THE AUTHOR

FREDERICK J. HACKER, M.D., is a psychiatrist and psychoanalyst, and a world-renowned authority on aggression and terrorism. He is president of the Sigmund Freud Society in Vienna. He holds double professorships in psychiatry at the University of Southern California Medical School and in psychiatry at law at the U.S.C. Law Center. He is chief of staff at the Hacker Clinics in Beverly Hills and Lynwood, California, and director of the Institute for Conflict Research in Vienna. Dr. Hacker has written and published in both English and German for learned journals on a variety of psychiatric subjects and has written a highly successful layman's book on aggression.

WE DELIVER!
And So Do These Bestsellers.

Bantam Book Catalog

Here's your up-to-the-minute listing of every book currently available from Bantam.

This easy-to-use catalog is divided into categories and contains over 1400 titles by your favorite authors.

So don't delay—take advantage of this special opportunity to increase your reading pleasure.

Just send us your name and address and 25¢ (to help defray postage and handling costs).